Advance Prais

"In *Winded*, Dawn Newton shares the story of her lung cancer, its delayed diagnosis, dark prognosis, and an unexpected drug that helped her live with it – not in remission but rather in temporary stasis. In this moving memoir, she grapples with her illness in the midst of a demanding life, all the while asking the important questions: how will I live now, how will my family manage, how will my children remember me, and – not to be overlooked – who will take care of the dog? The tone is forthright and unsentimental – even as she tries to understand her own fears. The writing is clear as the bell of determination and hope she rings for herself and others who face end-of-life issues while embracing life's full stride."

> — Anne-Marie Oomen, author of *Love, Sex and 4-H*, winner of the Next Generation Indie Award for Memoir, and co-author of *Lake Michigan Mermaid*, a Michigan Notable Book for 2018

"In *Winded*, Dawn Newton launches forth filament after filament, exploring the connections between body and illness, husband and wife, parent and child, teacher and student, writer and word, until her web stretches out in all directions, thrumming with life."

> — Adrienne Sharp, national bestselling author of *The Magnificent Esme Wells*

"If any woman should live like her hair is on fire, it's Dawn Newton. She's got three children, a husband, a new puppy and stage IV lung cancer. If any woman should be bummed about the lung cancer, it's Dawn Newton. She didn't smoke. If any woman has written a memoir about how her cancer will never go away, but neither will she let it take over, it's Dawn Newton. She's kept The Emperor of All Maladies at bay for six years with the help of the drug, Tarceva, and her optimistic East Indian oncologist. Aided by her mindfulness practice, she lives life in full. Reminiscent of Annie Dillard and Patricia Hampl, Newton's poetic memoir savors the beautiful details of life, in all its forms."

— Dedria Humphries Barker, author of *Mother of Orphans: The True and Curious Story of Irish Alice, a Colored Man's Widow*

"In this brave and intimate memoir, Dawn Newton lays bare the raw facts of her life, which includes, but is not reduced by, cancer. With her spare and elegant prose, Newton makes even the most ordinary experiences shimmer, reminding us that there is grandeur in every small moment and that each life is only a chain of such moments strung together, flickering and giving off light."

— Valerie Laken, author of *Dream House* and *Separate Kingdoms*

"I've read Dawn Newton's work for years now with pleasure and admiration. It is character driven and her portraiture credible, complex, and compelling. I think of her as a natural storyteller – one who writes a lovely sentence."

— Stuart Dybek, distinguished writer in residence, Northwestern University, and author of *I Sailed With Magellan*, *The Coast of Chicago*, and *Childhood and Other Neighborhoods*

"*Winded* takes your breath away, as Dawn Newton shows how fast cancer can bring a hectic life to a standstill. Bending down to pick up a book, she feels a twinge in her chest that reminds her of her pregnancies, when her children were "all acrobatic in the womb." The sad discovery of the twinge is evidence of stage IV lung cancer. Newton faces down the odds with everything she's learned as a writer, teacher, and mother. Along the way, she invades her daughter's privacy, gets the family a puppy, teaches her son how to use his EpiPen without her. Full of raw honesty about our fears and feelings, *Winded* is a gifted portrait of the artist battling for life."

— Mary Kay Zuravleff, author of *Man Alive!*, *The Bowl Is Already Broken*, and *The Frequency of Souls*

Winded

Winded

A Memoir in Four Stages

Dawn Newton

Dawn Newton [signature]

November 26, 2019

Apprentice
House Press
Loyola University Maryland

First Edition

Casebound ISBN: 978-1-62720-244-2
Paperback ISBN: 978-1-62720-245-9
Ebook ISBN: 978-1-62720-246-6

Printed in the United States of America

Design by Julia Trinkoff
Acquired & developed by Paula-Yuan Gregory
Promotion plan developed by Miranda Nolan

Published by Apprentice House Press

Apprentice House Press
Loyola University Maryland
4501 N. Charles Street
Baltimore, MD 21210
410.617.5265 • 410.617.2198 (fax)
www.ApprenticeHouse.com
info@ApprenticeHouse.com

for my cancer cohort —
Grace, Leigh, and Nancy

Contents

Foreword

We met in 1981, searching for apartments in Baltimore. Dawn had recently finished college and was to begin the prestigious Master's program in creative writing at Johns Hopkins University. I had just completed two years as a "disease detective" at the Centers for Disease Control and Prevention and was embarking on a clinical epidemiology fellowship at Hopkins School of Hygiene and Public Health. I kept running into her, and was conscious that, like me, she was wryly observing other prospective renters who appeared much more organized than either of us and who would surely get the best deals.

We arrived simultaneously at a large sunny two-bedroom apartment on St. Paul Street, the converted half of the second floor of what was once a large beautiful home. It was perfect for two people who didn't want to spend a lot of money, walking distance from Dawn's program, and an easy bus ride for me to the downtown campus. With a few inquiries, we discovered that despite the 10-year difference in age, and the cultural difference between Midwestern earnestness and New Jersey frankness, we were meant for each other. Both of us had grown up sharing bathrooms with multiple family members and had been first generation college students who found ourselves continually amazed at how far we had travelled from our homes and our parents' experiences.

The apartment was spacious and often sunny but fit the typical student lodging profile of that era. Furniture was mostly cheap or non-existent. Book shelves were home-made, and there were stacks of LPs near the turntable. Turning on the lights at night sent the pesticide-resistant cockroaches scrambling – an auditory and visual spectacle that never failed to elicit a surprise-revulsion response, even though we should have come to expect it in that old Baltimore kitchen. All of this was more endurable than the heat, or lack thereof.

Our landlady listened patiently to our complaints when the cold weather demanded full winter gear to be indoors comfortably. She insisted that the renters on the first floor were too warm and was reluctant to raise the temperature. We would pass the thermostat in the hall on the first floor as we mounted the stairs to our arctic apartment. The thermostat was surrounded by a locked metal cage to prevent manual adjustment of the settings by tenants. Cold and frustrated, we resorted to placing bags of ice on top of the cage. It felt like a miracle. A heat wave! We could roam our apartment in cut-offs, t-shirts, and skimpy pajamas. Sometimes, it was actually too hot – but we didn't mind that. Of course, we knew it couldn't last, and were not surprised when someone snitched. Somehow, we made it through the winter, cheered by the weeks (or was it days?) of unusual warmth. Then came spring…

By that time, I had reconciled with Bobby, my boyfriend of 10 years, intermittent fiancé, and now husband of 30+ years, partly through Dawn's intervention. "He sounds so nice on the phone," she would say, while entreating me to at least talk to him. Of course, she hadn't known me when he broke our engagement, causing me to "hold the mayo" as one friend put it, and seek the Hopkins fellowship as an alternative to the one planned at the Mayo Clinic in Rochester, Minnesota. She found him charming both on the phone, and later when he came to visit. Who knows what would have happened if I hadn't seen him again through her eyes, and was able to be re-charmed?

It was a year of figuring things out for both of us. Dawn's college friend, Tim, now husband of 30+ years was spending his year following their Michigan State graduation traveling in Europe, and his letters did not bring any certainty about their status upon his return. I'd like to think that we wasted little emotional energy on our respective future partners, but that might be another story. The year helped to solidify our career paths. Dawn was always a writer and that identity was strengthened through a year dedicated to writing, sharing, and revising. I worked on my analytic skills and became comfortable calling myself an epidemiologist as well as a physician. At the same time, I felt lucky to be a part of Dawn's world. I read and inexpertly critiqued her work and that of her classmates which she shared with me. Dawn told me her classmates were jealous that she had someone who wanted to read her writing! I guess that is what most writers want.

The year on St. Paul Street went quickly. Most of my family and friends were on the east coast, so we had a string of visitors, and when it was just Dawn and I, it was a comfortable arrangement. I don't think we had a TV, but we had long talks and plenty of music and singing. Dawn is the middle of 3 sisters, who often sang in harmony. Dawn has a beautiful voice and I guess her sisters did too. Her daughter, Rachel also has that gift. We were a family of singers as well, and often sang together sitting around the dining room table after big holiday meals. I know Dawn was a good teacher by how patient she was with my attempts to harmonize with her. I'm not good at staying on tune but she put up with me, and I eventually learned one of her family standards, an Andrews sisters-like rendition of Boogie Woogie Bugle Boy.

After our time in Baltimore, there were years when babies and children dominated our lives. Dawn and Tim returned to Michigan, and Bobby and I ended up in Nashville. We were all busy with work and family and had a hard time keeping up. Dawn visited once, before Nathaniel, her youngest was born. I would sometimes get a long hand-written letter from her, maybe with a book she thought I would like. I would be more likely to write a brief email and send a list of the latest books I had read. We had phone calls about once a year, usually between my September and her November birthdays. We shared stories of hyperactive children and seemingly fruitless attempts at control. I remember talking about her decision to stop taking antidepressants during pregnancy and breastfeeding. She wanted to avoid unknown risks to the babies and was willing to face the risk of a less stable mental state and the emergence of the internal "voice" full of self-criticism. I felt more like a mother then, wanting her to avoid anything that would make her life harder, including pregnancy. But I also understood and shared that deep desire for children and family.

My parents' generation grew up familiar with death. Both my parents' mothers died when they were very young, and both also lost a sibling. Things were different for us. I was one of 7 siblings, all of whom were healthy, as were our combined twelve children. Both my parents and in-laws reached "old age." I had few personal encounters with death among my family and friends. My mother and mother-in-law both died in their 90s peacefully at our respective childhood homes, within months of each other. Shortly after that, things began to change. My youngest brother required emergency surgery for a leaking aneurysm, my brother-in-law was found to have a malignant brain cancer, my sister developed a disturbing heart rhythm, and my sister-in-law was diagnosed with multiple myeloma. Of course, I was then in my 60s, and had been mostly lucky up until that time. Now, I felt like an orphan, and the last vestiges of childhood had disappeared.

Dawn's call came around this time, the year after my mother's death. She told me of her diagnosis of metastatic lung cancer, discovered during a hospitalization for progressive shortness of breath. Through a heart-breaking lack of communication, she was not told the cause of the fluid that had built up around her heart and lungs until several weeks after her hospitalization, and in a way that did not engender trust. At the time she called, she was scheduled to have a "port" or temporary intravenous line placed so that she could start chemotherapy, but her sisters were pushing her to get another opinion. She also reported getting a test for specific lung cancer markers that might change the optimum treatment choice but did not have those results yet. Bobby and I agreed that she should go to a cancer center. Bobby was a basic scientist and cancer researcher and was able to recommend Dr. Shirish Gadgeel at Karmanos Cancer Institute, who agreed to see her quickly.

The treatment of lung cancer has changed dramatically in the past 10 years, for a subset of patients. Targeted treatments are available for an important minority of patients that have specific genetic mutations identified in their tumors. The chance of being one of these patients is higher if you are female and a life-long nonsmoker, like Dawn. It turns out that Dawn's tumor had an epidermal growth factor receptor (EGFR) mutation. EGFR is one of a family of receptors that are important in Bobby's research. Dawn didn't need a port or intravenous chemotherapy, and was ultimately prescribed erlotinib or Tarceva, a pill that targets EGFR, and which she has been taking for the last six years.

The medical misadventures Dawn documents are a reminder of the complexity of today's practice of medicine. I used to think that physicians as patients had the worst luck in hospitals – they always seemed to have something avoidable go wrong. Then I realized that physicians might just be better at spotting what goes wrong, and that many patients have avoidable adverse experiences. Of course, the problem of medical errors is now well recognized, but persists. When there are so many different people and systems involved, it is hard for everything to go without a glitch. Dawn is an engaged patient and astute observer, who maintains a healthy skepticism about instructions. She knows medical systems through her personal history of asthma and depression, and her children's illnesses, most notably, Nathaniel's severe allergies. Some patients treat their bodies like I treat my car – I don't understand it and just want it fixed. She is a sophisticated patient, who tries to understand how her body has betrayed her. I think this serves her well, and she is a better navigator through medicine's complexities than many patients.

Dawn's experiences are also a reminder of things going right. She is living proof of life-saving advances. Her memoir illuminates the difference one person can make in words delivered to a vulnerable patient, and how trust can provide a measure of comfort during the ensuing weeks, months, and years. Dr. Gadgeel was able to give Dawn hope without exaggerating the seriousness of her condition. It reminded me of the family talk we all had with my brother-in-law's neurosurgeon, at the time of his hospital discharge following surgery for his glioblastoma. Dr. Olivi was kind and caring, and expertly attuned to answering the questions my brother-in-law was ready to ask. He had no need to push ahead to discuss all aspects of that devastating diagnosis at that time. It was clear that he would be available when Alan wanted to talk more.

Dawn has been working on her book or several books since her time at Hopkins. I'm not sure if publishing a book was on the "bucket list" she made for herself when she was told her prognosis, but her diagnosis must have served as a driver as well as gripping subject matter for this memoir. It was probably 30 years ago when I read a draft of Dawn's first novel – a mystery set in Michigan. I thought it had enormous promise, both because I could hear her voice, and because it gave me a completely new sense of Michigan, one I still carry with me. My childhood was dominated by the Delaware River, terribly polluted in the pre-Clean Water Act era, but beautiful nonetheless, and always a destination or necessary detour for bike rides, runs, and car trips. We were also not far from the Atlantic Ocean and I always considered lakes a bit dull. After reading her book, I could picture a childhood surrounded by lakes, neighborhoods in which everyone had a lake in their back yard or down the street, and summers spent walking or biking to the lake where there might be a lifeguard and where one could spread a towel and bask in the sun. I'm not sure what happened to that book, but I always hoped I would see the next version and a published copy.

Dawn understood that she might live five years, and she resolved to do just that. Her 5-year plan included Rachel getting launched after college, Connor's junior year abroad and graduation from college, Nathaniel's graduation from high school, and a family trip to Paris. I like to think this memoir was also on that list, as something she is doing for herself, but also for us, especially for her children. I loved reading it because again I could hear her voice, both the earnestness and the sarcasm, and sometimes that muffled laugh that just seems to burst out of her when discussing life's absurdities. I liked the clever transformation of her persistent negative thoughts into John Boehner's disapproving looks at Obama. I can appreciate her wanting to be with her long dead parents on her "first cancer birthday." I still have that urge to call my own long dead mother when something noteworthy happens.

My brother-in-law talked about how the "gift of cancer" brings everything important into focus. In the close to four years he lived following his diagnosis, he urged all of us to appreciate our lives and make the most of our time here. Yes, it sounds like such a platitude. Michael Pollan wrote about trying to describe transcendent states on hallucinogens – it can't fail to sound like a Hallmark card, despite the profound experience. I see Dawn's 5-year plan as her version of placing the bag of ice on the thermostat. Who knows how long it will last? But, let's celebrate the warmth, and yes, bring all the important things into focus. Another miracle! It is the miracle of the everyday, which in Dawn's words could feel "…so ordinary and extraordinary at the same time."

—*Marie R Griffin, Nashville, TN Jan 8 2019*

I. Tempest

October 29, 2012 – December 17, 2012

Hurricane Sandy

The wind from Hurricane Sandy swept into Michigan and onto the campus of Oakland University, a college nestled within a suburb of Detroit. I wheeled my teaching bag behind me as I walked to my van after night class ended. The wind wrestled with the bag, and loose papers inside an open pocket fluttered. Although the air felt warm swirling around me, it was strong enough to make me worry about Nathaniel, at home alone in East Lansing, and about my van being buffeted across the dark lanes of I-75 on my evening commute, especially in the tundra of open space south of Flint. Yet before tackling the journey, I needed to make it to my vehicle.

The walk had become more difficult. My lungs couldn't take in enough air, and my legs didn't want to lift and move forward. I needed a puff on my inhaler. I lurched around the bend at the base of O'Dowd Hall where a construction fence fashioned an orange skirt ruffle at the ground level. There, under the gleam of the parking lot lights, the dust on my van glowed. My shoes clumped against the pavement of the side-walk, and the rolling sound of the teaching bag wheels continued until I reached my destination.

Once in the van, I rummaged through my purse for an albuterol inhaler. Two puffs. The attack subsided almost immediately.

After I got onto the expressway, I called home. I made my commuting call twice a week, usually to my husband Tim, but this week, Nathaniel answered. Tim was in Chicago, Connor had just started his first semester at Kalamazoo College, and Rachel had play rehearsal that evening in Detroit – and would then be staying over with her boyfriend in Hazel Park. Nathaniel remained alone in the house. I needed to get home to him.

I told him that class had ended, and I was on the road. We joked about his not starting a fire in the kitchen. He reminded me that since he'd recently turned fourteen, he could take care of himself. But he begged me to stop at McDonald's when I got off the expressway at Marsh Road near home. I told him he was fortunate that the golden arches rose right next to my path. I refused to make detours this late at night.

As I drove on I-75 heading north toward Flint, lights from suburbia fading in the rearview mirror, the wind began toying with my van, pushing against the sides. A few strong gales shoved the van first toward the center of the lane and then toward the shoulder, pushing me back and forth. I clenched the steering wheel. Ahead, to the right, the face of an archetypal Jesus shone down from a sign advertising the Dixie Baptist Church, an I-75 landmark that had been around since my childhood. Jesus beamed beatifically onto the expressway. I wondered how many people on the East Coast in Hurricane Sandy's path would pray to him that night.

When I came in the door near midnight with hot, greasy fries, Nathaniel smirked his thanks and began inhaling his food. I went through the house, extinguishing all the lights he'd switched on to bury the dark. I climbed the stairs to the second floor, each step requiring labor.

As I reached the top, where the dusty bookshelf I'd made in high school rested against the wall, I spotted again the paperback copy of *Catch-22* that rested there.

I'd noticed it a few days earlier during the previous weekend. I'd driven to Kalamazoo to visit Connor for Parents' Weekend at Kalamazoo College. Because it was his freshman year, I wanted to take him out to dinner at Food Dance, the trendy restaurant in town. We sat together in an open room, enjoying the clatter of plates and the tantalizing food choices. Our first dinner as parent and college student.

That night, on my journey back to Lansing, Tim called from Chicago. We talked briefly, but he had a dinner to attend. When I arrived home,

I'd climbed the stairs in my house, breathing heavily as I reached the top. Thinking of my inhaler next to the bed, I noticed Joseph Heller's *Catch-22* on the landing bookshelf. I reached down to retrieve it from a lower shelf and felt an odd wobble in my mid-section, not unlike the flopping sensation I'd felt when pregnant with my children, all of them acrobatic in the womb. Yet this sensation radiated higher, in my chest.

I'd experienced the movie version of *Catch-22* before reading the book, and I appreciated the film's comic moments – the Simon and Garfunkel characters, the Bob Newhart role of Major Major Major Major. The funny parts helped me tolerate the anguish of the film's dramatic narrative. Now, each time I climbed the stairs and saw the book's spine on my bookshelf, I forgot the comedy, remembering the repeated flashbacks to the scene in which Yossarian, the main character, tries to keep his friend warm in the cold, windy sterility of his memory. He keeps flashing back to the moment in which he utters reassurances to the comrade with whom he's endured a plane crash. He wants to provide comfort.

And then he lifts the garment covering his friend. To tuck it in at the side. Or so I thought, as I watched the movie the first time. Or to lift the friend up? I couldn't tell.

Yossarian raises the material higher, and when he looks beneath it, he finally realizes that half of his friend's chest is gone. As a viewer, I experienced the same realization simultaneously, knowing then, that all the optimism in the world won't save the man. I felt sucker-punched by Yossarian's discovery, wounded by the hope maintained throughout the earlier flashbacks.

Now, as I stumbled to my bed on a second late night, this one much windier than the first, I tried to forget about Yossarian. Yet I couldn't forget the sensation in my chest from the weekend. I needed to call my doctor in the morning.

I drank coffee in my pajamas and held the phone to my ear as the automated menu explained which number to press for the nurse queue. Impatient, I lectured myself about cutting things close. I'd allowed myself

5

to return to bed after I dropped Nathaniel off at school that morning – fell onto the tangled sheets, exhausted. But the clock read 11:00 AM now. School got out at 3:00 PM; I needed to pick up him and my friend's daughter, Mohra.

The phone nurse finally came on the line and listened to my symptoms, asking me a few more questions about my shortness of breath and then cutting me off with an apology. They couldn't see me in the office. My symptoms so closely resembled those of a heart attack that I needed to go to the emergency department at the hospital. Of course, she realized my fear about the trip being time-consuming. "Try the St. Lawrence campus instead of Sparrow Hospital downtown," she said. "There might be less of a wait."

At the hospital, in the triage room, the nurse took my pulse ox, 97% saturation. She seemed surprised that I'd come to an emergency department, and I felt self-conscious, thinking I'd overreacted. "You've been sick, right? A cold?"

No, I told her. No cold. No drainage. Just the shortness of breath. And a weird sensation in my chest when I bent over to pick things up.

The resident who followed the nurse listened as I explained my situation again – the funny palpitation on the evening that I came home from Kalamazoo, the shortness of breath on Oakland's campus on Monday. No cold. No drainage. She nodded and didn't interrupt, and her intense listening soothed me. She sent me for a chest X-ray. An hour later I learned that I needed a CT scan to follow up on the X-ray. They shuttled me off for the scan.

I tried to reach Tim but couldn't get through. He'd been away for almost a week and hadn't mastered his new iPhone before he'd left for Chicago. I fretted, wondering if my previous calls and texts had entered some mail void on his touch screen, though I knew from his schedule that he was likely driving the rented van back from Chicago with his coworker Julie. Tim worked for the American Board of Emergency Medicine. The exams he helped to create and administer certified emergency physicians who worked in emergency departments across the country, analyzing symptoms, ordering medical tests, and providing care. I was in an emergency department attended by a resident who would one day take the Board's exam. But I didn't care if an exam question in the organization's item bank matched my symptoms. I just wanted to reach someone who could pick up Nathaniel and Mohra from school.

I wasn't angry or worried, but I recalled the panic I'd experienced when the kids were younger, before cell phones existed, when things happened while Tim was away and I had to deal with them on my own. The time my middle son got chicken pox ten days after his sister (making his case the more difficult, dangerous case) and I spent hours in a rocking chair, holding his feverish body. The time the ants in our cape cod attic spaces hatched, and large, full bodied, winged, black ants began pouring out of a crack in the crevice of a living room bookshelf, flying around the room above the heads of my children. Something always went wrong when Tim went out of town. What would the problem be this time?

The hospital staff brought me a turkey sandwich. When it became clear that I couldn't leave anytime soon, I called Madhu and told her that I'd contacted the middle school so they could send Nathaniel home on the bus, and she should do the same for Mohra. She remained silent as I explained my predicament and then wished me luck in her quiet voice. I contacted my brother-in-law Terry and told him that he shouldn't alarm anyone, but if he heard from Tim, I needed to reach him. He promised to check on Nathaniel later in the evening.

When the resident returned, she explained that an odd spot appeared in my left lung on both the X-ray and CT. Maybe pneumonia. I'd had pneumonia as a child several times, back when treatment included oxygen tents augmented with ice delivered by wise-cracking attendants who made kids laugh when they delivered the cold. I told the resident it didn't feel like pneumonia, and she nodded her head in agreement. "We want you to have an Echocardiogram," she said. "But we don't have the equipment here. We're sending you to Sparrow Hospital downtown, and they'll do the ECHO in the morning."

By the time the ambulance arrived, I reached Nathaniel, who'd made it home on the bus without incident. He took my news about the hospital visit well, responding in his usual monotone. Tim finally called, alarmed to hear the news. He hadn't received my texts. He and Julie had just entered Michigan on I-94. He would drive straight to Sparrow after dropping her off. "What happened?" he said. "I didn't even know you were sick!"

I tried to explain the details, but the nurse told me the EMTs were arriving, so I had to cut it short. The EMTs entered with a stretcher and gathered my belongings – my coat, my purse, and the sack of papers I'd brought along to grade – cramming them all under the wheeled stretcher and transferring me. The nurse swaddled me in a heated blanket and sent me out into the wind, where paramedics loaded me into the back of the vehicle and latched me into place.

In Washington, D.C., the federal government had been closed for the day as Hurricane Sandy pushed through the region. Off the coast of Chicago, in the waters of Lake Michigan, a buoy recorded near-record waves of 21.7 feet in height.

As we pulled out of the ambulance loop in Lansing, Michigan, the rear of my dirt-shrouded van appeared through the window, languishing in its parking spot. I wondered how it would get home.

ECHO

My morning nurse wore a plastic headband with springs attached. Each spring sported a yellow and black plastic critter which jiggled and bounced as she walked. The springs matched the corkscrew quality of her hair, curly and yellow-orange. She'd woken me for the Echocardiogram (ECHO). Yes, she confirmed, she had transformed herself into a bee for Halloween. Wearing the headband was the only way she could be silly on the cardiac floor since the hospital had moved to color-coded scrubs for nurses, aides, and respiratory therapists. I knew that Nathaniel, my allergy boy, did not plan to wear a costume to school that day or to go trick-or-treating in the evening either. He had outgrown the joy of collecting a bunch of candy he couldn't eat anyway because of his severe allergies to milk, eggs, and peanuts.

My bumble bee nurse got me up and prepared, ready to be wheeled off to the ECHO station. Throughout the halls, I saw bits of Halloween – a costume here and there, mixed in with the scrubs, and orange pumpkins in variations of plastic, ceramic, clay, artificial vines with rust and magenta leaves twining around pumpkin bases.

The ECHO tech explained that she would celebrate with her daughter later. No doubt other parents would enjoy the daytime celebration at the school, but what she anticipated most was moving with her daughter and the flashlight from house to house later in the evening.

She rolled the Doppler around my chest as she spoke. The foam wedge she'd tucked behind my back earlier kept me in a propped position with my body angled toward her and the thick wand she held. With her other hand, she squeezed warm jelly onto my breast plate, moving it up to my neck and collar bone and then down to my breast plate again and

9

near my ribs. The Doppler searched for my heart and lungs. The tech kept her conversational patter going, not revealing in her voice any irregularities she might see, instead apologizing for how much gel the imaging required, promising that she would give me lots of towels to wipe myself. After a few more glides of the wand, she handed me lots of towels and called for transport. Then I rode once again through the orange, autumnal halls to the cardiac care unit on the fourth floor.

Back in my room, I nibbled at breakfast, eavesdropping on my roommate's phone conversations. She wanted to get home to her children, so she could take them trick-or-treating or at least spend Halloween with them. She needed the doctors to discharge her. Later, she confided to me that she had congestive heart failure and came to the hospital frequently. Her prognosis wasn't great, but she would live for a while. She worried about her children and her boyfriend's children. She'd met her boyfriend when his wife died of congestive heart failure. I felt overwhelmed by the magnitude of the sorrow they'd experienced. I realized that I'd heard her voice the night before, on the phone, speaking to a young child. Via FaceTime.

She explained that she had lots of fluid in her heart and took a drug known as Lasix to drain that fluid. But she'd been in the hospital long enough. When the nursing staff came in, she reminded them that she needed to see her doctors for discharge. I found her manner edgy at times, but I felt a dogged admiration for her emphatic manner of commanding attention. A male nurse came in and began teasing her; she told him he was the only one who understood her.

Tim had arrived the previous night when he got back to town, and I sent him home to Rachel and Nathaniel. He returned around 1:00 PM, after I'd finished the ECHO, and we exchanged only a few brief comments before a man entered the room and walked purposefully toward my bed, handing me his card. Ronald Pacis, D.O. Cardiologist. He was a hefty man with a large neck and solid arms, almost like a body-builder's, with dark hair and serious but friendly eyes behind his glasses. "I read your ECHO and came right over. You have fluid in your pericardium – that sack around your heart? And fluid in your left lung as well."

He waited for me to process the information. I liked his style, which struck me as no-nonsense, but helpful and explanatory. I nodded, wanting him to finish.

"The pericardium is a sack," he repeated, "kind of like a net, around your heart. But it's small – really small. Which poses a problem. With all the liquid, the sack is filling up and squeezing the heart." He illustrated the squeezing action with his fist, fingers and knuckles pulsating. "The condition is called tamponade. We need a cardiac surgeon to get in there, make a small hole in the pericardium, and drain that fluid so the pressure comes off the heart. We're going to try to get it done today. I'll send a surgeon by." He looked at Tim and back at me.

I felt relieved that the solution to my problem appeared so obvious to a medical doctor, even though I didn't understand the underlying cause for the pressure.

"Why does the fluid build up?" I asked.

He shrugged. "We don't always know. Often the buildup results from a virus. Sometimes it's congestive heart failure." I kept looking at his face, but I thought of my new roommate, wondering if her condition had started with tamponade. Wondering if she could hear our conversation. "But we'll know more when we go in there," he continued. "Sometimes the cause is something really random, and it never happens again." He did his exam and told us to sit tight; he would send a cardiac surgeon.

I was prepared to go with the flow. And sit tight. Because soon I'd hear the whistle of a fast-paced train that would stop in front of me, chuffing, waiting just long enough for me to get on board before it careened through a darker landscape. But for the moment, I would sit tight. I'd already notified the English Department at Oakland University that they should cancel my classes for the day. I had no place else I needed to be for Halloween.

Chest Tube

The voices grew louder, and when I forced my eyelids open, surgical scrubs materialized in the form of human shapes. Two nurses continued to yell. "Dawn! Wake up! Dawn!" Later I would learn that clock hands had passed midnight and Halloween had slipped away.

I lay on a bed in the recovery room. "There she is!" one nurse said as I opened my eyes more fully. I'd entered the fog of anesthesia on the last day of October, and I'd come out on November 1. The cardiovascular and thoracic surgeon had already visited. He'd suctioned out more blood and fluid than he'd ever seen once he opened my pericardial window, he told Tim.

After the nurses checked my vitals, a transport team took me to a different room on the cardiac unit. Tim and the new nurse explained that I was now hooked up to a chest tube.

On the left side of my chest, white gauze and tape covered an area from which a thick, clear rubber tube emerged. Through the clear walls of the rubber, I saw the swirl of pink and red filaments and yellow fluid, like sea anemones behind the glass of an aquarium tank wall. The tube ran toward the floor, connecting to a large container at the bottom of a pole next to my bed.

The container resembled a coin bank I'd had when I was younger, where each type of coin had its own chamber, making the stacks of pennies, nickels, dimes, and quarters appear formal, precise. This container had chambers as well, although I didn't know their purpose yet. Later I would learn that the contraption was a chest drainage unit; my release date from the hospital was directly linked to how much or how little fluid rose in the chambers of the device. Hatch marks at various intervals on the unit indicated liter amounts. I'd spend the rest of my hospital days waiting for the volume of fluid in the unit to ebb, or better yet, stop completely.

I knew the waters rose now in New Jersey and people there likely marked the height of the waters swirling around their homes and businesses, just as others had during Hurricane Katrina. We shared a need for recession. Outside the hospital, the wind still gusted loudly, and although I'd travelled five floors up from the surgical unit in the basement to the cardiac unit on the fourth floor of Neumann Tower, leaves rose from the ground and spiraled high in the air, visible under the spotlights of the building from the window next to my bed. The clock read 3:00 AM, and I told Tim to go home and be with Rachel and Nathaniel. He'd called them earlier along with my sisters and his mom to report that I'd come out of surgery safely. We'd decided not to tell Connor yet because we didn't want him to lose focus during his first term of college.

Still doped up from the surgery, I tried to wedge my back against the left bedside rail, leery of the tube that looped over the Stryker bed panels, wondering where the ocean of fluid in my pericardium and lung cavity had come from. But the painkillers pulled me back into a foggy dreamscape of sea creatures, and I drifted back into ignorance.

My goal that next morning was to order breakfast. Someone from the hospital had explained that patients ordered their own meals through a menu-style system. According to my medical chart, I needed to limit my sugar intake to 2 sugars per meal, but beyond that restriction, I could have whatever else I wanted, within reason. Within reason meant only one entrée.

I wasn't hungry but desperately wanted coffee. According to the dietician, I should order it with breakfast, which would arrive approximately forty-five minutes after I placed the order.

Other things would fill my time. Blood draws. Bedside chest x-rays. Doctors' rounds.

The cardiac surgery people came to report that even though they'd taken care of most of the fluid in my chest on Halloween, the chest tube collection device would capture the residual, which should taper off and disappear. They'd taken a biopsy when they'd opened the pericardial window, but the results hadn't come in yet. They explained that 50 percent of the time, pericardial and pleural effusions resulted from admittedly frightening causes: tuberculosis, cancer, a rare infection. However, 50 percent of the time, the cause of effusions was indeterminate — the result of some random virus that would never occur again.

They planned to spend some time trying to determine a specific cause, but their primary goal was to drain my lungs and then remove the chest tube. We would do everything possible to reduce the fluid and when the fluid output remained below a certain level in a 24-hour period, they would remove the tube. That was how the process worked.

The cardiologist's people stopped in to share their congratulations that the surgery had gone well. The cardiovascular and thoracic surgeon had done a biopsy, but they didn't have the results yet. When they listened to my chest, my heart sounded good. They would return.

The hospitalist from my internist's office came in and listened to my chest as well. My own internist didn't do rounds, so I tried to accept this hospitalist as a substitute, even though we had no established rapport. I missed my own doctor, who had a humorous way of addressing issues. This doctor asked few questions. One day at a time, she said.

The infectious disease team members who arrived next had been referred to the case because of the large amount of fluid that had been removed from my pericardium and lungs. Had I travelled outside the country in recent weeks? Had I been around anyone with tuberculosis? I didn't travel much, I told them. I managed a soup kitchen about five times a year, with clients who usually didn't have access to health care. Guests sat at folding tables in the gym; coughing sounds came from all four corners when we served the meal. We used bleach when we cleaned.

In between visits from doctors, I tried to create order. Tim had emailed my chairperson to tell her that my surgery had gone well. He'd left it at that, to give me options. I needed to figure out a plan for my Monday and Wednesday classes. I didn't want to get a substitute or cancel them for very long. I'd spent the first half of the semester teaching students how to give each other feedback in the small group setting; now we were supposed to begin larger group workshops in both classes I taught. How could I hand that task off to a substitute?

Worrying about classes provided me with a convenient distraction. I found it easier to plan my return to work and revise the syllabi for my two courses than to face the more immediate question of when I would be able to go the bathroom on my own. When the chest tube would come out. When they would determine why my lungs and pericardium had drawn in and concealed so much fluid.

I'd learned how to order my food from the new guest menu Sparrow provided, but I remained reluctant to eat. I'd entered the hospital in the constipation phase of my irritable bowel syndrome cycle. Now, after surgery, my intestines felt swollen, my gut heavy. The nurses kept pestering me to go to the bathroom, yet when I finally agreed, they wheeled over an industrial-looking commode with stainless steel handles. My chest ached at the prospect of using it.

They pulled the curtain between my bed and that of the roommate I hadn't yet met. Then, holding my tubes of oxygen, my IV line, and my chest tube, they shifted me from the bed to the toilet. I closed my eyes, trying to concentrate and ignore the voices of my roommate's visitors.

The commode on wheels fit snugly next to my bed – too snugly. Its awkward shape pushed into the folds of the curtain that separated the beds. I opened my eyes and stared down at the floor, noticing a man's shoes underneath the curtain. Brown, worn. Creases in the top. I had never gone to the bathroom in the presence of a stranger's shoes before. His visitor's chair backed up against my commode. I felt more defeated than I had since I'd entered the hospital.

They expected me to shit over some strange man's feet.

Six days into my hospital visit, I found my focus. I fell in love with a nurse named Danielle. Dani for short. She loved biscuits and gravy for breakfast, which her boyfriend made for her and his son on quiet weekends, sometimes before she left for her 7:00 AM shift on the 4th floor of Sparrow. During the week that I met her, she'd taken extra shifts to cover for a coworker, so she served as my primary nurse for four days in a row. I don't remember which day of my hospitalization I first met her, but I will never forget that she gave me more of her attention than I had any right to expect. She made it her goal to get my chest tube out and get me home.

She wrote on my designated white board which hung across from my bed that I could go to the bathroom on my own – I was NOT a fall risk. She taught me how to pull the suction tube out of the wall, so I could wrap it around the chest tube pole, wheel the whole contraption to the bathroom, and shit alone in peace. She told me that some people ended up naming their chest drainage systems, especially the pole part. I devoured the independence and permission she granted me, though I still joked about escaping, using the chest tube liquid for fuel.

Dani wore her long, blonde hair back in a ponytail, and in addition to biscuits and gravy, she loved Tim Bits from Tim Horton's. The week she pulled all those shifts, she craved them fiercely, and when I said I'd never had them, she explained that they were just regular old donut holes with a fancy name.

On the day my chest tube drainage output went up instead of down, I was so disappointed that I couldn't rouse myself to smile back at Dani when she gave me her usual afternoon smirk, wondering if she could get me to drink some apple juice with Miralax since my shitting, even in peace, remained minimal. When Dani noticed my lack of response to the Miralax prompt, she squeezed my arm, urging me to view the fluid increase as a mere setback. She knew my still unnamed chest drainage unit would cooperate the next day.

Outside the hospital, the wind had finally ceased its battering of the East Coast. The television flashed stories about the damaging effects of the storm, downgraded from a Hurricane to Superstorm Sandy, with consequences no less devastating in spite of the name change.

The election had geared up, with pundits predicting a change in the existing momentum for Romney. In addition to needing to get back to work, I needed to get out of the hospital to vote on Election Day. Each night I watched the news with dinner, concerned about my vote. I didn't hate Romney, but I'd devoted myself to Obama once I'd read his book *Dreams For My Father*. I'd rejoiced at his election in 2008 and wanted to see him reelected. Between Tim's juggling of his work, the kids, and hospital time with me, he ran to the Township Clerk's office and secured an absentee ballot. I didn't accept defeat with the chest tube; I just wanted my vote to count.

Nine days after my admission to the hospital, on the day the doctors decided that my drainage had decreased, they could take out the chest tube, and I could even go home as well, Dani helped the cardiovascular and thoracic surgeon's point person set up the drop cloth next to my hospital bed. The drop cloth served as a protective measure, meant to secure the waste and protect others from its potential danger. My chest tube waste included the tubing, the collection unit, any gauze surrounding the tubes and all the tape that anchored the tube to my skin. The cardiovascular and thoracic surgeon's people explained that they would snip the small stitches holding the tube in place, and then they would pull. They would give me warning. Dani looked on. "I love watching this real cardiac stuff," she said. And then, when she noticed my apprehension, she reassured me. "You've done all the hard work. Really. It will just be a tug."

I wanted a more specific description of what the tug would feel like. I didn't know what I feared, but the fear crept solidly into my limbs. The tube had resided inside my chest for days, and although it was an alien object, my body had adjusted to it. I feared its departure.

They told me they were ready, and we should count to three together.

And then, at three, I felt the tug, which produced an odd sensation but not a painful one.

I was now officially unfettered. Free.

When I look back at that moment of intense apprehension, I recognize that the fear of that tug masked other, larger fears. I still didn't know why the pleural and pericardial effusion had developed, and I should have persisted with my questioning, with my queries about the biopsy results. Instead, in that moment, I worried about the pain of the tug, a tug no sharper than that of one of my babies being tugged from the womb. The tube was out. I would go home.

I never went back to tell Dani thank you. By the time Christmas rolled around, when I'd thought I'd be sending a gift to her and the other nurses on the floor, I had instead just begun to deal with a startling diagnosis I'd never anticipated.

For some reason, it was important to me back then to leave that success we shared alone, to keep it unadulterated by the truth. I'd had a pericardial and pleural effusion of enormous proportions, but the doctors had fixed the problem, and I'd survived. With Dani's help, I'd ditched the chest tube and walked out of the hospital a few days after Barack Obama was reelected President of the United States.

The truth of what caused my effusion, what led to the chest tube in the first place, did not seem important on the day Sparrow discharged me. As Dani had wrapped up the drop cloth with my chest tube waste, we'd celebrated sweet success. Yet sometimes, I want to find her and tell her that a Tim Horton's shop has moved in just down at the corner, a short, brisk walk from my house. And sometimes, when I order a coffee and see Tim Bits on the menu, I want to bring her some. I want to return to those hours when it was just me and Dani, the Miralax, and the chest tube. When I had only small goals.

The Facebook Message

When Rachel walked into my hospital room three days after the surgery, the pale, puffy tissue around her eyes transformed her green jeweled irises into small chips of clouded gray rimmed in red. "Hi!" She created a lilt in her voice to greet me, but I could sense her true mood.

"You broke up," I guessed. She nodded, and tears slipped down her face. I scooted to the left side of the bed, close to my chest tube pole so she could slide in next to me.

Stroking her hair, I told her how sorry I was, though neither of us was surprised. She and Nick had argued a lot since she'd moved back home after college. She complained often about the problems with long-distance relationships. Since he lived only an hour and a half away yet didn't travel to meet as often as she did, the distance struck me as a natural cause for a break up, in place of boredom, waning attraction, or lack of effort. Still, only six weeks had elapsed since they'd performed together in a production of *Spring Awakening* in Lansing. We'd been jubilant because of Nick's success in the role of Moritz, the neurasthenic adolescent, and pleased for Rachel with her smaller chorus role.

As Moritz, Nick sang "I Don't Do Sadness." Unfortunately, the lyrics of the song became the message Rachel heard distinctly from him after my emergency cardiac surgery.

Two days after my release from the hospital, a few days after the break up, I sat wrapped in a quilt on my family room couch with Rachel across the room, her laptop engaged. She inhaled sharply, gulping air in a prolonged gasp. "No!" she choked out.

She shook her head back and forth. "No," she wailed louder. In spite of her reputation as the family's drama queen, I always tried to take her

19

expressions of emotion seriously. She and I were of the same ilk, in many ways, aside from the drama. We liked to process "orally," my term for analyzing our feelings in detail, dissecting them with the hope of learning some truth about ourselves or a situation. At least that's what we told ourselves.

But I could be a bit dramatic, too. "I told you not to go on Facebook after the break up," I wailed in my alto, a register lower.

She dropped the laptop to the carpet and pitched forward onto the family room floor.

"Oh, my God, this can't be happening."

I untangled myself from the quilt and held my right hand under my left breast at the incision site. Later I would think of Sanford, the father on *Sanford and Son*, who always clutched his heart and moaned "This is the Big One, Elizabeth," to manipulate his son. I should have gone that route. Instead, I reached with my free hand toward the laptop, grasping the edge of it and pulling it over to where I sat on the couch.

I didn't recognize the photo in the profile picture of the person who had sent the message.

"Who is this guy?" I said.

"Someone Nick's brother knows – a guy named JJ."

Rachel remained crouched in a ball on the floor. The private Facebook message JJ had sent her read like a tabloid article or a clip from *Entertainment Tonight*. It began with a reassuring comment about how he knew Rachel was a nice person and didn't deserve to hear the bad news from him. But he wanted to tell her about what had been going on between his own girlfriend, ex-girlfriend now, and Nick. He guessed Rachel probably knew that the two had been friends for a while. But in truth, they were more than friends, which was why his ex-girlfriend had just broken up with him. This ex-girlfriend had gone to Nick's house and slept with him just a few days earlier. While Nick and Rachel were still together.

"It's not true," I said. "This guy's just some weirdo, yanking your chain. You need to talk to Nick. Or just stop opening up your Facebook."

She still lay on the floor, tears running. "I can't believe it." Her shoulders shook with sobs. I was less patient than usual, my mind grappling with how to create order in my postoperative life; the situation had become more of a soap opera than I needed.

"This is ridiculous. You need to call him," I said again.

"No," she groaned from the floor.

"I'm calling him," I said, uncharacteristically decisive. I grabbed my cell from the table and hobbled up. With a blanket pulled around my shoulders, I stumbled to the next room. The action felt like a pre-emptive strike on my part, and a voice in my head took me to task, telling me to stay out of it. To remain sympathetic but uninvolved. Yet I'd been the star of my own reality show for a few weeks and I refused to give up the stage. I didn't want any drama to sweep over me unless I could be a part of it. Center stage. "You're making this about you," the voice inside my head told me.

No, I wasn't, I argued back. I didn't have the energy for drama.

"Don't call him!" she yelled.

I went to the dining room, a kitchen away from her, searching through my cell phone, trying to figure out where Nick's name was in my contacts. I opened the door to the sunroom, and a wave of cold air from the closed-off room came at me.

Back in the kitchen, Rachel shrieked at Tim, imploring him. "Don't let her do it!"

My hands shook as I highlighted Nick's name and pushed Send.

He answered on the second ring. I told him why I was calling – that some guy had sent Rachel a weird Facebook message and I needed him to clear it up, regardless of their status.

Because I'd just gotten out of the hospital. And I didn't want any more drama.

He knew about the message, was so sorry JJ had sent it, sorry that I was ill, sorry, really sorry, about everything. He would call her.

21

I came out of the cold room feeling both relief and guilt, knowing I'd gone too far but feeling justified. Rachel sat crying quietly at the table. I told her Nick would call her in a few minutes. She looked up, surprised.

"What did you think I would do?" I said. "Ream him out? I wasn't going there. Besides, I don't believe it's true. He'll straighten it out."

Her phone buzzed, and she drew in a long breath and moved toward the stairs. "Hello?" she gulped into the phone. She nodded, inhaled, and climbed the stairs to her room, a refuge providing privacy, the phone pressed to her ear.

I looked at Tim. "I've only been home from the hospital two days," I said. "I didn't want to deal with the drama."

"I know," Tim said.

During the spring of Rachel's senior year in high school, I committed an unthinkable crime as a parent. She had earned the coveted role of Marian, the librarian, in *The Music Man*. She'd fallen in love with the musical at an early age and had even dressed as Marian, the librarian, one Halloween in fourth grade. She'd gotten her dream role.

Her senior spring had been a promising one in so many ways – she'd gained admission into a selective and notable musical theatre program at a relatively inexpensive in-state school. A new boyfriend had spent part of the winter and early spring bonding with our family – playing video games with my sons, watching *Transformers* with us, debating whether Megan Fox was merely attractive or a classic beauty, and making pudding with Rachel.

Her first boyfriend had been a nice enough guy who drove her to and from school each day, relieving us of a time-consuming chore. When he came to our house, he tolerated our presence for only brief periods of time, always testing boundaries.

But Nando, the new guy, had been in the cast of their high school production of *Working*. He'd described her solo as Kate, the housewife, to my husband in artistic, admiring terms. Each time he visited became family party time. Nathaniel hung around for chances to join in; Connor developed a fondness for The Strokes based on Nando's recommendation. I celebrated my anxious daughter's security and happiness in this new relationship.

But both were fleeting. By the time Tech Week arrived for the show, Nando struck all of us as remote and aloof. Rachel became distracted by his distance and his seeming interest in a freshman chorus girl who clearly had a crush on him. I told Rachel she needed to talk to him, but she wouldn't. She dealt with her anxiety by raising her head in a typical Marian posture, feigning indifference. She didn't want to reveal weakness or appear vulnerable.

I didn't want her to explode and sabotage her hard work. Whether I cared about her welfare or took on the role of imperious stage mom or a bit of both, I convinced myself that someone must address the uncertainty of the relationship before performances began.

So I stepped in. I went to the school at the end of rehearsal one afternoon, located Nando, and took him aside. I told him to break up with her if that's the way things were headed.

That she didn't need to blow her success in the only lead in high school she'd been granted just because he didn't know how to handle his changed feelings. "Tell her tonight," I said.

That night after play practice, they drove around for a bit, and he broke up with her. She came home but didn't cry. The next day, the fishbowl effect of high school theater kicked in, but she held her head up and enjoyed her run as Marian in spite of heartbreak.

I don't know why I overstepped the bounds of wise parental practice on those two occasions with my daughter's boyfriends. It would have been far wiser to let Rachel solve her own problems. I can persuade myself that I watched out for her, protected her feelings and her future, but how do I know that I didn't act simply to become the drama queen myself, entering the fray to add to the combustion?

I tell myself that I acted in part because these young men, however immature they may have been at the time, affected our whole family when they became a part of us. And perhaps I didn't give Rachel enough credit. I didn't believe that she might have enough strength and bravery to handle things on her own. It's a good story that I tell myself. Sometimes I believe it. In subsequent conversations with Nick after the Facebook message, Rachel learned that he had, in fact, slept with JJ's girlfriend. Rachel buried the drama but spent honest time sorting through emotions, sometimes travelling to Hazel Park to challenge Nick face-to-face. "You told me to talk to Nando afterward, and I never did," she told me. "I needed closure this time."

For a while, I had only two contacts in my cell phone beginning with the letter "N" – Nathaniel, my son, and Nick. A year after Nick broke up with Rachel, a full year after my surgery, my kids asked me why I kept Nick's phone number since I could so easily make a mistake and send him a message intended for Nathaniel.

I kept his number because he answered the phone when I called two days after getting out of the hospital. He answered, and he called my daughter as I'd requested. Like Nando, he listened. Maybe he feared a lunatic mother, but he listened nonetheless.

Statistics I
(What I Told My Students)

I returned to the classroom on Wednesday, November 14, 2012. Five days after the visiting nurse okayed me for driving. Six days after my discharge from the hospital. Eight days after Barack Obama was re-elected President of the United States of America. Fourteen days after Halloween surgery. On that day, I told my students not to worry about anything. Not about how we were going to catch up. Not about whether we'd have any additional class cancellations.

And especially not about my health and well-being.

I shared the science that so many doctors and health professionals had explained to me in the hospital. Approximately 50 percent of the time, pericardial effusion and cardiac tamponade were caused by something unknown. A virus. A fluke. Something of idiopathic origin.

The other 50 percent of the time, the cause was something serious — tuberculosis, lupus, cancer, or a rare but deadly germ. The doctors in the hospital had pursued potential causes and had found nothing that raised their suspicions.

I now belonged to the healthy group. I was one of the 50 percent who would never know what caused the problem. One of the lucky 50 percent.

Biopsy Results

Someone from the cardiologist's office called after I'd had a routine post-operative ECHO. The person on the line said she needed to know the pharmacy to which she should FAX the furosemide prescription. I needed the prescription to empty the fluid remaining in my lungs.

The ECHO appointment I'd kept on the day before I returned to teaching had been, I thought, my last crucial appointment before I put the hospital and surgery experience behind me. I had no reason to think I needed any more follow-up. But I knew about furosemide – Lasix – from the hospital roommate I'd had before the cardiologist diagnosed my tamponade. She took it for her congestive heart failure. Why were they prescribing it for me now?

I gave the woman from the cardiology office my pharmacy information and hung up, knowing I hadn't asked the right questions. I needed to make another phone call.

I dialed the thoracic surgeon's office and told the person who answered that I'd had surgery on Halloween but had never gotten a biopsy report. My own internist had tried to find the results on her computer the previous week; the report didn't seem to exist. Could a nurse please call me with those results? The receptionist promised to research the issue.

A few hours later, the phone rang. The person on the line said the doctor wanted to see me. Could I make it in that afternoon, at, say, 2:00 PM?

I knew the news would be dire. The biopsy results had been elusive all along. I'd finally relaxed, believing that I belonged to the 50 percent of the population that had pleural and pericardial effusion for no discernible reason. I was one of the lucky ones who didn't have cancer, or tuberculosis, or a crazy infection that eluded the infectious disease doctors.

As I awaited the appointment, Rachel returned from her work shift at Best Buy, and I was forced to tell her about my unexpected doctor's appointment. I needed her to pick up Nathaniel and Mohra if I didn't get back in time. I didn't want to burden her, but I suspected I wouldn't be home for a while – I might stop off at her dad's office after the appointment. I needed her to pick up her brother and pretend that everything was fine. Because who knows. Maybe it was.

She would handle it. "I love you!" she said.

Since I'd interacted with the thoracic surgeon only at the hospital, I didn't realize that his office at the Sparrow Professional Building occupied the same space that my OB/GYN practice had inhabited during my final pregnancy. In previous days, the room had contained a different energy and clientele. Women with various bowling-ball sized bellies, sometimes with men, sometimes alone, and occasionally with car seats containing newborns.

The people in the waiting room now had passed fertility age. Less joy and anticipation permeated the room. From my vantage point in the corner, I saw the thoracic surgeon in the back hallway behind the reception desk and the door to the inner office. I imagined he saw me and quickly looked down. Paranoia tainted my perceptions, I told myself.

After the nurse led me into an exam room, I climbed on the table. I wanted to kick at the surface underneath my heels like my kids had done a dozen times at the pediatrician's office, their anxiety escalating as the dreaded vaccination time drew near.

The thoracic surgeon entered, greeting me. He wanted to see the incision first, and he peeled off the bandage my visiting nurse had taught me to create with gauze and tape. He was slow and thoughtful as he examined the goop of muropricin I'd squeezed onto the three-cornered tear in my skin he'd created for the chest tube. "You don't need that stuff," he said. "The skin will heal on its own now; antibiotic cream just makes it messier. The wound looks good."

I didn't tell him that I hadn't comprehended until after my hospital discharge that I actually had two incisions – one for the pericardial window itself, a slice under my left breast, and the hole where the chest tube had entered my lung further down. I didn't tell him that I'd asked my visiting nurse about the weird waxy strips under my breast, material like leftover gummy adhesive from a bandage. I confessed to her that I'd tugged at the strips when they began to peel off like licorice. She explained that they'd probably used a substance to seal my breast flap back in place. I'd felt foolish that I hadn't understood the two incisions.

He leaned against the counter. "Have you seen an oncologist or anything?"

The word "oncologist" clattered onto the floor. I exhaled, the pain in my chest returning.

Then I tried to conjure belligerence, watching his face. "*Should* I see an oncologist?"

I don't remember which of us referenced the biopsy first, but he began saying words like "smoking" and "growths." He said a word I didn't recognize – "adenocarcinoma." The words began to merge together in my brain, becoming like a haze filling the room. I couldn't determine from his voice and his posture what he wanted to communicate. If I were a pregnant woman who needed to pee, I'd just skate over everything and exit, step out of the fog and inhale clean air. But I needed to stay put. Sit tight, as the other doctor might say.

"I need a copy of the biopsy report," I said.

He touched the lapel of his white coat, looking closely at my face. "You want a copy?"

I wanted to scream the answer, but I simply nodded.

He reached into his coat and pulled out a folded sheet of paper. He didn't even know what kind of cancer I had, whether there was a tumor in my lung or elsewhere. But I needed to see an oncologist, and he would try to get me connected with the very best one at Sparrow.

"Three of us failed you," he said. "You don't know how strange it is for me to give you this news. I don't tell people they have cancer. They learn it from someone else. Three of us," he repeated. "But we're going to fight this thing."

I didn't know what "this thing" was. I studied the biopsy report, trying to discern.

"I'm sorry," he said. "You're young. We're going to fight this. My office will be in touch to get you the oncologist appointment. He's a good doctor. You'll like him."

In the days to come, the doctor who gave me the bad news would become the buffoon in the story of my diagnosis, a bumbling practitioner who tried to cover his ass in a communication snafu of mammoth proportions in my small world. His statement, "You don't know how unusual it is for me to give you this news," struck me as self-centered, lacking in empathy.

Over the next few years, however, I would reflect on my meeting with him and finally view it from his perspective, recognizing a well-intended individual's attempt to correct the communication failure that had happened after a windy Halloween night when he'd encountered the mess in my chest. Sparrow had been implementing an electronic medical record system during my stay. Routines were interrupted. Yet surgical staff had addressed my emergency situation; when improvement took place, the question of causes receded, just like the effusion.

But on that day in Pridjian's office, I left the exam room, my biopsy report in hand, carrying to my husband's office a thin, nearly weightless sheaf of paper that had become a new burden we would now need to explore -- the wrong side of fifty percent. The biopsy report I held was dated November 2, six days before I left the hospital.

Dr. Gadgeel

When Shirish Gadgeel entered my exam room at the Barbara Ann Karmanos Cancer Center and began talking on that snowy Thursday in mid-December, the exam table paper unfurled into the room as if from the scroll of an ancient scribe. Instead of anchoring that paper on the table as a patient, I sat in a chair and became a student again at age fifty-three, rapt, absorbing the story Dr. Gadgeel sketched on the parchment in front of me.

Cells. He began with a crude graphic of cells. Cancer begins with cells in a simple, elementary fashion, so that is how Gadgeel's teaching began. Along the way, he added words and acronyms: adenocarcinoma, pleura, squamous, EGFR, NSCLC, and COPD.

His Fellow had entered the room earlier, apologizing for the delay, telling us Gadgeel would be with us shortly. When Gadgeel arrived for the appointment, he apologized again for his tardiness, admitting that he had squeezed us into an already packed clinic day.

His boss had requested that he see me. He wondered why. I explained that when I learned of my diagnosis, I'd contacted an old friend and roommate, Marie Griffin, a physician at Vanderbilt University who headed up the Master in Public Health program. Her partner, Bob Coffey, also a physician, worked as a cancer researcher at Vanderbilt and knew several oncologists across the country. They'd urged me to go to a National Cancer Institute (NCI) in Michigan – Karmanos or the University of Michigan, especially after the miscommunication with Sparrow about the biopsy results. An official NCI-Designated Cancer Center would be more aware of drug trials and cutting-edge research.

We all had qualms about Sparrow after the delay of the biopsy results, and when we learned that my insurance favored Karmanos over the University of Michigan, Marie and Bob made the connection for me with Gadgeel.

I'd also contacted Marie and Bob in part because I'd learned from the Internet that nonsmokers diagnosed with lung cancer often had cancer mutations. When I had typed in one in particular, the epidermal growth factor receptor (EGFR), I learned that a doctor at Vanderbilt had, in fact, discovered the epidermal growth factor and its receptor, and I suspected Bob knew about all the attendant research.

As Dr. Gadgeel continued to speak and write key words on the examination table paper, I realized that he used the writing surface as I did the blackboard when I talked to my students about writing. Not to record a pre-established body of knowledge but as a prop to tell a new version of a story. Writing down words and phrases for emphasis. He drew arrows. He extracted energy from the information he recorded and brought it into the room, infusing the air.

Yet every few minutes, he paused to say, "Are you with me?"

Are you with me?

His voice grew louder. He made marks and gestured. He pulled on the examination table paper to provide more space on which to write, the action filling the room with sound and an intense sort of intellectual industry.

White space. As a writer, I loved white space.

Dr. Gadgeel spoke of the mutation I'd learned about, the EGFR, and explained that cancer mutations now drove drug research in treatment called "targeted therapy." He was a master teacher, determined to educate me. Perhaps I would die, but I would learn well what would kill me. The Fellow stood on the sidelines, nodding his head, listening intently to his mentor and looking up at me from time to time to smile encouragingly.

Dr. Gadgeel tilted his head to the side, directing a question both at me and the Fellow.

"And why is it that we don't have pathology results about a possible EGFR or ALK mutation?"

I remembered other paper – a summary the other oncologist had given me, his handwriting neat and sparse in the blanks on a form. My treatment plan, a plan we would put into action assuming that my cancer exhibited no mutation. Calcium. Xgeva. Chemotherapy, specifically a cocktail that would include Avastin, Alimta, Cisplatin. Another pathology request to test for mutations. "They sent away for it at Sparrow," I said, remembering.

I didn't like to make judgments based on first impressions, but the Sparrow oncologist had struck both Tim and me as resigned. His gentle eyes conveyed empathy, even a somber spirituality of sorts, but his voice felt wooden as it presented my case as hopeless. One person, he said. He'd known one person who had beaten stage IV non-small cell lung cancer. He'd examined me the day after Dr. Pridjian had handed me the errant biopsy results. He ordered a PET scan, which I'd had done the day before Thanksgiving, and then brought me back to his office to deliver the results. I learned that "adenocarcinoma" in this case meant stage IV lung cancer, the stage indicating that I had metastases. He showed Tim and me the PET scan on his computer, pointing to the spots in my bones where the cancer had found residence outside of my lungs. Those spots caused some of the pain I had attributed to osteoarthritis.

We would look to the pathology report for some hope about mutations, he said, but in the meantime, I should set up some educational appointments on chemotherapy and make an appointment with Dr. Pridjian for the installation of a port in my chest.

Six to eighteen months, he'd said.

I looked at the PET scan, thinking about those two numbers, *six* and *eighteen*. If you subtracted one from the other, you got twelve months, a whole year. Aloud, I said I was glad I wasn't crazy. I suspected something had been toying with my body, and the bright spots confirmed my suspicions. Evidence.

He looked at me with sadness. "Much better to be crazy than to have cancer."

If the Sparrow oncologist served as solemn undertaker and priest, Dr. Gadgeel took on the role of ambulance driver, careening around corners and barreling through intersections.

"Call them," he said to the Fellow. *Them*. Sparrow. The Fellow would call the oncologist I'd decided not to see anymore.

As the Fellow left the room to check with Sparrow, Dr. Gadgeel continued to review potential causes, asking questions and offering facts. It seemed doubtful that my parents' smoking provided a major factor because it had happened so long ago. My childhood acute and chronic asthma also provided no clear links verified by existing research. As an aside, Karmanos did participate in a study on Chronic Obstructive Pulmonary Disease (COPD) to investigate potential links between COPD and lung cancer. Would I participate? We discussed workplaces and the chronic sinusitis of my mid-thirties. He tried to explain the complexity of determining overall environmental causes, although the environment certainly played a major if ill-defined role in all respiratory illnesses.

The Fellow re-entered the room, visibly energized. "She has the mutation!" he announced. He held out a FAX and listed off some genetic codes, clearly pleased with his role in delivering the news.

Gadgeel's eyes, always alive, grew wider. "This changes everything!" he said. *This changes everything!* He returned to the exam table paper, writing down the words, EXON 21 and EXON 19, creating arrows pointing to EXON 19.

When we left the room, several hours had passed, and the staff outside prepared to leave for the day. I'd given blood for the COPD trial and answered questions. I learned about the drug I'd be taking.

Erlotinib. Trade name, Tarceva. It wasn't a cure, but because I had the EGFR mutation, this drug might keep my cancer controlled for a while.

We called the kids, who were back in East Lansing, to give them the news. Then we drove to Eastside Marios, the place where we'd celebrated

Rachel's graduation from Oakland University eight months earlier, this time celebrating with my sisters the alternative therapy path I would take – targeted therapy, not chemotherapy. We told everyone over and over again about Gadgeel's energy, and the time he spent teaching us about the disease. The way the air in the room changed, the way it vibrated with some palpable new rhythm when the Fellow entered with the mutation results in a triumphant flourish, the way Gadgeel had said, "This changes everything." Those words of cautious excitement or possibility.

Gadgeel had examined the X-rays and determined I wouldn't need radiation, either. No infusions. No radiation. A single pill to take once a day. And calcium injections every six weeks, XGEVA, the same thing the Sparrow oncologist had written on my treatment form. No promise of an extended life, but no resignation.

As a lifelong introvert, I leaned toward individuals who shared my introversion and knew better than to judge a spirited style of communication as evidence of overall superior performance.

And yet, I saved that exam table paper. It was my Dead Sea Scroll. When I touched it, my fingers glided across the surface, smooth and familiar, and a crinkle whispered in the air, soft, neither percussive or melodic, but significant.

Before I'd travelled to Detroit to meet Gadgeel that day in December, I'd looked up his publications on PubMed. I found the short prose essay, "Hope and Realism: The Perfect Balance?" that he'd published a year and a half earlier in the *Journal of Clinical Oncology*. It talked about a former patient of his and described how he'd tried to find a balance in what he could offer her but how he felt he'd inevitably failed in his attempt. When we'd parked our car in the ramp for the Detroit Medical Center on John R and emerged from the parking lot elevator to approach the entrance of the conjoined hospitals, I'd thought about hope and realism and the way the words of his article had emerged on the page from my printer, black and definitive against bright, white paper. When we'd trudged to the hospital door, skirting the snow piles marked with debris that lined the extensive parking lot, I'd carried the article in my purse.

I didn't want to make a god out of him, yet some sense of awe was inevitable. He was a Buddha, a Vishnu, a Mohammad, a Jesus. Or my mother, the only god I'd really prayed to for years, since her death at age sixty-four, over twenty years earlier. But I worshiped him most for what he refused to promise me. I believed only in his version of hope and science, his balance of hope and realism.

He never told me that he would cure my cancer. He never exhorted me to hope.

Just as the Sparrow doctors never failed in their treatment of me during or following my surgery and pleural and pericardial effusion. They had erred only in the communication arena.

When I saw Dr. Gadgeel after our December meeting, two months after I started Tarceva, he took Tim and me into his office at the Farmington Hills campus of Karmanos to view my scans on the computer, to point out where, in my lungs, the cancer had receded. I realized for the first time as I stood next to him, staring at the images, that he was shorter than I.

Because, of course, he appeared much taller. When I saw him, every three months, even on the long clinic days when his energy flagged, and he had delivered bad news, signed patients into hospice, or viewed the shadows darkening the CT images before him in a way that made his soul shrink, he infused the room with an immense and magnetic humanity.

Dedria and Diplomat Specialty Pharmacy

We sat in the greenhouse area of Harrison Roadhouse, just outside the main bar, an area with a clear-windowed roof through which we could see the December day. Dedria said she came there sometimes with friends for happy hour. I'd never been, even though the bar occupied a prominent corner adjacent to Michigan State's campus just down the road from both Spartan Stadium and the Breslin Center, where the Spartans played basketball.

We rewarded ourselves with lunch because we'd both turned our grades in for the semester. I'd done mine for Oakland University the evening prior, just before the 5:00 PM deadline. Dedria had finished hers as well for Lansing Community College (LCC).

I'd told her about my diagnosis when she'd called a few days before. She knew nothing about my Halloween surgery and hospitalization; there hadn't been time to tell anyone outside of my daily circle. Because of our respective paper-grading loads, Dedria and I connected only at the end of the fall semester and then again in the summer.

Dedria was the gift I'd received from my three years of full-time work for the Writing Program at LCC in the early 2000's. Although we'd both worked adjunct prior to that time, our paths hadn't crossed until 2002, when the Writing Program hired the two of us for full-time positions – a coup we celebrated by becoming friends and across-the-hall office colleagues.

When we occupied our offices at the same time during the day, we left our doors open and called to each other across the hall. Sometimes

Dedria shrieked in dismay at something she read on her computer, often from the online version of *The Lansing State Journal*, the newspaper for which she'd been a journalist. I'd rise from my chair and step across the narrow hallway into her office, to look over her shoulder, searching for what had provoked the shriek.

Or I'd be sitting in my office chair, reading some student's short story and moan about how the student writer had decided to kill off the first-person narrator at the story's end. Dedria would cross the hall and help me address the issue in my commentary to the student.

I don't remember when I understood the significance of our office doors facing each other across that hallway. But I was reminded of my childhood growing up in Waterford, Michigan, a suburb of Pontiac, looking out our kitchen window across the narrow driveway while doing dishes with my sisters to see one of our neighbors standing at the kitchen sink, doing dishes. Lifting a sudsy hand from the dishwater to wave, maybe later coming out to stand next to a fence between our yards and chat. Dedria had grown up in southeastern Michigan also – in Detroit. We were neighbors, through and through.

We talked about our children. Back then, Dedria's youngest son, David, played football at East Lansing High School, the school my eldest, Rachel, would eventually attend. My family had just moved cross-town from Lansing to East Lansing, our house a short block from Dedria's.

Over the three years that we spent together as full-time teachers, I watched Dedria handle the weight of the full-time load – four classes per semester, mostly composition sections with externally evaluated portfolios – much better than I did. She graded more efficiently than I, diagnosing common writing problems, writing comments faster, discerning more quickly the direction in which a student should move for revision and expansion of ideas based on the material already on the page.

At times, I could barely absorb students' arguments let alone find ways to redirect them.

I'd always struggled to handle the paper load when teaching composition, but when I'd done it years before at James Madison University in

Harrisonburg, Virginia, at the young age of twenty-six, no children had tugged at my attention.

I eventually resigned from the prized full-time position, not wanting to dilute my offerings to either my children or my students. I tried to switch to academic advising at LCC, a career choice which seemed to fit much more naturally with my strengths and skills, allowing me to work with a population of individuals I loved. But I'd made the mistake of not coordinating the switch while I held a full-time union position. And though I spent a few rewarding years as an adjunct advisor, roaming between various LCC sites to help students figure out curriculums and classes, I couldn't get any traction on even a semi-permanent part-time position, so I gave up on the field of advising also, working to build a nearly full-time position as a creative writing teacher at Oakland University in Rochester, a school not far from where I grew up in Waterford.

When Dedria and I met now, we liked to talk about writing, teaching, and the books on our nightstands. We worked hard now to make our friendship last, even though she'd stayed in the Writing Program and I'd left, too overwhelmed by the grading load and the burden the externally graded portfolio evaluation system put on writing structure.

But at the time of our lunch that December afternoon, since Dedria didn't know the whole story of my pericardial surgery, recovery, and surprise cancer diagnosis, we talked quietly, still laughing, but more somber than usual.

I picked at my salad. When I left her that day, I'd be driving to Flint, I explained. Only certain specialty pharmacies dispensed the drug my oncologist at Karmanos had prescribed. I'd tried to obtain it through a place called Curescript, out of Florida, but after days of fruitless phone calls and emails, I'd begun searching for an alternative source. A specialty pharmacy in Flint, less than an hour away, carried the drug I needed.

I didn't need to worry about shipment dates. I could simply drive over to get it. The city of Flint happened to be the half-way mark on my commuting drive to Oakland University.

But I wouldn't drive to Oakland for that next semester. I'd been scheduled for only one class, so I'd asked my department chair to find a temporary replacement. I'd stay home and adjust to the side effects of my targeted therapy, a daily 150 milligram dose of Tarceva.

Dedria reluctantly shared that one of my former colleagues, a full-time faculty member in the Speech Program, a sister program within the Communications Department, had died unexpectedly the week before. Mark Gallup, one of only two full-time speech faculty members. An aberration with his heart. In his home, with no one around. At fifty-one years old, he was two years younger than I.

When I'd left the Writing Program and trained to become an advisor instead, he'd always smiled and greeted me when he saw me in the halls near the advising center. I appreciated his treating me like a person who had a history with the college, even though I'd had to start all over again building a reputation as a go-to employee in advising.

Dedria wondered how Tim and the kids had been dealing with the diagnosis. I explained that we'd had to delay telling Connor. Since he thought I was recovering from cardiac surgery, we allowed him to live with that story until he finished his term just before Thanksgiving.

"They're trying to make sense of it." I leaned forward. "I don't know how to get everything ready for when I die. Tim's not prepared to take over everything he'll have to do. I have so much to teach him! Yes, that sounds patronizing, but he needs to show his love for the kids more. I need to teach him how to do that!"

Dedria reached her hand across the table and put it over mine. "It's okay," she said. "He doesn't have to know it all just yet."

We said goodbye in the Harrison Roadhouse, and I drove straight to Flint. I located Diplomat Specialty Pharmacy, where they prepared my prescription and gave it to me with detailed instructions about taking it one hour before eating or two hours after meals.

I opened the container and shook out a plain white tablet of Tarceva. I unscrewed the cap on my bottled water. I placed the pill on my tongue, took a gulp of water, and swallowed.

II. Putting Things Away

January 2, 2013 – December 19, 2014

Statistics II

- Approximately 222,000 new cases of lung cancer are diagnosed each year.

- Approximately half of the people diagnosed with advanced lung cancer die within 12-14 months.

- Approximately 85% of all lung cancer cases are non-small cell lung cancer (NSCLC).

- The five-year survival rate for people with stage IV NSCLC ranges from 1 to 10%.

- Ten to fifteen percent of people with the EGFR mutation for advanced NSCLC live with their cancer controlled for five years or longer on Tarceva.

Hairnet

The second time I wore a hairnet to cook food, Nathaniel said it looked creepy. "Please take it off." But I didn't want to get hair in the Russian Banana fingerling potatoes that I'd fixed in honor of Connor's time at home over break. Fingerlings, boiled, cut up in banana-length thirds, fried in garlic, onions, and Nathaniel-friendly margarine. Nathaniel's discovery from his trip to Banff with his father. Who wants to raise a fork and find a frail, broken strand of hair peering out from behind a frond of onion?

You're not supposed to lose your hair on Tarceva, at least not all of it. And maybe I wouldn't lose it all. But the volume continued to dwindle. I could feel the thinning when I reached up to put the ends in a pony-tail or when I combed my wet hair in the morning, touching it only long enough to find a part. The strands – short and brown, long and gray – tangled together to make a little matting not unlike a fur ball. I resented the grooming behavior I had to engage in surreptitiously while in public – scanning the surface of my shoulders and arms, collecting the single units, manufacturing my own matted ball and transmitting it to the wastepaper basket. Sometimes while driving I opened the window, let the strands loose in the air, my contribution to the environment. Biodegradable.

"I'll take it off when the meal's done," I said. "I'm protecting your potatoes."

"I know that," Nathaniel said. He kissed me on the cheek. "But it still looks creepy." He told me that if I eventually shaved my head, he'd shave his, too. I told him I wouldn't hold him to it. One day, in the spring, I picked him up from school, my hair still wet. He reached over and ran his fingers through my hair on the side he faced, and his eyebrows rose when he saw what had collected on his hand. I'd been telling my family members that my hair had begun to fall out, that tons of it disappeared in the shower, but they didn't believe me. Yet here was proof, at the end of a tiring day. He wadded it up and tried to toss it back at me. One more clump of hair for me to ferret out of the upholstery.

In the shower, after I massaged shampoo into my scalp, I held my fingers under the shower head, pointing them downward so that the pressure of the water could beat the strands encircling my fingers and hands off my skin, beat them down with the water toward the drain and the hair catcher. Sometimes I looked at my hand poised there, fingers artfully spread, and imagined that if I stood there long enough and turned off the water, spiders could come and make webs there, my hair ready-made silk for them to work with. But it broke easily and didn't have the strength of a real web, so I kept the shower on, letting the water pulse at the strands. Then I stepped out of the shower and left the hair collecting in the drain.

Mammogram

I stood in line at the imaging window to sign in for my mammogram, a bit exasperated because the office had moved and no one had bothered to tell me when I made the appointment on the phone. In spite of leaving an hour in advance, I'd arrived late, having driven to the other location to find a note on the door and a woman in the elevator moving files. I only get a mammogram once a year, I wanted to tell the woman at the counter. Someone should have told me. She spoke too fast when she answered the phone, and I wanted her to slow down, so people understood. I quieted myself by looking around, taking in the fibrous scent of new carpeting, new chairs. On the floor at the feet of two women, a baby rested in a car seat.

I tried to ignore her – I assumed she was a she because of the pink blanket behind her head. I avoided babies now. I turned back to examine the polo shirt of the man ahead of me in line. Off to the right, a door opened, and another man came out with a boy, maybe twelve. It took a minute to recognize the man's face, but then I realized I knew him from my hospital stay.

I'd met him in those hours before my surgery on Halloween, before I knew about my tamponade, long before I learned about my cancer. His girlfriend, my hospital roommate for twenty-four hours, had congestive heart failure. She was the mom who'd told each shift change that she needed to be out of the hospital to take her four children out for trick-or-treating. Her boyfriend said "fuck" a hundred times when he was talking on the phone to a relative, and at one point, after my nurses moved me to a chair, he sat at the edge of my freshly made bed and asked me about my situation. He told me his wife had died from congestive heart failure

46

and he'd met his girlfriend in the process and now cared for her and their respective kids. Tired and anxious, I'd known little about my situation at that point. I wanted him to go away.

While his girlfriend yanked out her I.V. in anticipation of being released, she told me that living with a chronic illness wiped her out. As a rule follower, I felt awe at her forwardness in removing her own tubing; in the moments after she'd pulled at the tape, I imagined an arc of blood shooting into the space above the two of us. When they released her, in time for the afternoon parties at the elementary schools and the evening of trick-or-treating, a few hours before my surgery, she gave me the flower arrangement she'd gotten from her ex-husband and a fan she didn't need any longer. She wished me luck.

I wondered if she were still alive. I didn't want to know, but I wished I could summon up the courage to tell the boyfriend that I wanted to thank her for the fan and her kind gesture in giving it to me. Yet I felt cowardly rather than courageous. I turned my face away from the boyfriend and the child with him and looked back at the baby. "How old is she?" I tried to sound dispassionate, casual.

"Seven days," the mother said.

"A week," the other woman said. "Last Monday."

The mother counted her fingers. "Eight days."

I watched the baby's face, observing how distinct each feature was, the way her fingers flailed. "She's really pretty," I said. And then, "They aren't always." As if I'd had a dozen.

"I know," the woman said. "We couldn't believe how perfect she came out."

When I expressed to my friend Sharon my deep sadness about not having my novel published before I died, she seemed puzzled. "But you're a writer, whether the book is published or not. Why do you feel a sense of failure? You've done other things; you are a mom. Why the novel before you die, and not, say...." She looked in the air, searching for alternatives that someone with an end-stage disease might focus on. "Grandchildren?"

I winced. "I can't even go there," I said. "At least the novel I can talk about."

"Oh," she said.

I reached the front of the window, and I also feigned boredom in the conversation with the mother. But the administrative clerk took a phone call, so I couldn't help it. I turned back.

"What's her name?"

"Madeline," she said.

"Nice." I remained at the window, but another version of me walked toward the car seat.

Reached down and touched the skin at the baby's wrist. Inhaled.

The clerk, now off the phone, spoke. "The tech will call you back in a minute." I surmised that even though the office moved, the tech would still be Donna. I doubted she would remember me, but a few years earlier during the pinch and press of the mammogram machine's plates against my breast tissue she'd told me about her husband's sudden death and how she had to remake her life, lobby for more work hours, and re-envision her future.

The door opened and Donna called my name. She walked me down the hall and showed me the new room, reminding me to take off every-thing from the waist up and use one of the moist towelettes in a packet to wipe off any deodorant or anti-perspirant I might have worn. She moved into the other half of the segmented room, pulling a yellow curtain. "I'll just ask you some questions." She covered a few basic ones and then said, "Any changes to your health?"

"Stage IV lung cancer." I had a hard time saying it without feeling apologetic, without telling people that there was no need to be silent or grim on my account.

She remained quiet for a moment. "That's a pretty significant change."

I tried to sound nonchalant as I answered the rest of her questions. No breast surgeries, per se, I told her, although they made an incision under my left breast for the pericardial window.

"You had surgery before the diagnosis?" she said.

"It's a long, complicated story." I resisted the impulse to tell it to her.

When she asked about my periods, I told her that I'd made this mammogram appointment and one with my gynecologist out of habit, not knowing if the appointments were necessary. If I were dying of one kind of cancer, did it matter if I developed another?

Donna put a pastel pink sponge pad on the machine to cushion my breasts from the cold, hard metal. "It's nice that they provide these," I said.

"Pink is warm and comforting," she said. She talked me through the adjustments I needed to make in my posture, the angles at which I should raise my arms and place them on the grips, and the direction in which I should step toward the machine. She placed my breasts gently on the pink surface. She hesitated, looked up in the air to retrieve some thought, and talked about how the new machine, the Hologic, didn't need plates anymore.

I wanted to tell her that I'd read statistics about how lung cancer kills more women than breast cancer does. But did it matter, really, which cancer killed more women? What I wanted to know most was how she felt these days, now that several years had passed since her husband's death. Instead I remained quiet and observed the shiny surfaces of the Hologic.

We finished. She showed me how to get out of the labyrinth in this new office. When I exited to the waiting room, the women and the baby still remained seated. I avoided them and thought about the fan my hospital roommate had given me that Halloween she escaped the hospital for trick-or-treat.

Away, Not Down

My friend Bill and I talked once about the way two people in a relationship negotiate the level of order and cleanliness in their shared household. Individuals could range from obsessive neatniks to slobs but they needed to adapt as a couple – find an acceptable, shared level of chaos or rigor. His new partner told him that he needed to learn how to put things away. Doing so wasn't difficult, Bill said, but he had to practice. "He puts things away," Bill explained. "I put things down."

I loved him for giving me that simple line, gravestone-worthy: "I put things down." Bill opened up for me a new way of viewing my inefficiency in operating a household.

At some point, I had forgotten how to put things away. At first blush, I blamed it on my children. How could one maintain order in a household with three offspring? But I shouldn't blame the disorder entirely on children. I recalled stacks of papers in some of the apartments Tim and I lived in after we got married and set up household in Virginia. Before we had children. Perhaps I'd never known how to put things away.

But I had a slew of circumstances that fostered chaos in my life: my love of books and paper, the tempestuous infancy and toddlerhood of my eldest child, the deaths of my parents in 1993 just thirty-six days apart during my pregnancy with my second child, and the incorporation of many of my parents' totems into my own home. My movement in and out of a series of jobs, and the birth of two more children. Depression. Part-time work. Stacks of papers to grade. Mail.

I'd started, when my kids were young, to write a children's book about a family of packrats – hoarders, as the A&E show would have it. My Aunt Aggie had been a milder version of one of those hoarders, living in a small rent-controlled apartment in Mt. Clemens, the town in which my mother had grown up. The gene for hoarding was related to the cleaning and grooming gene, I'd heard, just like the gene for trichotillomania, a condition that played a role in a novel I began years ago. Both projects, interestingly enough, the children's book and the novel, lived lives of their own in a bin somewhere in my basement, a hoarder's paradise.

When I took the semester off after my initial cancer diagnosis, my sister Linda came up to East Lansing once a month. To help me organize. We plowed through paper, old bills, and stacks of clothes. We donated, shredded, and carted items to recycling. We made a good start.

But only a start. After a semester, I went back to work and then did another three semesters of teaching, accumulating more handouts and copies of student work, because in order to give feedback, I needed to touch paper and write in margins. I had a paper problem.

Or maybe a hoarding problem.

Yet viewed in my friend Bill's terms, the problem wasn't about paper; it stemmed from the bad habit of "down" instead of "away." After I used a pair of scissors, my brain jumped forward to another task. Letting the dog out before she peed on the carpet. Or calling in a refill on my son's prescription. The end result was that the scissors went "down" and not "away." My brain didn't even register the omission until a week or more later, when I looked at the counters and wondered why so much clutter filled my life. All those things put down.

I'd been living with a new partner, too. Cancer. Its unpredictable, non-linear nature overwhelmed at times. A pain throbbed in my back – had the metastasis at the base of the spine, supposedly healing, become active again? My brain felt like cotton – should I blame the cancer drug I took each day, my sleeping pill, or some undiscovered growth, lurking in the shadows?

Urgency built as I batted at the haze in my brain and searched for focus. I couldn't leave things undone, couldn't shift the burden of cleaning up to others. I needed completion. I needed to put those scissors away. Now.

Indian Food

During my first appointment at the Farmington Hills campus of Karmanos, my second appointment with Dr. Gadgeel, I found the December 2012 issue of *Karmanos Hope: A Publication of the Barbara Ann Karmanos Cancer Institute* on a table in the patient lounge. The article, entitled "Kitchen Cures: Can natural agents help destroy cancer cells?" featured a discussion about curcumin, a component of the spice turmeric. Used in many Southeast Asian recipes, turmeric reportedly had anti-inflammatory properties. I knew the spice as a staple in Indian food, which I ate as often as possible, although Tim didn't care for it as much as I did.

My friend Madhu had shared various dishes with me over the years at her children's naming ceremonies and other family functions. My friend Shashi had started dropping off Indian food shortly after my initial cancer diagnosis. She purchased it for herself and her husband from a woman who made it in large quantities. Shashi would bring to the door a few containers, usually a hot and spicy dal and a vegetable dish with some bread. When Rachel got home from her shift at Best Buy, we paired the two dishes with cottage cheese, mostly for me, to offset the heat, and ate our food with a pitcher of water nearby for fast relief.

During the semester I stayed home from teaching, I had more time to read. Madhu loaned me her cookbooks, which I piled up next to my bed, *Climbing the Mango Trees: A Memoir of a Childhood in India* by Madhur Jaffrey. *Classic Indian Cooking* by Julie Sahni. *1,000 Indian Recipes* by Neelam Batra. *Ismail Merchant's Passionate Meals: The New Indian Cuisine for Fearless Cooks and Adventurous Eaters*. Tim and I loved

Merchant and Ivory films. *The Remains of the Day. Howards End. The Bostonians.*

I pored over the books and sprinkled post-it notes throughout them, marking recipes to xerox. I wanted to learn the language of Indian food. When I'd dined at the Indian restaurant previously, the names of the dishes didn't leave an imprint. But now, with my advanced cancer, I felt compelled to know the names of things – especially trees, flowers, birds, and Indian dishes.

Spinach was saag. Aloo was potatoes. Gobi was cauliflower. Paneer, a kind of cheese. Bhindi, okra. I loved absorbing the language of food that frequently contained turmeric. Even if this spice form of turmeric might not filter through my food and into my body in a concentrated enough form to address my cancer, I felt powerful ingesting it. I felt a sense of control.

I bought new turmeric to replace the ancient tin container from mother's house and some garam masala as well as some lentils and chick peas. I began ordering takeout Indian food every time Tim left on a business trip. Chicken saag. (My father and I had shared a love of spinach.) A dish of raita, the cooling cucumber yogurt that made everything go down more smoothly. Basmati or saffron rice. A portion of mango custard. And sometimes an order of naan bread, which I loved to sweep through the sauce of my saag. When I learned of a sweet version of naan bread, peshwari, stuffed with coconut, raisins, and nuts, I enjoyed two different versions, the one prepared by Connor's favorite Indian restaurant in Kalamazoo, Saffron, with plump, white raisins, and another with reddish-pink coconut flakes made by my local restaurant, Sindhu.

My friend Ann, whose multiple myeloma was confirmed around the same time that I learned of my cancer diagnosis, came to visit me during the February when I was off work. She made her New England molasses cookies using an egg substitute for Nathaniel, her godson. The scent of cloves, cinnamon, and ginger filled the house.

Then we went to the Indian restaurant and inhaled a different set of spices, eating saag and biryani and mango custard. Envisioned our cancers dissolving.

Recording the CD (February 23, 2013)

I.

Before my sisters and nieces arrived, I needed to collect the sheet music from where it lay scattered throughout the house. Ideally it all would have rested on top of the piano in the living room in tidy order, but I didn't usually do things in a tidy, orderly way. I could retrieve one piece of sheet music from the floor next to my bed, on top of the furnace vent, blocking the warm air, where many things I wanted to have a look at ended up. Another piece of sheet music probably lay on the family room coffee table. "Close to You" likely sat on the computer desk, since I'd been looking online for other versions that might begin in a different key.

My sisters and I had decided to record a CD with our female off-spring. The six of us would rehearse that night after they all arrived at our house and ate pizza, once Rachel came home from her shift at Best Buy. My niece Devon had arranged it, because of her work with the Michigan State University A Capella Choir, Ladies First, that she'd belonged to during her years at the University. During her time with the group, they'd recorded a few CDs, so Devon knew of a reliable studio nearby where we could purchase recording time and the help of an audio technician at a reasonable price.

II.

We didn't have a dishwasher in the house in which I grew up. My father always said, "I have three dishwashers." One of us set the table and another cleared the table. One of us washed the dishes and two of us dried. We dried because my dad didn't like the drainer on the counter

54

with dishes. We stored the drainer back under the sink when we finished drying.

Linda liked to wash, so Lori and I usually allowed her that pleasure, knowing that since she was the oldest, she would probably get what she wanted anyway. We ran the wash water as warm as we could tolerate it with lots of detergent poured under the stream of water as the sink filled. We filled the second sink with rinse water, which always grew cold too quickly. The idea was to dip or dunk each dish into the rinse water and transfer it to the drainer, but sometimes we just let the water out of the second sink and rinsed dishes and glasses under the faucet. Doing so, we knew, was a waste of water, but it struck us as more hygienic.

While we washed and dried, we sang.

III.

Our selection of songs for the recording session the next day reflected our mixed generations of experiences. "Edelweiss" was a song my mother taught us, with harmony and echo features, long before we ever watched *The Sound of Music* on television or performed it in school. We picked "Tell Me Why" for a similar reason – we'd known the song and harmonies before we ever learned about the concept of public television or watched with our offspring an episode of *Barney*, the purple dinosaur who sang it to the kids in his mock classroom in front of the television viewers. Since we grew up in the Carpenter era, "Close to You" felt like an homage to Karen Carpenter with her mellow and haunting voice.

My sisters and I had piled on the couch a couple of times each year to watch *The Wizard of Oz* whenever the television programmers put it on the viewing schedule. Our daughters grew up with a new generation of wicked witches, a new musical with unforgettable characters and songs with heartbreaking melodies and powerful lyrics. "For Good" was a favorite of ours from *Wicked,* and we decided to sing it for the CD in part because Rachel, Devon, and Emelia had grown up in the heyday of *Wicked* popularity. Idena Menzel and Kristin Chenoweth became icons for young women everywhere.

Our last two choices were unusual but suited our family histories, both together and separately. "Walk Hand in Hand" was an older wedding song that two of us had sung at two sisters' weddings. In an odd statement our mother had made a few months before her fatal heart attack, she mentioned to two of us at a funeral that she hoped we would all sing at hers. When she died less than a year later, "Walk Hand in Hand" was the song we could put together as grief over her death and my father's overwhelmed us.

The final song, "Love You Forever" came from the Robert Munsch book of the same title. Since we all raised our children in roughly the same decade, we'd all read the book to our kids, each of us, unbeknownst to the other, creating a melody for the lyrics Munsch provided in the book. We wanted to record the three distinct melodies with the three mother-daughter pairs.

IV.

The three of us would have learned the names of the notes and the treble clef in elementary school, in music class and then band class. The teachers taught the EGBDF – Every Good Boy Deserves Fudge – mnemonic device to help us all learn the lines of the clef; some of them back then even recognized that girls might deserve fudge, also. The spaces, FACE, didn't need a mnemonic because they spelled a word.

Back then, I was fascinated that the lines of a musical staff could be so straight and precise, unlike the ones I made with my pen, squiggles and wobbles, even though I'd begun to earn good grades in penmanship. But the music teachers often had a special device with which they wrote notes on the board. A metal ruler with brackets and wires for holding five evenly spaced pieces of chalk with which the teachers could recreate music staff lines on the board.

From our mother we'd learned to sing by ear at an early age, before we knew about notes. She'd grown up in a large family with talented singers, and although her older sister, my Aunt Aggie, knew how to play the piano, my mother did not. But she knew how to sing, how to find an alto or second soprano harmony for nearly any song. She had the ear.

As a clarinet player in the fifth-grade band, I cemented my knowledge of notes and their lines and spaces with whatever I hadn't figured out in years of music classes singing "Oh, Suzanna," "Kookaburro," and "The Boll Weevil Song." Lori cemented her knowledge of the notes when she took up French Horn. Linda studied choir and drums, continuing to play drums into high school, focusing on the percussive marks in the music, often depicted by little x's in place of notes on the page, but it didn't matter whether she cemented the note names or not. She'd inherited our mother's ear.

V.

After pizza, we stood around the piano and played notes. Linda said we needed to remember that she couldn't read notes. I never really remembered that detail. We'd sung trios for holiday music at our home town church at Christmas and Easter for several years when we were in college; Lori, still at home for part of that time, arranged it with the choir director there. Linda and I almost always sang harmonies; she could find her notes with her voice, and after she repeated them a few times, I could see where they fell on the music staff. Since our mother had taught us how to harmonize by ear, we probably sang first, figuring out notes and intervals later.

Lori was the only soprano back then, so she usually sang the melody line, while Linda and I crafted parts. But Lori had studied both choral music and French Horn in high school and had a natural musical gift that went beyond what Linda or I had studied or applied, so our three-part harmonies grew from a conglomeration of our skills, some of them mathematical and analytical, some of them intuitive and physical.

Devon had prepared a document for our time at the studio the next day which laid out which songs we would sing when, who would be on which microphone, and whether the music would be pre-recorded by our accompanist or played on the spot. I appreciated her organization, although the document filled me with fear as I tried to round up emotions that felt like something akin to performance anxiety.

As we leaned over the piano again, Rachel came into the house, returning from work after a long shift. She grabbed a piece of pizza and admitted to a scratchy throat. We moved from the piano, where I was accustomed to rehearsing, to the computer, which provided so many other contemporary options in terms of soundtracks and bits of songs. We searched for the words for "Edelweiss." I realized that we were making music with the six of us, three of us from a different generation who'd grown up in the same household and learned music without accompaniment. I wanted to enjoy simply the experience of singing with my sisters and our daughters, but all three of the daughters had developed their music skills in a newer generation with better tools, tools that I needed to understand, if not master.

VI.

We always sang when we drove on family vacations during our childhood, even our father. We never flew anywhere, always driving to some place in Michigan, stopping along the way to eat cheese and smoked salmon at a roadside table. We started with "Henry the VIII" and "Finnegan" before moving to our dish-washing songs – "I've Got Spurs" and "Ragtime Cowboy Joe." My father, like my mother, had grown up with six brothers and sisters, and though they weren't known for singing, several of them played the piano. My father's pitch was perfect for summer hands-on-the-wheel crooning, and his solo male voice mixed well with ours. His other musical talent involved whistling with vibrato, which he did frequently on weekends when he worked on projects in our house and garage, his melodious whistle appearing and disappearing under the whine of the table saw on summer days.

VII.

When we practiced "For Good" from *Wicked*, I was stunned by how little flexibility my voice had as I tried to maneuver it around my chosen section of the melody line, the part where Elphaba talks about learning so much from Glinda and feeling her handprint. And things weren't much better when I worked on the harmony. I knew how to find a harmony with my voice, had done so for years when singing along with songs on the radio. But now I couldn't even hear a harmony in my head, even though I'd listened to the *Wicked* soundtrack for years.

I should have practiced ahead of time. Lori had thought to practice. I was too worried about setting things up, making sleeping arrangements, and coordinating schedules.

"So what key are we doing the Carpenter song in?" Lori said.

"I don't know the key names like you and Rachel," I said. "But I think it might depend on who starts the song and who finishes it?"

Gradually, the strands began to weave together. I'd thought "For Good" would be my favorite, but when we sang "Close to You," a recent addition to the list, our voices blended together in a familiar way, the voices of our daughters rich, youthful, energetic. I looked at my sisters, each with her head tilted or dipped with a note. Listening became the most important item on the agenda. Listening and remembering. And watching their faces.

In the final hours of preparation that night, the daughters made a last-minute decision to do a trio of their own. They unearthed Rachel's old sheet music to *Anastasia*, pulled out Rachel's keyboards, and chorded their way through the music from the movie video they'd all loved as kids. "Journey to the Past" was added to our list, and as Linda, Lori, and I watched Devon, Rachel, and Emelia come up with their last-minute arrangement of a song for the next day's recording, we were happy to be upstaged, outsung.

VIII.

As my mother lay dying in a hospital bed in William Beaumont's Cardiac Intensive Care Unit, my sisters and I sang to her. We tried to sing softly, knowing there were people recovering or dying in nearby rooms, people who might not care for music as much as we did. But we also took note of the sturdy doors which separated each of the rooms from one another, hoping that the doors and the basic set up of the Unit would allow for more insulation, keeping the sound we made inside the room.

IX.

Melanie Seal, our accompanist, arrived at the door on the morning of our recording session. I'd dropped music off to her earlier in the week. I had the piano tuned so infrequently, but I'd known it should be tuned before we recorded the songs; I hadn't remembered to get my own vocal instrument in working order, but I'd remembered the piano. The tuner was the person who gave me Melanie's name. I had told him about my diagnosis and my desire to record a CD with my sisters, and he said he thought he knew someone who would be on board with the idea.

We only had an hour and a half to prepare for the recordings. Working off Devon's agenda note, we huddled around the piano, working at the harmonies and the entrances and exits, our voices excited. I still sounded awful on the *Wicked* piece and tried to hit my notes straight on without scooping, but my whole voice seemed like one big scoop. Linda, Lori, and I complained to Melanie about how old we felt; she cheered us on with praise and encouragement, telling us how great we were doing. With time elapsing and our voices becoming strained, we ended the rehearsal with a plan to gather things together for the studio — music, agendas, water, throat lozenges, Kleenex.

X.

She lay in a coma with little brain activity, the doctors told us, but all three of us knew that the brains neurons contained amazing communication properties; who knew what my mother's brain could hear and absorb from notes that we sang that day, words we whispered to her? And who knew, too, what part of music benefitted the listener and what part benefitted the performer. What did we gain when we put our voices together in song? Was there a way to qualify those moments of unity and harmony?

XI.

We arrived at the house off of Pennsylvania and Kalamazoo, giddy with excitement, wondering what the studio would be like. As we entered the space, the microphones captured my attention. So prominent in the space. I'd only rarely sung with a microphone, but I respected the power. Devon's friend who ran the studio taught us how to use the headphones. When I put them on and turned to look through a window, I realized I could see to the other side, a room where Melanie sat at the keyboard. She learned how that particular keyboard changed keys and learned the adjustments for the songs we planned to sing. We practiced a few of the songs, practiced listening to each other through the earphones. I could hear my sisters' voices through the black caps over my ears, magical ear muffs transporting me from the winter snow gear of my childhood to this technical world which I inhabited for this new kind of singing.

For one of the numbers, people agreed that I should handle the cut off because of where I stood in the room; I realized then how little I liked to take the lead, how inadequate I felt in the role of that kind of direction. I could orchestrate the activities in a classroom or in my children's lives, but I was afraid to commit in the world of music. Yet we made it through to the next song, and then we made the decision to start the takes. As we worked in the actual moment of recording, I felt the thin wisp of air between my lips and the surface of the microphone, the weaving of its textured surface almost like a living interface. Like plants, soil, roots. Fertile.

When our three daughters took their turn to record the *Anastasia* song, my sisters and I had the chance to go up to the booth where the audio technician sat, overlooking the studio. It was there that I realized how red the recording studio was, large sections of a dark red wall with gray sound-absorbing material. We looked on as they sang their arrangement, their mouths closer to the microphones than ours had been, more comfortable with the proximity, their younger bodies shaping the notes with their hands and faces. My sisters and I closed our eyes to the beauty of their harmonies and the interplay of their rising voices, and I imagined that we each remembered our younger selves, the way we'd found music in our bodies and souls all those years ago. We had one more song to record, and then we'd be done with our adventure, but I knew we each still felt the flush of that first excitement, the quiet, focused sound we heard in our earphones.

XII.

As adults, my sisters and I each took our turns being involved in our respective churches' music programs. We involved our children, depending on however much they wanted to be involved or depending on whether or not their love of music required a performance aspect. I viewed my mother's gift of music to my sisters and me taking place largely in our home and in the homes of relatives who allowed for moments of song during family get togethers. Yet my key memory of my mother in song resides in an image I carry from young adulthood, when my three sisters and I still came home for Christmas Eve church service, during which our congregation dimmed the lights and sang "Silent Night" by candlelight. The pieces of the memory are distinct. The flame passing from person to person in the pews as we tipped the unlit candles to the lit ones and passed the flame along. The organ beginning the accompaniment, holding a soft quiet note during which the click of the light from the circuit breaker panel sounded at the same moment the overhead lights went out. The organ gaining volume, moving forward, and the slow song beginning. My mother peeking out at each of us, one at a time, from above her candle, her chin firm, mouth shaped in vowels of heavenly peace.

Before Clover

On April 18, 2013, the back yard puddled with rain. The wind rumbled like the rolling boil of water in a large pot that someone forgot on a stove. Rolling. Rolling. Outlined against an undecipherable sky, cardinals sat in the maple's branches. While the sun shone, doleful gusts swept through the trees, rattling vents in the bathrooms overhead.

I wondered where our new puppy, Clover, would go to the bathroom. I was afraid of dying. I was afraid of raising a puppy and facing moments of indecision about where to put her crate, where to take her in the back yard, whether she should stay in the crate while travelling in the car. A puppy should solve everything, yet on this windy day before we're scheduled to adopt her, after a night of bad dreams, sad dreams, in which a dog's head fell off and I climbed a set of stairs to find a suite of rooms where no one lives, I was afraid. Afraid of separation. Because I didn't know when the separation would occur. Afraid I wouldn't have enough warning, so I'd end up standing at the top of a stairway, surrounded by empty rooms in which no one lived.

I shouldn't be angry at the wind, which might very well sweep pockets of rain water out of the grass, but its tremolo frustrated me, a cold, insistent sound when I was so tired of cold, tired of the long winter that started for me back on Halloween. My feet cold, still, after all of these months. Cold under layers of blankets. Cold from Tarceva.

The wind grew louder and the sky darker; the window panes shook in their frames.

The top floor of the house in the dream stood empty.

CT Scans

I imagined a legion of women, some wearing hats and turbans, thin and frail, others large, like me, hair intact. Still others in wheelchairs pushed by relatives.

We started drinking shortly after we arrived for our scans and appointments. Absopure spiked with Omnipaque, the liquid used as one of two contrasts for the CT scans. The bottles held twenty ounces, but we needed to drink only to the bottom of the labels. The liquid tasted like stale water. The staff members verified that we were not allergic to iodine, personalizing our water bottles with labels bearing our names and birthdates.

We were women with stage IV lung cancer, nonsmokers whose cancer carried the EGFR mutation, permitting us to take a pill each day to prolong our lives. We came to this suburban building, the Lawrence and Idell Weisberg Center at the Farmington Campus of Karmanos Cancer Center, for our quarterly scans and appointments with our oncologists.

And so the preparation began. Sometimes we sipped, sometimes we gulped, me and my legion, knowing we had an hour to drink, to pee, and to have our blood drawn by a lab tech.

When I first started with the scans, I loved having Angel do the draw, Angel with the combat boots who called herself a vampire. She was a sure hand with the needle, not like the guy who came after whose first poke faltered so badly that he cursed his luck aloud as the vein on the left side of my hand remained stubborn and unwilling to produce any sort of flow. "I should have trusted my original gut," he said when the inside of my other arm responded more positively. "I was on a roll, today, too."

I learned to tell whoever drew the blood to save the best veins for Steve and Donna, who performed the scans. They needed good veins to run the IV for the second contrast used in the CT scan. As I sat in the blood draw chair, I absorbed again the details of the black-and-white photos of the campus of Cranbrook, home to a Science Institute, an Art Museum, and a private school down the road in Bloomfield Hills.

Back in the waiting area, I noticed the subtle placard stating policy: *In the event of a respiratory or cardiac arrest in an outpatient setting, Karmanos will initiate CPR.*

At this branch in Farmington Hills, the light streamed through the pentagon-shaped wall windows on the northern side of the building. The overhead lighting was more subdued, suspended in small fixtures from the tongue-and-grooved pine ceiling. The large waiting room offered an array of comfortable chairs, some a cushy burnt orange leather, others a dark royal blue woven fabric. A banner above the reception area read "The Detroit Red Wings Support You," and the hockey stick graphic to the left was fashioned out of pink ribbons. Signatures slanted left and right under the words. I tried not to feel slighted since my lung cancer wasn't represented by the color pink. The wall behind the coffee area displayed small clay plaques with rectangles of copper- and silver-engraved metal underneath each plaque to identify the donors being recognized with the art.

When I first came to the Center, I noticed the east wall of the Rosenhaus Patient Waiting Lounge where a wall of water separated the open waiting area from the hallway leading toward the examination and treatment rooms, the water forming a sparkling curtain against a backdrop of green and blue tiles. At some point, the waterfall stopped flowing, and I hadn't asked about the cause, even though there was likely a simple answer to the question, like "Bacteria developed." Or, "The pipes broke, and we haven't gotten around to fixing them." Or maybe "Someone on our board complained about the ecological waste of the water." I knew from experience that causes aren't always clearly defined.

Once I finished drinking the water and Steve or Donna escorted me to the CT room, I took one last sip of water while they quizzed me about recent surgeries, my last period, whether or not I could possibly be pregnant. They reminded me of Metformin interactions. If I took that particular medication, I couldn't take my usual dose for forty-eight hours after the CT scan, or a reaction might occur. I had to sign a statement acknowledging receipt of this information.

Then I lay on my back, my arm extended with that plump vein I saved for them, the best one, so they could pop the I.V. in. And they reminded me that after they took the thoracic CTs without contrast, they would run the IV, and the metallic taste might fill my mouth as I experienced a warm faux urination. Then I raised both arms above my heads like I was at one of my kids' weddings, throwing myself into the Macarena or the Cha Cha Slide. Or like I was preparing my grandchildren for swimming class, modelling the chicken-airplane-soldier poses.

The machine, mercifully quieter than the MRIs I'd endured, began its whir, and a man's voice chanted the drill:

Breathe in.

Hold your breath.

Breathe.

After the practice runs, the machine started for real, the CT cylinder not only rotating around me but clicking now, too, the tray-bed on which I was positioned rolling me in and out of the whirring, clicking ring.

I was always thankful when Steve or Donna said they were good to go, because I got to pee again, right away, and then I got to have a cup of coffee, my first of the day. Dr. Gadgeel arranged things early on so I could get everything done in just one day: the bloodwork, the scans, the appointment. Unlike people who lived in the area, I had a one-stop extended visit every three months; I didn't have to go home and come back the next day after scans. One-stop care. Which made it much easier with respect to the driving/commuting factor but also provided the advantage of receiving the report about the scans right away.

Because once I'd been scanned, I knew that the next thing to face was the interpretation of those scans. The drug would stop working at some point, and I knew that. I thought I knew when, because given my cancer's mutation type, my EXON 19 deletion, I hoped to get five years of controlled cancer on my daily pill.

But five was really just a number that I gave myself, just a way of shaping my hopes and expectations. I still didn't know what the scans would reveal. Until Dr. Gadgeel came into the room and said, almost before greeting me, "The scans look good," I could only drink my coffee, stare out the lovely pentagon-shaped window wall of the Lawrence and Idell Weisberg Center, or look at the waterfall, and imagine water, flowing down the wall.

Breathe in.

Hold your breath.

Breathe.

Mobility

The bird inside the McNamara terminal at Detroit Metro Airport walked with confidence over the gray carpet. Her strut reminded me that I forgot to say goodbye aloud to Clover before leaving on this trip to see my friend Marie in Nashville. As my bird-watching companion, Clover looked for a place to squat while I stood in the grass, holding her leash and surveying the branches above me. A fat robin who'd appeared lately in the branches sent me to Google in an attempt to understand robin pregnancies. I wondered if the female's belly became large like a human's because she was ready to lay those blue eggs, or if she was just stout because some robins, like people, were built that way.

If the bird in this terminal rose above me and hovered just above my head, she could deposit something in my overpriced yogurt parfait from the coffee shop. This bird acted more forward than our backyard bird. More like Clover. Clover had grown comfortable, Tim said. After four weeks of living with us, she wandered the main floor of the house with more confidence, less timidity than she did in the beginning. She began to demonstrate her strength.

When I held the leash and stood at the top of the frost-slick rise in my backyard on that Sunday just before Mother's Day, I didn't know that her one playful tug would be powerful enough to send me to the ground, my crocs sliding on the soggy grass beneath me. I closed my eyes and winced. My bad ankle had bent underneath me as I fell, and I also felt a crick of pain in my spine, which held a healing-but-still-cancer-sclerotic spot at the intersection of the lumbar and sacral regions.

Once I hit the ground, Clover rejoiced to have me there, available for licking.

My hands clutched at the grass underneath me, the grass I'd watched green up over the last few weeks. I hoped it wasn't a break. I called for Tim, knowing he wouldn't hear a sound, with the windows closed up. I'd called out only to articulate in some dramatic way my frustration with my situation. I hated the sound of my voice. Angry. Pleading.

"Fuck Cheryl Strayed," I'd told Rachel weeks earlier. I'd been trying to get her to understand that I needed more help from her. That even though she struggled with her customer-service-oriented job at Best Buy and confusion about her future and an accompanying desperation to get out from under our roof and be her own person, I had my own issues.

I'd requested a summer section of Introduction to Poetry and Prose, and I didn't want to let it go. I'd finished my semester of respite. We needed the income.

"Her mother died of lung cancer," Rachel had told me. "She has had the same experience that I'm having. And I've loved the 'Dear Sugar' column for a long time."

I understood how hard it must be to have a mother dying of lung cancer. But this mother dying of lung cancer needed help at a very physical and practical level. Help with the dog. Help with the house. Help with the younger brother's activities. "I'm right here!" I wanted to say to her. "I'm not dead yet. Help me, please!"

What I couldn't admit to then was my total jealousy of Cheryl Strayed and how she had gained my daughter's fervent allegiance. I was jealous that some other woman had written about how much she missed her dead mother. I had missed my dead mother for years, had slogged through parenting, and was trying even now to slog through an unrewarding writing career and part-time work that barely paid the bills, in spite of the joy it often gave me. I wanted Rachel to take care of the dog and clean the upstairs bathroom. I didn't want to hear her discuss the solace she found in the words of some best-selling writer's trauma.

She doesn't remember my saying those words, "Fuck Cheryl Strayed." Perhaps I never said them aloud. Perhaps I just imagined a four-syllable litany and repeated it while scouring the sink or taking the dog into the backyard or making stuffed peppers for dinner.

On the weekends, I rose first. I liked to go to bed before midnight and rise early enough to enjoy the day when it could still be called morning. Clover had expanded the capacity of her bladder, which eliminated any middle-of-the-night hassle but made my morning rising even more urgent. The task of going out with her each morning seemed to default more and more to me. Since Tim put her in the crate at night before he went to bed and long after I retired, I never knew how long she would last – how long I could lie in bed once I awoke. Anxiety about potential messes in the crate forced me out of bed on weekend mornings.

On the day of my fall, rain fell lightly. Without thinking, I'd slipped into my Crocs, attached Clover to the leash and walked into the back yard. The two of us stood on the rise. She tugged. The pull, combined with the gravity and the plastic of the Croc soles against the wet grass, sent me into a tumble.

I lay on the grass. Let out a burst of air. Felt Clover's soft tongue against my face. But the people in the house still slept, so I had to crawl back up to a kneeling position and test my injured foot against the wet grass, trying not to whimper. I rose, clenching the leash in my hand, and called for Clover to follow me as I limped back to the house.

After twenty-four hours of ice, a visit to the doctor, and the requisite X-ray, I became the proud owner of a fitted boot for my sprained ankle and a respite from Clover potty duty.

A few weeks later, I took Rachel out to lunch for her birthday and presented her with one of her gifts, a copy of Cheryl Strayed's *Torch*. An apology. To her and to Cheryl. For what I'd said. Or didn't say. Or thought.

Burgundy Skirt

Purple rhododendrons fluttered in the breeze, lacy at the edges. On the back deck, from a spot overlooking the trees, a salamander crawled on a brick just under the downspout. He skittered on the edge, his moving a kind of flicking. A cardinal chittered in the trees next to Marie's house on Laurel Ridge. The wrought iron railing curved around the deck.

Rachel would be auditioning that night for *Bonnie and Clyde* back in Michigan. She told me she didn't know what she would do if she didn't get the role of Bonnie.

I'd driven her to so many auditions over the years, waiting in the car or at a nearby coffee shop. She would likely wear the burgundy skirt, a pencil skirt, paring it with a nude shirt that appeared more blousy and delicate. Nude heels. Or maybe she would just wear flats because she didn't want to tower over Adam, who was serving as Clyde for the auditions and would likely be cast because he'd proposed the show to the theatre.

She wanted so desperately to be the outlaw. The good girl who wanted to be bad. Perhaps I'd spent too much of my life encouraging her in the role of the good girl. She'd called me last night, here in Nashville at Marie's house, and told me her outrage at her current director's statement that he couldn't give her any more time from that show's rehearsals for callbacks to another theatre's future show auditions. She'd only missed one of his rehearsals, but she felt scolded and irresponsible. And my first thought was, "Oh, no. He's frustrated with her. She's going to get a bad reputation, a reputation for being 'difficult' in our Lansing venues."

What was so wrong with being outraged every once in a while? Why did I want her to be the good girl? To be nice? We all knew that men were assertive and women were bitchy. Why couldn't I just let her be bitchy? She should have the opportunity to play Bonnie, the good woman transformed to bad, throwing herself into the keening notes of "Dying Ain't So Bad."

In the musical revue she performed in during the spring, she sang "At the Ballet" from *A Chorus Line* with two other women. During her solo, her voice rose at the end of the line and repeated. Plaintive, it moved higher and higher. Her sage green eyes were ringed with a darker rim of black around the iris, so they always looked smudged in a dreamy sort of way, her hair now always in ringlets when she dressed up because she'd worn it straight most of her life and she wanted curls now, wanted to be different. My head carried snapshots of dresses she'd worn for auditions: the blue dress we ordered for the Belle audition in New York and the beige shoes we picked up from Payless at Great Lakes Crossing in Pontiac, just hours before our flight to New York. The seafoam green dress we purchased at Macy's when I vetoed all of the others – not classy enough, too high-waisted, the material too cheap.

I'd never been a fashion plate myself, rarely had opinions about what was stylish and what wasn't, so why did I hold such strong opinions for my daughter's clothing selections?

She was the child who'd projectile vomited as an infant, cried for hours each evening in a colic phase lasting months, screamed her lungs out in the infant car seat all the way from Virginia to Michigan, when she was just a month old, when I sang every ballad and show tune I could think of so she would hear my voice from her car seat behind me where I sat, immobilized in front of the steering wheel. My firstborn whose face gave me an intense rush of pleasure each time I opened her bedroom door in the morning, to lift her body from the crib.

I was away from home, taking a break from it all, yet part of me wanted to be back there, waiting somewhere to get the call about how the audition went. I yearned to be part of the transformation process when she moved from good girl to bad girl. Or good girl to better girl. Did I care so much about the details because I want to be a part of the process or because I wanted her to get it right? Was it her transformation I cared about or my own?

Being at Marie's house in Tennessee put me back in our rowhouse apartment in Baltimore, when I was the same age that Rachel was now, trying to figure out my future, trying to figure out if I could live the life of an artist. I admired Rachel's effort to work the problems out, but at the same time that I observed her efforts, I feared that my own chances to be that artist had crumbled. So many missed opportunities.

Marie would be home from her clinical work soon, and we would do something fun. The night before, when I'd arrived, she and Bobby had taken me to a club for seafood night, and we talked about a book they thought I should read about cancer, *The Emperor of All Maladies*. On Sunday, before I left, Marie would take me to Ann Patchett's new Nashville bookstore, Parnassus Books, to buy Mukherjee's book. We planned to walk in the Botanical Gardens at Cheekwood, one of the city's treasures. Since Bobby had left town for a meeting somewhere, Marie and I would talk like we used to when we lived together in Baltimore. Talk and talk and talk, so I could empty all of the crazy thoughts in my head, all of the good girl/bad girl, what's-wrong-with-me thoughts that wound through and tangled in my brain. Marie and I would remember being thirty years younger and trying to figure out where we stood in the world.

I would be here, making peace with the cardinal, and the salamander, and the smell of spring, but I would also be there in Michigan, with the dresses, the shoes, and the young woman trying to transform, to be transformed, who ached with every note of dying she sang.

The Talk (June 23, 2013)

I remembered concretely only one time that my mother expressed extreme disappointment in me as an adult – when I was on the phone with my friend Penny, and it was Valentine's Day. I'd returned to her house after graduate school in Baltimore and lived with her as I paid on my student loans from college and graduate school and determined my next plan of action. I stayed on the phone too long after I got back from work at the stock brokerage firm, and when I hung up the phone, my mother said something about how long I'd tied up the phone on Valentine's Day. Maybe my father was trying to call her, she said, but how would she ever know because I'd been on the phone so long.

With her comment, she implied that I was selfish, and of course, I was. She owned the house, the phone. In addition, the two of us had planned to go to dinner, a date which had been delayed by the call I took.

Perhaps because I knew I was wrong, I distracted myself by thinking, "Why do you want him to call? He is bad news for you. I thought you were over all that." Maybe I even said those words aloud, although it would have been unlike me to be so frank in such a moment.

I wanted her to be over the divorce, three years old. I wanted her to be the independent woman I knew her to be, not to express aloud any need or want or longing. How naïve I was.

And "naïve" was the word I liked to use for Rachel – it was so much kinder and truer than the word "selfish." I was hurt sometimes by how easy it seemed for her to express her own needs and wants on a daily basis and how little attention she seemed to pay to mine. I assumed denial was at work – that it was much easier for her to see her mother at the stove, cooking in a normal fashion, folding clothes, driving off to work, than it was to think about the fact that even as her mother did these things, malignant cells were replicating in the hidden folds of her organs, tissues, and bones. Taking her down.

Rachel occupied a difficult space, living at home with few friends around, slogging at a low-paying job, marching through hours of daunting auditions followed by unpredictable rehearsal schedules, if she were fortunate enough to be cast in shows for which she auditioned.

But I needed understanding. All I asked for was understanding. When she opposed, challenged, relented, and then challenged again, she apologized and explained that she was different, that her life was different. She was so busy. Too busy to plan ahead and reserve an hour to make a salad every now and then, or schedule a few days to take the dog out in the morning, or do the three hours of afternoon damage control Clover needed to keep her from chewing through her anxiety and the rubber of her puppy toys?

"We need a team approach," my husband said.

After she left the family meeting, off to a rehearsal, my older son said, "She's not on board yet, but we can get her there." Yet I knew that she wasn't the only one who needed to get on board. They'd all been dragging their heels. She might have been my focus of the moment, but I needed them all to be on board. To be honest, maybe I expected more from her because she was female. I didn't want to think I believed that only females were capable of true nurturing, but maybe I did. Or maybe I expected more from her because of her place as the oldest.

I wanted her to be on board without even thinking. Automatically. I wanted her to value the time we had left; I wanted her to have an aching desire to ease my load. I didn't want the hurt of disappointment. Or the chill of judgment I might subject her to once my hurt set in.

75

Soup Kitchen on Connor's Birthday (June 29, 2013)

I'd been so anxious about the upcoming soup kitchen that I'd forgotten to wish Connor "Happy Birthday!" when I awoke, remembering only when he pulled up to drop me off at the church door and said he couldn't believe he was twenty. To my knowledge, I'd never before forgotten to wish one of my children "Happy Birthday!" the minute they fell out of beds or emerged from their rooms. I tried not to view my omission as a loss.

Soup kitchen was always anxiety-producing, but that day's stint proved more challenging than usual. I'd learned ahead of time that the meal would be easy – some sort of goulash. Yet with the number of volunteers at eleven, a number on the low side for volunteers, everyone helping would need to work hard at each stage of the process – the cooking and baking, the serving, the cleaning up. After only an hour or so, when the dishwasher began to act up and Tim started to get anxious because he led the dishwashing team, the day became an endurance test.

I worried about losing my capacity for empathy. For four years I had managed to stay positive when dealing with Tom, the elderly guest, mostly now in a wheelchair, who liked to talk, demanded attention, told jokes and asked people to cart him to the bathroom upstairs, even though there was one down in the basement, next to the kitchen and gym, where the guests ate. The church personnel had emphasized to us at the manager meetings that we didn't have to accommodate him – it was nice to be nice, but ultimately, the church just might not have the resources any longer to deal with his handicaps.

But because I often saw Tom drag his leg in a manner reminiscent of the way my father dragged his with multiple sclerosis, I'd been able to be kind and patient in my dealings with him. (Let's be honest – I often had the men deal with him, or Charlie, our friends' teenage son, so how patient did I really have to be?) But as I stood there after the meal was over, my bones aching, my chest heavy with whatever pain had hung there since March, I found it increasingly difficult to listen to him. I wheeled him to the elevator and got him to the next floor, and another man stepped in to help him to the bathroom. But my mind didn't want to hear him go on about the veteran named Bruce who let his meal get cold at the restaurant the night before in order to help somebody in need. I couldn't feel moved at all by the tears that came to his eyes, making his face all watery, making me think that yes, it must be multiple sclerosis because my father would tear up just like that in his final years after a lifetime of rarely crying.

When the church doorbell rang, and that other man stepped in after I unlocked the upstairs bathroom, I was so thankful to have an excuse to walk away from Tom. Yet perhaps I wasn't frustrated with him. Perhaps I was mad at Brandon the janitor, who came downstairs at 11:10, twenty minutes before serving time, and asked if I could unlock the door upstairs myself and let the guests in because he had things he needed to do.

I should have said, "No. I have things to do! They told us in the managers' meeting that it's your job to unlock the door, so you need to do it."

But he'd distracted me when he said, "Are you new here? I've never met you before." I told him I probably looked different. What I really wanted to tell him was that I'd known him for over three years. In that time, I'd managed the soup kitchen to the best of my abilities on my quarterly stints, even though managing clearly didn't play to my strengths, even though I wasn't an extrovert or a linear thinker. Instead I said, "Yeah. Go ahead. I'll unlock the door."

My psychologist liked to impress upon me that my judgments, however small-minded they might make me feel, were just thoughts. They didn't define me. They didn't make me an evil person. They didn't hurt anyone. Still, I hated having them. I wanted to be always and only generous-hearted. I had long believed that it was important to serve others. I wanted to teach my children to value service. I wanted to believe that managing the soup kitchen was an important and valuable way to spend my time. I probably assumed that if I served others, I would do so joyfully. But with my bones and muscles aching, I wondered about why I retained so little energy at the end of each day, regardless of the day's tasks and what that depletion meant about my cancer. Being fatigued didn't seem like a benign phenomenon.

I woke from my post-soup-kitchen nap and immersed myself in a television movie, examining Donald Sutherland's face as he came on the screen for scenes. His facial features were so malleable, capable of contorting into the evil pyromaniac Donald Sutherland from *Backdraft* or into the equally disturbing SS officer in *1900*. And yet if his face was in a line of people stumbling into the gym for Saturday soup kitchen, would it stand out? It was a face like Tom's. Most faces displayed some humanity, humanity to which I must try to connect.

Connor wrote about Tom in one of his college application essays, casting him in only a positive light. Tom, the disabled man at the soup kitchen, cracking jokes, needing just a bit of attention. If Connor had stayed home to work the soup kitchen on his birthday, he might have been the one wheeling Tom up to the bathroom, perhaps allowing me to retain my empathy.

But I was happy he didn't serve on his birthday, happy he was in Kalamazoo, with his tennis teammates. I realized that my empathy might flag, just as my energy flagged, but until it became impossible to do so, I needed to try to learn from the people around me while at the same time recognizing both my frailties and my own humanity, which might get buried sometimes but surely never disappeared completely. As I watched Donald Sutherland, I texted Connor "Happy Birthday!" telling him that I hoped he'd had a great day.

Return to Work

After I spent the winter semester off work learning how to adjust to Tarceva and its minions – the skin rash, the fatigue, the occasional diarrhea, the hair loss, and the hair growth – and after I acquired a puppy with my family, sprained my ankle, and trekked to Nashville to see my friend Marie and unload a brain full of confusion, I prepared to return to work.

I didn't know what the future held for me in terms of cancer growth, but I'd finally made it to the point in my employment at Oakland that I'd planned and lobbied for – a summer section of the Introduction to Poetry and Prose class, which would be followed by the dream schedule I hoped to spend the rest of my work life following: three sections of creative writing in the Fall Semester and three sections in the Winter Semester each academic year.

The salary was not what I'd hoped for, approximately $30,000 per academic year, about $5000 per section, and because I was an adjunct, I wouldn't have the benefits unless I paid for them, nor would I have a guarantee of a certain number of sections per year. My work load depended on enrollment, and I would need to sign a contract each semester. But I believed I could handle the paper load of the three-class-per-semester creative writing instruction better than the four-class-per-semester, mostly-composition load I'd taught previously at Lansing Community College. And though I'd loved advising at LCC and missed the students a great deal, I knew that however much advising might mesh with my interests, my skill set, and my love of students, landing a full-time job, or even a stable part-time job, in the advising field was no easier than landing a tenure-track teaching position. Clearly, with a cancer diagnosis, I could no longer work multiple jobs at different universities.

I began that summer semester at Oakland on Monday, May 6, 2013, knowing I'd hit the jackpot when it came to students. Only six students, one of whom I'd had before. Getting back on the horse in temperate weather every Monday and Wednesday evening was the gentlest reintroduction to college teaching that a mother with stage IV lung cancer could have. I'd be teaching poetry again, along with prose. I often thought I was a more playful teacher when it came to poetry because I didn't have all of the concepts seared in my head like I did with fiction.

Bobby. Stacey. David. Brian. Ricky. Annie. For seven weeks we wrote hard, workshopped hard, enjoyed the sunshine and the bees on the campus lawns, and laughed more than I'd thought possible. I'd felt compelled to be honest with them about my diagnosis and they'd been respectful, encouraging, and kind. On the last day of class of the condensed summer semester, June 19, when we decided to have our final reading inside because of the heat, in the lobby of South Foundation Hall with the odd 70s plastic bucket seats, I thought I would cry. Their writing was so human, and I would miss them.

However, I welcomed the luxury of another two months off. Another respite, after which I would return to work again, in the Fall of 2013, to those three golden sections. A Monday and Wednesday Introduction to Poetry and Prose class, just like the one I'd taught that summer. And two Intermediate Fiction Workshops, one on Monday night and one on Wednesday night.

When the first Monday night section met, I followed the pattern I'd established in the summer and told the class I wanted to be transparent about my illness, and because of the ubiquity of cancer, I wanted them to have the opportunity to drop the class if they had any traumatic experiences with cancer that they didn't want to relive.

When the class concluded for the evening, one student remained – a tall, thin, silver-blonde young man wearing a neck brace. His name was Jeremy, and he had osteosarcoma.

For the next thirty minutes we sat in the South Foundation Hall classroom, swapping cancer discovery stories. I learned that his parents had found his cancer when he was just fourteen. A bone in his leg had snapped one day at a soccer game just after he'd kicked the ball. It was an athletic event, at which any injury could potentially occur. Yet he hadn't kicked the ball particularly hard, nor had he come into contact with any of the opposing team's members. When I met Jeremy, he'd been dealing with the osteosarcoma for seven years, and here he was in front of me, preparing to be in my class for an entire semester.

He didn't like to write or read about cancer. He wasn't a big fan of religion, and he wasn't fond of hearing from people that they were praying for him. I shared with him my own difficulties with prayer because I refused to believe in a god who picked winners and losers. We parted for the evening on an energized note, although we were both tired.

On my drive home, I turned over in my head what he'd shared. I was saddened by his health situation and its unending battles with his bones but overwhelmed by his courage. As he'd sat there, his jaw and face jutting out from the neck brace, I saw the determination in the angle of his head; I hoped I could teach him as much as he would likely teach me.

Tarceva Moment (September 18, 2013)

The gas station had formerly been a B.P., and when I stopped in the first time, before I knew about the hookah lounge in town, or anything much about hookahs, I was startled by the pipes on the back wall behind the cashier who took my money for gas, wondering why a gas station would carry what I thought was drug paraphernalia.

The station had since changed to a Mobil, and the last time I'd stopped in, the hookah pipes had disappeared. The man behind the counter was young, with glasses and short hair, and smiled politely when I asked for the restroom. He nodded to the corner, a few steps from the cash register.

I was having a Tarceva moment, even though I'd travelled less than two miles from home, had just left there, in fact, and had gone to the bathroom several times before I left.

One of the major side effects of Tarceva was diarrhea, and it was referenced prominently on the drug information insert. Dr. Gadgeel told me when I first began taking the drug that most of his other patients carried a bottle of Imodium AD with them at all times. As someone who had suffered from Irritable Bowel Syndrome for many years, particularly the constipation side of the Syndrome, I had struggled only rarely with diarrhea. But I was not immune, and Tarceva was a powerful drug.

On that day, I had no money. It had long been a rule of mine, probably passed down by my mother, that I needed to buy something when I used the bathroom at an establishment.

Okay, so maybe I'd cheated at McDonald's from time to time, sneaking in and out the side door, knowing that in the course of my lifetime with three children, I'd paid my fair share to the establishment and deserved to use their toilets from time to time. But anywhere else, I bought when I used something. I paid a user's fee.

As I sat in the restroom, thankful for the empty store, I thought about how I would face the man outside. What I would say. Maybe there was an ATM, and I could get money out to buy a bag of chips or a Coke Zero. But the account contained only a few dollars, less than ten if I counted the check that was supposed to hit today. The credit card was maxed out until the next payment hit. I couldn't afford to pay my user's fee.

I felt quasi-relieved when I opened the door and looked around at the rows of Cheetos and Planter's Peanuts and Campbell's Chicken Noodle Soup and realized there was no ATM. It was just as well. Except that I still felt I should buy something. And since the worker was in my field of vision and since he had, after all, provided me with a solution to a problem, a solution he had provided for free, I needed to thank him. Part of me wanted to spell it out – tell him that I had to stop because I had this occasional odd side effect from Tarceva, which could hit at any time, and I carried Imodium AD everywhere I went.

But what was the point? He knew how long I'd occupied that little room behind the bolted door. And still, he smiled a disarming smile and said, "Have a Nice Day" as I passed him on the way out.

I thanked him for the service.

Tarceva Refills

When I came down the stairs that Wednesday morning after my shower, having left Clover in the kitchen eating area for far too long by herself, she was gripping the medicine bottle sideways in her teeth, the torn-open end of the bottle dripping soggy tablets. The edges of the plastic were jagged, not sharp enough to draw blood, but thin, wispy and lacy, almost like the edges of cookies with too much butter spread out like doilies on the Air Bake sheet just inside the oven window.

Clover eyed me, not quite defiantly, with the pill bottle in her mouth, and then ran around the table, dodging between the chair legs, her tail catching the edge of a paper receipt on the table and flicking it onto the floor. A few more tablets fell out of the bottle.

"Clover!" I wailed. I wanted to sink to the floor.

I did sink to the floor. I squatted and began picking up each dropped tablet, moist with a chalky mixture of pill coating and saliva. "No, Clover," I tried to whisper fiercely, "drop it!"

She circled to the other side of the table, and I plucked up a few more tablets. Five. Six. Seven.

"That medicine will make you sick," I said. "Drop it!"

She darted past me into the family room.

I pressed my hand to the dirty linoleum and rose from my squat. Her box of dog biscuits rested on the corner of the nearby hutch. I reached my hand into the box. Her sensitive ears knew the sound of fingers fumbling against cardboard. I grabbed a biscuit. "Treat," I said, dropping it on the floor. I was a horrible dog mother. I frequently did the bait-and-switch routine rather than demanding complete and utter obedience. But this ploy might be my best chance at getting her to drop the bottle.

She dropped it.

I'd counted thirteen Tarceva tablets when I'd talked to Diplomat Specialty Pharmacy that morning to place my refill on the prescription. As I trailed after Clover, I counted aloud the pills I retrieved from the floor. Now I had eleven. I didn't even usually keep track; I felt fortunate I'd done the count recently.

My chest felt so heavy. No one else was at home. Tim and Rachel were off at work and Nathaniel was in school. My first class at Oakland didn't start for hours, but I still had the hour and a half commute and several hours of class preparation ahead of me.

I dug through my Clover folder on the counter and picked up the phone. When Joel, one of my favorites at East Lansing Vet Clinic answered, I described the event. "My dog ate my oral chemotherapy" was more dramatic than "my dog ate my homework."

"Bring her in," he said.

I loaded her into the car and drove the five minutes to the vet's office. After they took her weight and she did her usual submissive peeing on the floor, they ushered us into an examination room and had me repeat my story to Dr. Mortimer. The plan of action, they told me, would be to contact the poison hotline for animals to make sure it was okay to induce vomiting and to determine if there were other measures they should take to reduce toxicity.

We waited in the exam room, Clover and I. She looked and acted fine. Happy. Happier than usual because of the animal-loving staff members who lavished affection on her.

I texted Rachel and Tim to let them know what was happening and to ask them to be prepared as back-up care providers depending on how things went. I tried not to let my mind go further than that.

Dr. Mortimer and Joel returned with a go-ahead from the poison people to induce vomiting. They would use a drug called Apomorphine, a standard veterinary emetic which they would put in her eye. Once they saw the contents of her stomach, they would know what to do.

Taking her leash, they led her away. She was happy to follow; she was one of the happiest beings I knew. I'd gotten this dog to replace me in my family's affections after I died, and I'd be damned if I'd let her die before me.

Back in the waiting room, I lowered myself into one of the chairs, trying to concentrate on what I needed to get done before my class met that afternoon. If they sent Clover home with me, Tim could probably leave work and monitor her for a bit until Rachel got home from work.

As I sat there, looking at a stand of special leashes and treats, I thought of how often in the last year we'd all had to make alternate arrangements to our personal and work schedules because of medical issues. The act of figuring out alternative game plans reduced anxiety, but you could only prolong the suspension briefly before you needed to return to the real world and confront the frightening details of the present moment and its trauma. Yet I knew some people could remain in that other arena of quasi-denial indefinitely. Planning, but not fully confronting.

About forty-five minutes later, Joel brought Clover out to the waiting area. She wore a huge cone around her neck like a sound dish featuring her happy face poking out of the middle.

"She's going to be fine," Joel said. "When we induced vomiting, we got about one and a half tablets, so very close to what you thought she'd gotten hold of. Then we watched her for a while. Based on what the poison people said, she should recover completely. Just watch her. And she's going to need to keep this cone on for a while. Her eye might be sensitive because of the drug used to induce vomiting; we need to make sure she doesn't scratch at her eyes."

He handed me the leash, and I paid the bill while Clover batted at her cone in cat-like fashion. Then I loaded my youngest into the car with her new plastic head guard and drove home, where I handed her off later to my husband before I got on the road for Oakland with my stereo blaring so I could sing at the top of my lungs on I-69, letting my stress go.

Child-Proof Bottle

The Tarceva bottle sat upside down on its child-proof cap, the circumference of that cap hatched with uniform grooves to make grasping easier. The bottom of the plastic container was what Clover had chewed open into a near perfect circle, leaving a disk of plastic still connecting the circle to the rest of the bottle. Clover's teeth marks in the hard plastic appeared like lace, a pattern of wispy white, the clinging lid poised open like the maw of a ghost or the The Great Wave from Katsushika Hokusai's woodblock. Or like Popeye's opened spinach can, with its ragged edges. The malfunctioning can opener in my mother's kitchen made a similar design, separating most lids from the cans of my childhood but often failing on the last bite, forcing me to grasp the serrated lid and wrench it free from the rest of the can, regardless of potential injury.

Many of the words on the label were still legible, although much of the surface felt gummy, the adhesive under the label mixing with Clover's saliva to create a papier-mâché texture still tacky enough to bear a few of Clover's white hairs next to the number of Diplomat Specialty Pharmacy in Flint. My doctor's name, Gadgeel, M.B.B.S., Shirish. The drug name itself, Tarceva, in letters of rich magenta. The drug symbol to the left, a half circle of that magenta into which a brighter red lightning bolt intruded, the drug companies' shares of the pill's success hard to determine from names and imprints on a label. Genentech, Roche, Astellas Pharma U.S. Lightning bolt companies, all, creating the life-lengthening but not curative drug.

Five months after I started on Tarceva, the Food and Drug Administration approved it for the first-line treatment of patients with metastatic non-small lung cancer whose tumors have mutations in their epidermal growth factor receptors (EGFR). In particular, tumors with EGFR mutations that were EXON 19 deletions or EXON 21 substitution mutations. The date of that approval was May 14, 2013. I was EGFR, EXON 19. A woman on Tarceva.

Cancer Birthday (November 26, 2013)

I felt ashamed of my thoughts. It was my 54th birthday, and I had a headache. I sat in a booth at Mitchell's Fish Market, waiting for my scallops. The other booths were empty, and although it was early yet, the waitress confided that it was a slow week prior to Thanksgiving.

The Caesar salad was tasty, but I wished the waitress had brought some bread. I was hoping that the Excedrin and the Sudafed I took earlier, along with the coffee I drank, would dull the headache enough so that I could enjoy my moscato. I wished Rachel were with me. I was torn between the moscato – her drink – and the Riesling – my mom's drink. But moscato was sweeter, and cheaper by $1.00. Rachel had already told me she was sorry her dad hadn't scheduled a celebration for my birthday; she felt guilty for being so busy with rehearsals and Best Buy hours, which she'd had to switch to day hours to accommodate night rehearsals.

Perhaps I expected too much for my birthday. Or perhaps I loaded too much wanting into one day. I remembered my first married birthday down in Charlottesville and how much I cried. I don't remember much about what Tim did or didn't do; he'd prepared Orange Roughy. Whatever else he did, it wasn't enough for that day, wasn't what my mother would have done. The wanting made me feel greedy, and then, by extension, guilty. I knew our family schedule was complicated with the Thanksgiving holiday, Rachel working on Black Friday, and our last soup kitchen Saturday. But I still thought Tim could have worked harder to get a dinner planned ahead of time with Rachel's *White Christmas* schedule.

I knew I felt hurt too easily. I'd always gotten hurt too easily. My birthday fell this year on a Tuesday, and my family didn't realize that

Tuesday was golden because it wasn't a Monday or Wednesday night when I taught late at Oakland University. I was free on this cancer birthday.

I had escaped from the house. I'd run away so I could spend my birthday alone and pretend that it meant something. I know I should have been gracious and accepted something thrown together at the last minute, as Tim had suggested that morning, but I wanted to punish those at home with my absence. While they would never completely forget my birthday, I wanted them to celebrate my living for a full year since I first learned I had cancer. To celebrate the importance of the day as an occasion.

The voice in my head told me I was being a drama queen, like Rachel sometimes. But deep inside, I wanted to be a sullen teenager who stomped her feet and stormed away petulant, punching the cell phone power off. I was maudlin with self-pity and recriminations. I wouldn't do recriminations any more. I needed to ask for and expect less.

I ate my scallops, and a bit later, my key lime pie, listening to the satellite radio playing jazz – a saxophone and a piano. "Our Day Will Come." "The Girl from Ipanema." "You are My Sunshine" with do-waps. The key lime was pale yellow, with lovely swirls of whipped cream atop it, and a perfect circle of fresh lime, a diameter cut into it, so if it were a skirt, it could fit over a head. The candle I brought with me was blue- and white-striped, and as I lit it, I imagined my parents' faces, twenty-one years distant from me. Their mouths were shaped in the vowels and consonants of "Happy Birthday."

I blew at the candle, and the wisp of smoke rose and disappeared.

Ice Storm (December 2013)

The ice arrived on the Saturday before Christmas, and when the sky filled with crackles and hisses and yellow and green light, Nathaniel thought there were fireworks. The next morning we realized the sound and light show was caused by transformers. We had power, and our life for the next week would be easy, so much easier than the lives of the people in our area who celebrated Christmas in the dark, with candles, or if they were lucky and could afford gas, a generator. Our only inconvenience was a closed Rite Aid where I'd hoped to buy candy canes.

The translucence wrapped itself around each branch, a cylindrical sheathing of ice, so that each tree and bush glistened. People who eventually went days without showers would stop the pioneering acts they did – bringing wood in from piles, drying it in the bath tub, making eggs over the fireplace – to acknowledge that yes, it was a beautiful pain in the ass.

A man died of carbon monoxide poisoning, a by-product of gas released by his generator.

Clover tiptoed on the surface of sparkled white. Eight days later the power was still out in spots throughout the greater Lansing area, even as the temperatures rose and the sheathing sprung off the trapped surfaces like snapped bands. Like bodies bounced off a trampoline. Cars stopped at lights found segments of small ice cylinders falling to their hoods from the traffic signals. I thought of the Kevin Kline, Sigourney Weaver, Joan Allen, and Elijah Wood movie Tim and I watched a few years earlier, *The Ice Storm*. Based on a story by Rick Moody, the film presented characters who were devoid of morality, Tim said, an unusually harsh judgment for him. I loved the role the ice storm itself played as a character.

I tried to articulate to someone the guilt I felt as a person in the community who had experienced no ill effects from the storm. I didn't lose power, electricity, heat, the ability to bathe or to make food. What did I really know about what it meant to survive?

The Voice

My psychologist said that the voice inside my head was like that of John Boehner, the former Speaker of the House. John Boehner with a fake, sprayed-on orange tan, smirking at whatever Obama said during his State of the Union Address. Whenever Obama talked about his goals, his hopes, his plans – it was John Boehner's job, my psychologist said, to criticize it. To smirk and wrinkle his face into some inscrutable visage not suitable for framing, even on the forty-six-inch television screen my husband recently purchased to replace our old Magnavox because we could no longer see the Michigan State basketball players run up and down the floors anymore on our outdated non-HD television with our fifty-some year-old eyeballs. Your depression brings that voice alive, my psychologist explained. It's cruel to you and hard on you. It was the kind of voice, I realized, that would belittle me and tell me I'd never be able to survive a power outage like the one we'd just seen, and why didn't I go out and help those people?

I told him – my psychologist, not John Boehner or my husband or the voice – that I didn't know until we got the new television that John Boehner's skin was so orange. As someone whose skin changed color on Tarceva, I wondered what was up with that.

The voice's job, my psychologist said, was to smirk at me and deride my thoughts, questioning their value, worth, and accuracy. I knew this to be true. The voice was often present and always brutal. John Boehner was never supposed to affirm any thought, belief, or value Obama expressed. I told him once – my psychologist, not John Boehner – that I admired Obama for many reasons, one of which was my conviction that his exterior was not easily marred by the disapproval or even the hint of disapproval from others. I wanted to be like that.

I wanted the voice and its John Boehner orange-faced counterpart to disappear from the sound track and screen in my head. I wanted to be like Obama, unafraid of the voice, the face.

Swarthmore Pizza

The walk from the Swarthmore Indoor Tennis Facility to Swarthmore Pizza was only a short, brisk one, but we decided to take the car, giving other parents a ride. When we filed in, the tennis team members were waiting in line while the waitress cleared off a table large enough.

Connor asked Coach Riley for permission to sit with us instead of his teammates, and the Coach okayed his request. We ordered a thin crust pizza, and Rachel ordered a Yuengling.

In the booth that backed up to ours, another teammate sat with his parents, who came from New Jersey to see him play. The family had moved recently from Holland, Michigan, I learned from the mom during the match, although she'd been in the New York area for a few years, having transferred there for a job. Thus, she explained, Jeremy, her son, a transfer from Indiana University-Purdue University Fort Wayne (IPFW), was in the middle of a geographical displacement. Born and raised in Holland, attending IPFW, and then transferring to Kalamazoo, a Michigan school, he had multiple homes, or none, depending on how he looked at it.

In the middle of the room, the Kalamazoo College Men's Tennis Team members argued over who was hungrier and speculated about who would eat more, not really talking about the intense matches they just played. The coach reminded them that he wouldn't cover appetizers, and then he sat down in a booth by himself, pulling out a packet of receipts which he shuffled through, commenting to the team, less than an arm's length away, that the administration would be all over him about spending. I wondered if he needed the time to himself to process the matches and the long trip during which he'd been supervising the guys as they played tennis matches during their spring break.

A few feet from me an old desk held a computer. I had no eye for antiques, but it looked like a piece of furniture that could have had a new life somewhere if someone stripped and refurbished it. Yet it served a purpose in its present form. I kept looking back, noting the dust in corners of the piece, how unremarkable it appeared in its present condition.

Eventually, our pizza arrived, along with Rachel's beer, and Coach Mark Riley came over to our booth to sit down. He told us about the dinner his brother fixed for the guys -- his brother down the street in Philadelphia who had played tennis with Coach during college at Kalamazoo and now lived and worked in Philly. He told us some of the story of how he grew up in Philly; his father still lived there, in South Philly. I told him about the wife of his former assistant, who traipsed through the narrow walkways behind the Swarthmore courts all afternoon, entertaining her young toddler for hours as the match went on. Riley's former assistant was now helping to coach at Swarthmore. When the former assistant had asked her why she stayed so long at the facility chasing after their child in challenging circumstances, she said, "Because I didn't know if we would have the chance to see Mark again."

Coach Riley said that yes, they were definitely part of his family. He missed them, even as much as he loved Kalamazoo. We talked a while, and he commented on Rachel's Yuengling and the team's travel plans. He was fascinated that Rachel planned to pursue theatre in Philly and that her boyfriend would attend Penn Law.

I drove with Rachel hundreds of miles from Michigan to see a single tennis match, one in which I knew my son would not play, so that we could show our support for Connor and so that I could bring Rachel to visit apartments in which she might live with her boyfriend when she moved to Philly in August or September.

What I wanted to say to the coach, who knew about my diagnosis, was that while he might not be able to solve my son's confidence problems, he needed to continue to work with him, even if those problems didn't occur as a result of my diagnosis, even if college tennis was a business focused on winning. My son loved tennis, and he was a good player. He just needed confidence. I wanted to tell Coach that whether he played Connor in his lineup or not, Coach needed to be there for him emotionally. He'd developed a reputation not only as a winning coach but also as a coach who took interest in his players' lives, on and off the court.

We walked out to the parking lot, and the guys got into the van. Connor stood with us for a bit, giving us a few more hugs, thanking us for coming. But it was cold, and Rachel and I needed to get into our own beat-up van to travel back to our cheap hotel room and prepare for the following day, when we would meet up with her boyfriend and they'd look around Philly for places to live. I remembered what I'd heard Coach Riley say before – thanks for trusting me with your guys – as I pulled out of the parking lot of Swarthmore Pizza. I did trust him with my son, and I hoped he'd remember that his role as a mentor went beyond the wins. I tried not to stare back at my son in the rear-view mirror.

Command

We took our places at the side of the training room on the plastic chairs, allowing a leash length of space between us. From another part of the building we heard the faint yips and barks of the dogs boarding overnight at the Doggy Day Care and Spa. Janet, our trainer, stood in front of us, jean-clad as usual, answering a last-minute question.

Rose's owner wore an orange fluorescent fanny pack around her waist, treats at the ready. When I offered to dig out my old fanny pack for Rachel to use during puppy class, she said, "No." Emphatically. Today Janet wanted us to practice our sit-down command, the only one which we had mastered. While I remained on the sidelines, Rachel and Clover began, and after practicing a few sit-down commands, Rachel even threw in the stay-and-release command when Clover appeared to tire of practicing the other.

Last week, when Rachel kept repeating the down command as Clover sat, unmoving, Janet asked, "Do you think she knows what you're saying? What you mean?"

"I know she does. I know she understands," Rachel said. We were very proud of our puppy's comprehension, even if the behaviors weren't quite there. At that point, Janet stepped in and took Clover's leash. She gave her the "sit" command. And "down." Only once. With a long, calm stare.

After ten seconds, Clover slid back on her hind legs and assumed the "down." Rachel and I laughed.

This week, we were better at "down."

Janet didn't know who I was, didn't know that I was a close friend of her friend Barb. I didn't think she remembered that we'd met before, when she and Barb sold Three Hot Bitches t-shirts at the women's arts and crafts sales. I could reveal this information to her – Barb told me I should say hello. But I wanted to stay incognito and continue to observe her. When she talked to us, she looked directly at us, not up at the ceiling, as I increasingly did when I taught and had a momentary word-retrieval lapse. Janet explained things in a calm, matter-of-fact voice, and when she took Rose from her owner to illustrate a move, she was confident that she could handle the dog. It was that confidence that impressed me. I wanted some. Not just with Clover, so I could control her on walks, but for everything.

Perhaps I wanted to keep my identity secret because my dog was a submissive urinator. I had read about Clover's problem in the training manual written by the Monks of New Skete. Submissive urination was not an uncommon problem, but I always felt frazzled after Clover had peed and I had to make a mad dash for clean-up supplies.

Clover was a beautiful dog, but she was not perfect. She didn't listen as well as she could. And she peed. But I did feel some pride as I watched my lovely daughter work with my lovely dog. We needed to train Clover so she didn't run into the road. And we needed to train her so we could take her for walks to alleviate her boredom. In particular, I needed to be able to take her for walks, without losing control of her.

Janet watched as I joined Rachel and we gave Clover a command. Clover began to obey but become distracted by another dog and another owner. And then she peed.

Connor, Tim, and Nathaniel had brought Clover to her first puppy class when she was younger, and she'd absorbed a few things. But she seemed to have lost a bit of ground, and I suspected that I was to blame for some of her poor behaviors. I was not a natural at the training thing. I was too permissive. I felt that her peeing must be my fault.

"She is emotionally soft," Janet said. I winced.

She got that from me. I was emotionally soft.

EpiPen

Start with the trainer, the lighter-weight version of the EpiPen without medication inside. The key to using the EpiPen accurately is practicing first with the trainer. You will be anxious, but take those few seconds to practice and calm your nerves. When you're ready, switch to the real EpiPen. The black end is the tip, the needle.

The first step is removing the gray cap from the non-needle end of the EpiPen. Removing the cap loads epinephrine into the injection device. Next, hold the EpiPen in your dominant hand as if it were a dagger. Clench your fingers along the smooth cylinder and imagine yourself stabbing someone. The force of a clenched fist gives you accurate delivery. And courage. Somewhere close, Nathaniel is waiting. Maybe he went out to hit with one of the guys, so he's been on the courts, working up a sweat. Maybe he stopped at Tropical Smoothies, and they accidentally made his mango-strawberry smoothie with milk or whey powder. You probably won't know until later why it happened, but you're there. You came by to pick him up, just happened to be sitting in the parking lot listening to NPR. One of the guys saw your car, came running to get you.

Nathaniel knows the EpiPen drill, but he's too far gone, too woozy to do this himself. If you're the one holding the EpiPen, it means he's already got that locked feeling in his throat, his ears itch like mad, and his head is spinning so much that he's down on his knees, head bent forward, almost touching the blue court, just outside of the service line.

Call 911. Kneel down next to him; towering will just make him more afraid. Knowing the drill is one thing; he's never had to execute it. Even with all those times he guzzled down Benadryl after a too-rare hamburger or suspect sauce on a carry out order, he's escaped the need to use the EpiPen. He's become cavalier about the need to even carry it. He'll be mad at himself for screwing up and eating something or maybe mad at the person who told him whatever food was fine. Tell him to turn on his side. Tell him he'll be okay. Tell him you'll do it on the count of three, and then you'll both count to ten together while you hold the EpiPen in place. With your other hand, grip the muscle of his thigh just above his knee. His leg is bigger than the orange you've practiced on, so it will be easier to hold him still.

Count One. Raise the EpiPen in the air like you are Abraham ready to sacrifice his son.

Count Two. Take a deep breath.

Count Three. Think orange. Plunge the EpiPen into his thigh, right through his clothes.

Wait to hear the click, not the soft click of a pen, but a thicker, metallic-sounding click.

Don't pull back. Hold it there, and count to ten while the medicine enters his body. Pull it out.

Put the needle against the nearest hard surface and bend it at an angle so no one else is injected.

Watch his face. You'll hear the sirens in the distance. By the time the paramedics pull up, he'll be breathing easier. They'll make sure he's stabilized and transport him to the hospital for another dose of epinephrine and a follow-up exam.

If you were there to save him, you're lucky. Next time you might not be. Convince him that he must carry it everywhere, to Bubble Island, to Chipotle, to the girls' Varsity soccer game to watch that one girl he wants to impress. It can save his life, but only if he carries it with him.

It's not like an umbrella that he can forget in the car because being drenched is just a clammy inconvenience, at most the loss of a pair of shoes. It's an umbrella he has to carry from car to house to car to school. It's an umbrella you might need to force on him, like that zipped coat and those mittens when he reached sixth grade, an umbrella that you try to carry over him, thrusting it out, away from your body, more over his head than yours because you want to, need to keep the mist, the sprinkles, the spatters, the torrents away from him.

You have to get this right. I might not be there to help you.

Social Security Disability

Forty-eight chairs were lined up in three sets of back-to-back rows of eight. Most of the people occupying the chairs held cell phones in front of them. Behind me, to the right, a young boy read aloud to the adult who accompanied him, pronouncing words in the halting sing-song manner of a new reader who has earned enough confidence to forge ahead. On the wall across the room, a flat screen television posted the numbers being served. A91, B40, C61, D67, F557.

I was C63 today. The last time I came to this office, I was H something. In addition to flashing numbers, the screen flashed messages in black, white, and blue letters, in English, Spanish, and Vietnamese, the tone of each message warm and encouraging, the blue swirls in the background soothing. The people in the chairs were Caucasian, African-American, Hispanic, and Asian. Some with canes and leg braces. A woman rested an elbow in her lap, chin in open palm, and closed her eyes, shutting out the wails of a toddler as the screen flashed a new number.

When I applied for Social Security Disability Benefits, I thought it was a risk-free experiment. I'd read online about how difficult it was to make an application. I'd seen television commercials about how those applying for benefits might just want to hire a lawyer. I'd absorbed all the information I could about how the guidelines might apply to my own particular diagnosis of cancer. I was likely to be considered for a Compassionate Allowance, a classification that would speed up the process through which my claim would be considered. Yet the guidelines for non-small cell lung cancer (NSCLC) were very specific. To qualify for disability, one needed metastatic disease, and the metastases had to have progressed up to or beyond the hilar nodes. Hilar lymph nodes are located in the lungs, where lungs meet the bronchi. The nodes make up part of the lymphatic system, part of the immune system. My cancer had progressed beyond the hilar nodes before I was diagnosed. At present, my cancer wasn't in remission but halted by Tarceva. What did that mean in terms of a disability claim?

When I dragged myself to the Social Security office in Lansing at the end of the week that classes ended at Oakland University, on the advice of a gentleman I'd reached on the phone a few days earlier, it wasn't my hilar nodes I was concerned about. It was my brain.

I hadn't lost the ability to read and remember the specific details and twists and turns of my students' fiction and poetry works, nor had I lost the ability to learn their names within the first few classes of the semester. I just seemed to process all information more slowly. I felt pummeled by the six-hour adjunct teaching stint I pulled at Oakland each Monday and Wednesday afternoon and evening and similarly overwhelmed by the stacks of manuscripts and critiques I was supposed to be moving through on the days I wasn't on campus. I was numbed by the three-hour commute two days a week, the latter part of each commuting day in the late evening, so that I arrived home just before midnight.

I told myself how lucky I was not only to have my job but also to condense the teaching part of it into two, or at most, three days a week. But I still felt like I wasn't cutting it, wasn't giving my students the energy they paid for and deserved. It was my old problem coming back to haunt me; I didn't feel like I was good enough.

But I knew I couldn't quit working outright. We had two mortgages on our single home and loads of credit card debt. We had been paying on our Parent Plus loans for Rachel since her first semester of college; we would begin paying for Connor's Parent Plus loans in a few more years. I'd never earned a good enough salary to contribute in a meaningful way to our household income. And even though I was the one who paid all the bills and kept the checkbook balanced and borrowed from Peter to pay Paul several times each month, Tim fretted about our situation, proclaiming rather frequently that we were never going to get out from under the mountain that threatened to bury us. He made a good salary, excelled at the work he did. He spent very little money. I wished he could have had the opportunity to live in a household where he didn't have to carry so much of the financial burden. I felt I had failed him. But I also knew that I couldn't bear to live with him if I wasn't bringing some money in the door. I needed to provide some small pittance. Some good faith attempt to earn my keep.

The sign-in system at the Social Security office in Lansing was automated, so visitors needed only to enter their identification numbers on a touch screen computer in a kiosk near the doors and take a seat. A security guard sat at a desk on the back wall. The majority of the caseworkers themselves were not in sight, the bulk of them behind doorways and long secluded hallways off to the right and left of the lobby, although a few stood behind smaller, enclosed windows in the lobby area provided for initial screenings and smaller issues, presumably designated by the letters in our service numbers printed when we signed in. Clients were summoned to the back corridors after they were screened first at one of the lobby kiosks. The summons often came over the announcement system but was also posted on the television screen to help those of us whose hearing was challenged.

The first time I visited, after waiting an hour and a half, I'd learned that I should have been in a different alphabetical queue. When I finally got to one of the stand-up lobby windows and explained my situation, the customer service person winced and apologized. But I had an appointment with my psychologist that afternoon that I couldn't miss. I told the representative that I'd return later.

When I came back the next day, I made it through the first queue quickly. My number was called, and I reported to the back. I trudged down the quiet, cavernous hallway, looking for the specific window front they'd mentioned with my call number. Each window area had chairs, so at least in this second stage of appointments, I would be seated for the interaction.

I spoke to Mr. Lee, who responded politely to me, asking me questions, and explaining the process. There were two different applications we needed to fill out. One was for regular Social Security, which was dependent on how much income I had earned over the course of my life and whether the Social Security Administration would determine that I was eligible to receive a benefit early – before age 65 – as a "disabled" individual. The second application was for supplemental disability income. I told him I wasn't likely to be qualified for the second based on my husband's income; this aspect was based on need, not on earnings put into the system.

When I told him how I'd come to the office the day after my teaching semester had ended and that I was embarrassed to be making a claim, he quickly interjected, "If they approve your claim, this is YOUR money. You paid into the system. You have earned this money."

He talked about his wife, a teacher, and her struggles to get a permanent position. I confessed that I never expected to be in my fifties without a secure income and a sizable retirement in the bank. I explained that I'd tried to move to a different field, the field of advising, before my diagnosis. Ironically, it was the insecure nature of my semester-to-semester employment that allowed me to legally apply for disability. I wouldn't be offered a contract for fall semester until well into the summer, even though my classes in the online registration system at Oakland were already beginning to fill.

By the time I left, he'd buoyed me with encouragement. I didn't know if I'd feel a net loss or net gain to my dignity, but at least I'd taken action. I walked out through glassed-in offices with windows for difficult conversations, chairs holding heavy burdens. In the lobby, people still waited, although faces had changed, some heads bent, eyes closed. I knew well the posture of waiting. As I stepped out into the April day, I felt for the first time that season the lightness of spring.

Mother's Day 2014

The three women of the house set out from the back deck to take a walk. The Gentle Leader Head Halter gave Clover's face the appearance of a catcher with mask intact. As soon as she stepped onto the lawn, she began to rub the side of her face onto the blades of grass, like a swimmer, alternating sides to breathe, swiping first one side and then the other of her face against the ground. Clearly she preferred not to wear the device. Rachel had begun to walk Clover a few times a week, and on the advice of the dog trainer, we'd purchased the device to give us more control when walking her. It helped me to contain some of her strength. But Rachel was the one who took charge of getting the halter properly fitted, along with Ryan, her boyfriend, whose dog Mia had used one when she was younger. The straps for the nose piece had to be adjusted with one clasp. The clasp at the back of the head by Clover's ears required a different adjustment.

I'd slept in, waking to a lovely spring day. Later in the afternoon we would have dinner somewhere, but everything else about the day exuded leisure. Rachel knew I wanted to practice walking Clover and had a few things to point out to me.

We let ourselves out the gate that bordered the back of our yard and the side of the neighbor's and crossed over to the sidewalk that led to the neighborhood behind our house. Rachel showed me how to hold the leash in my right hand with Clover on my left side so I could use my left hand to create some slack in the leash, what dog trainers called a "loose leash." "And when she pulls, you stop and correct her," Rachel said. "You don't keep walking if she's trying to yank you along."

I loved handing over control of the dog, along with its concomitant anxiety. I wanted to just inhale the spring air and the faint scent of lilacs. We would be switching halfway through the walk – I would take over then, trying to mirror Rachel's movements.

We talked about her plans for the move to Philly – the lease she and Ryan were considering and potential dates when she should quit her two jobs in Michigan to pack for her departure.

I had just finished my year at Oakland, and though I was still exhausted from the semester, I was excited about my upcoming residency in Nebraska, happy to be out from under the weight of so many student manuscripts, although the final days of faces, pizza party celebrations, and class readings made me realize again – always again, those epiphanies – how much I loved watching students grow and discover themselves.

As Clover gamboled forward, sniffing the borders of the sidewalk and the concrete, stopping to examine each stray wisp of paper or remnant of animal waste, Rachel and I talked about her practices for Godspell and how much she was enjoying time with other cast members in the ensemble, especially the two adult children of her high school choir teacher, Jeff English, who had supported her through all of her high school singing adventures.

It was time to make the switch. Rachel moved to my right and handed over Clover's leash, which I held in my right hand, my left guiding another length of the leash to create some slack. Now Rachel would observe as I controlled Clover. She'd been such an independent child, always wanting to explore and be active, yet always wanting to involve me in her movement forward. The frozen waffle child. I couldn't just make the breakfast waffles for her; I had to lift her up and let her ferret the Eggo waffles out of the box in the freezer. Then carry her to the counter where the toaster sat and watch as she dropped the two disks into the toaster slots. Lower my body enough so that she could push down the lever on the toaster. Then put her on the ground and let her gather the syrup and the butter. Collaborative learning. Back then I often thought that I was just giving in to her stubbornness, allowing her to push me around, but I came to understand that I was letting her test not me, but the boundaries around her.

We turned the corner to head back down the street that would take us to our sidewalk. Clover stopped at the corner of yard where dogs lived behind a fence, sniffing at the slats. "How do you know when it's okay to let her just stand and sniff for a while and when you should make her come along with you because you're the boss?" I asked.

Rachel shrugged. "Play it by ear. The key thing is that she shouldn't be pulling you." Clover lifted her head and padded back to the sidewalk. I moved closer to her, adjusting my left hand to create more slack in the leash. At some breakfast table, a little girl poured syrup onto her toasted frozen waffles, the Log Cabin bottle at an awkward angle, the syrup emptying too quickly, swamping the waffles and the bottom of the plastic Tupperware plate, golden brown and shiny in the morning light.

Excerpts from *The Nebraska Journals*

June 10, 2014

When Marty picked me up at the Omaha airport, he asked me what I had in my suitcase – the lighter one, as it turns out – to make it so heavy. He then said he'd better think next time before he helped out his younger brother with his taxi business. I tried not to apologize for the weight of my bags. The van smelled of smoke, and there was a large crack in the windshield. "Figure out what lane you want to be in!" he yelled out occasionally through the front of the car. Or, "Hey, Mister!" His brother Ron, more than a dozen years his junior, the actual owner of Tree City Taxi Service, had flown out to Florida earlier in the week to see his twin sons graduate from college. Marty was taking me to the Kimmel Harding Nelson Center for the Arts in Nebraska City, where I had a two-week residency to work on my writing.

"My left hearing aid has been going in and out all day," he said. "So if I ignore you, it's just because I can't hear you." Then he asked me if the Convention Center was up ahead, because he didn't know his way around town and needed to get back on the right highway for Nebraska City.

The navy van carried a thick smoke scent in its upholstery, but Marty never reached for one of the packs of cigarettes on the floor to light up.

He told me he'd worked as a police officer for forty-one years, but he'd retired just in time because now everything was about drugs – meth – and it was just too hard. Four years ago this month, he told me, his son had disappeared in Alaska, from a reservation. He was an F.B.I. agent, stationed there with his family not far from the Russian border. He'd studied Russian languages in school, had even taught for a while at a university, but he needed to support his family, so he'd signed up with the F.B.I., who needed his expertise at the Alaska/Russian border.

One day he disappeared and the only thing they found was his car, abandoned on an Indian Reservation. His wife and three kids moved away, back where her mother was.

Over the course of our ride, Marty shared with me his opinions on a wide-ranging list of subjects. He hated Obamacare and wondered what I thought about the Guantanamo Bay detainees being released. He tried to convert me into being a carp lover, especially after I told him that my husband had always described carp as a nuisance fish. He told me that in Nebraska, lots of people liked carp better than catfish, and I needed to try it. When we drove over the Missouri River, he told me that he'd dragged lots of bodies out of it in his days with the police. Suicide and murder both.

June 11, 2014

I sat in a lovely, taupe wingback chair with ottoman in my Nebraska lodgings, the day stretching ahead of me and lots of projects to tackle, but I was missing home. I thought it would be a good idea to have some quiet time to get my head in order and make decisions without having to chauffeur Rachel and Nathaniel around, without having to let Clover out and play her silly mind games when I was cooking and she wanted attention so she rang the bell to go potty even though she didn't really have to go out to pee.

I was sad because I knew Connor had returned home from college the previous day, and I wasn't there to welcome him. He would be fine; they would all be fine, but I was afraid that they would learn how to live without me. That was the Catch-22. They needed to learn to live without me, but it would make all of us sad. Except for me. I'd be dead. But I was sad now at the thought of them learning the rhythms of a life without me, forgetting to call my name through the house, forgetting to set aside tasks they thought only I could do – putting Shout on stains, making orthodontist appointments, editing and proofing cover letters for job applications. When I was no longer alive, I would no longer have a purpose or a function. I knew that I could be alive in memory, just like my mother and father were alive in my memory, but I didn't know if that would be enough. Marty reminded me of my father – he grew up in a family of eight, while my dad grew up in a family of seven. He was younger than my father would have been – more the age of my father's younger sister, my Aunt Kay.

My mother had been in my thoughts lately because of the "Hold Tight" story I was revising. I could conjure up her smile, but I couldn't hear her voice very well any more, and that made me sad. Perhaps I needed to think about what I most wanted my family to remember. And I needed to make up some good-bye boxes. Or not good-bye. I'll be with you?

June 15, 2014

I woke this morning after a night of troubled dreams, featuring one long one in which I'd missed the first class, a science class, of the semester. I was a student, not a teacher. I kept trying to get the first-day assignment done, but people distracted me. And I couldn't get back to my place for a printer.

The dream made immediate sense when I awoke. I was in Nebraska City without a printer, rushing to complete deadlines, both self-imposed and external. I'd stayed up late several nights in a row reading Richard Russo's *Straight Man*, a book steeped in academia.

On the way back from the bathroom, I popped across the hall into my studio to look at my email, not wanting to distract myself from the goal of texting Tim a "Happy Father's Day" wish. I had an email from my student Jeremy. It was from his e-mail address, but it was really from his mother. She wrote to tell me that Jeremy had died the day before, that his seven-year battle with osteosarcoma was over.

I'd talked to him last at the beginning of the summer semester, just six weeks earlier, after his mother, Andie, had emailed me that he was at risk of losing his financial aid because of the Incompletes he had on his record. I promised her that I'd call him and figure out a remedy; I texted him from Kalamazoo, where I'd attended Connor's match, and told him I'd call him from the road.

We talked about the frustration he'd tried to articulate to me in the hallway outside of my classroom on the last day of classes at Oakland University. I frequently sat on a bench in the hallway, talking to students, on my break in between my two classes in the same room, and he often walked by on his way out of the building after his workshop with another professor. On that last day of class, a hectic one for me because I had to deal not only with the goodbyes for the semester but also with some emotional turbulence between students in my evening class, I was tired, sad, and distracted.

He was frustrated that he didn't know what class to take next. "Can't you be my advisor?" he said. What I wanted to say was, "Yes, certainly." But I was only an adjunct, and while I could steer him in the right direction, I wasn't official. In addition, I was feeling empty and lifeless after the long year of teaching. I didn't know if I could come back. I didn't want to make promises I couldn't keep.

As I held the phone to my ear on I-94 and I-69, I tried to offer support and listen to some of his confusion and frustration. We talked about his Incomplete in my class from the fall semester and I realized that he'd been too doped up with drugs back then after his hospitalization to remember that I'd laid out in an email what he needed to do to finish the class. "You mean it's all in an email somewhere?" he said.

I told him that yes, and I could forward the old email to him. But the work I'd outlined was with the assumption that he'd want to finish the class completely to earn the best grade possible. "You did enough work in the class that I can give you a passing grade," I said. He was grateful. That's the option he wanted, he said. He needed to take care of the Incompletes so that he could proceed with his summer classes. We hung up, promising to touch base in the fall, when I returned to teaching.

But now Andie's email told me that he was gone. Standing in the Nebraska apartment I shared with my resident apartment-mate, Josh, I hated myself for not being able to hear the coming of death in his voice on that day a few weeks earlier. How had I convinced myself that he was going to be okay?

June 16, 2014

Yesterday, along with my sadness about Jeremy, I felt nostalgia and sadness as well, knowing that I wouldn't be able to attend the wedding celebration of a student I'd tutored years earlier. Amrita, whom I'd met when she was still in grade school, had gotten married, and a special celebration was being held back in East Lansing. If I were home in Michigan, I would be at that celebration.

Today, I thought of Andie, Jeremy's mother, and how heavy her body must be as she carried it from room to room. The lyric from a *Godspell* song, "When wilt thou save the people? Oh, God of mercy, when?" kept running through my head, Matt Eldred's voice as that of Jesus a mourning query. But I wanted to banish the song because Jeremy struggled with religion, especially the Christian kind, and he would laugh at me if he knew I'd thought of that song. The God of *Godspell* was such a Christian God. Not Shashi's gods, whom she'd shared with me in our talks about religion. Not even my own liberal Lutheran God. Some sort of fundamental God, Rachel said. She told me that during the performance she had to stop listening to the rules Jesus teaches early on in the show's rehearsals and decided to focus on the relationships among the disciples instead.

I was in the southeast corner of Nebraska, and Jeremy's mother, Andie, was in Ann Arbor with an email account with her son's name on it and a long list of tasks to do.

June 16, 2014

Funeral:
Monday June 16th at 3:30 PM
Congregation Beth Israel
2000 Washtenaw Avenue Ann Arbor 48104
followed immediately by burial at Arbor Crest Cemetery

Shiva (2 days only):
Monday after cemetery until 9:00 PM
Tuesday from 4:00-9:00 PM

I honor you, Jeremy Wagner.

June 17, 2014

In three days, I would depart from Nebraska for home, and already my mind was moving back there, away from the quiet here, the isolation, the space. I was thinking about Rachel and Jeremy's mom, and Shashi and Amrita. And art. As I'd tried to write during the week, I'd gotten news of Jeremy's death. I'd thought of him just days before I got the email, in fact, while reading Russo's *Straight Man*. I wanted him to read it. Wanted him to know that someone who was in academia shared a lot of his frustrations and doubts about the workshop process and had actually made fun of that process in his novel.

I thought of Rachel and how she was trying to juggle her work and her art and her need to have closure before she left for Philadelphia. I should be sobbing about her departure, or maybe just thinking about it more, and I wondered if I was avoiding. How could I be so nostalgic about Amrita's wedding celebration when my daughter was moving away, and I would see her only a few times a year? I suppose what I was afraid of was that, like me, she would fill her days with activities and then I would drop her off in Philadelphia, and that would be the end, not of our relationship, but of the time when I had lived with her as an adult in the same house.

She did not get nominated for a Lansing Thespie. I was sorry that she didn't get recognized, sorry that she had to observe other people have more success and deal with the disappointment. But I knew well how that worked. Being in Nebraska in the residency program, I saw all the people who were younger than I, and I thought, once again, about how you never knew what your life was going to be. You thought you had some control, but really you didn't.

Jeremy tried to make meaning out of his writing and make sense of the process in his final days. There was no making sense of it, really. I should probably spend the rest of my time on the planet doing something other than "making art" that no one would absorb. But I would need something to fill my time when Rachel went to Philadelphia and Connor went to France. However meaningless it might be, however small the audience it garnered, the writing felt like an appropriate way to put my time in. To process my thoughts. Articulate my desires.

June 19, 2014: Workshop at the Assisted Living Facility

Richard was 93 years old. He'd never broken a bone until he broke his hip. Had two wives, both of them deceased, one a nurse, one a dental hygienist. He served on his church council for over thirty years. A mixture of Presbyterian and United Church of Christ.

Rosemary wrote about clothespins. Etching designs in her mother's clothespins and giving them to her children so they could have something of her. Cathy, the aid, said she was a beautiful woodworker. At first, Rosemary felt like I was telling them how to write without just letting them write. But when I told her my exercises were intended as a starting point for people who couldn't think of anything to write about, she seemed to be on board. Wrote about how her grandson died in a plane crash and they found his clothespin, the one she'd made for him, in a jewelry box. They went to Oscoda, Michigan, to visit her son, and she wrote about how beautiful it was on the water and looking at the pines. How she lost track of her son because he'd climbed up into a tree.

Roy wrote about his mother canning and how good it smelled. He asked if I knew the Augusta Barn Theater in Michigan, and I told him about Rachel and musical theater, that we'd gone to the Barn Theater to see one of her friends. He'd been a stage designer and actor there.

Mavis painted Elvis guitars. She was a lover of all things Elvis and wrote about the time she'd seen Elvis.

Barbara was an elementary school teacher, and she liked to teach her kids that they should not just write without worrying about punctuation and spelling. I told her that I agreed with her for the older kids. The younger kids should just write, I told her – from Kindergarten through second or third grade. Use the invented spelling and not worry about punctuation. Barbara wrote about her father coming home from work and picking up a book to read to them – *Little Women* – and how all of her sisters cried when Beth died in the book.

Ann was a gardener. She wrote about gloves, and shears, and pruning dwarf pear trees.

June 20, 2014

The part of me that has forced myself to open this journal and write is responding to that traditional, restrained voice. "Okay, you want journaling? I'll give you the Kimmel Harding Nelson version of 'What I Did on My Summer Vacation.'" I wanted to say in one sentence what I learned at Kimmel Harding Nelson. But the complexity of the education seems like something not easily teased out in a sentence.

I went for peace. I went to have the thoughts in my head slow down so I could hear them. I don't just struggle with the mean voice; I also struggle with the sheer volume of thoughts, some of them just related to scheduling. Being away from home has allowed me to omit a huge vein of strictly procedural and tactical thoughts.

Leaving room, unfortunately, for some of the harder thoughts, like, "What if they get used to not having me around?" or "See? They can cope on their own."

But I knew that having relationships with people was not about the service they provided. So regardless of the services I provided for my family, perhaps they were capable of handling them in my absence, secure in the knowledge that I would return and do those services again. Yet my absence at this point in my cancer life felt too much like a dress rehearsal or a trial run. At times the separation made me too sad, and when I got word that Jeremy had died, the notion of absence gained so much weight and heft. In reality, I might have never seen Jeremy again, had he remained alive. But I would have known he was out there, plugging along. Getting his college degree, one or two classes at a time. I was angry with myself for believing that he wasn't going to die, that he was going to be able to finish his degree. Why didn't I understand that he was losing time? I felt guilt about not checking in with him again. I valued my phone call with him. I valued hearing his voice and talking about writing workshops. I valued thinking last week before I knew he'd died that I'd like to talk to him about the view of the workshop Russo presented.

Today I was leaving Kimmel Harding Nelson and reuniting with my family, which would bring me so much happiness. But the departure was not without a loss. There would be the absence of Josh, who had been so much a part of my days for the last two weeks. Josh with his cool T-shirts, his stories about centipedes fighting cockroaches, and his love of beer and art. His soulful eyes that made eye contact in a way this morning that was just too much to bear. Kimmel Harding Nelson was about presence and absence. But it was also about decision making. The decision not to publish my novel with the smaller, non-literary press that offered me a contract (I liked Josh's language – it wasn't the right time for me to publish the book). Other decisions were still elusive. Did I think it was more meaningful to work on the memoir or the new novel? The people who approved my residency application here at Kimmel Harding Nelson allowed me to work on both. Yet after meeting the folks at the Ambassador Assisted Living Facility, I felt awkward about my "assisted living" novel. I didn't want the people there to inform my characters, but I did want to show that the lives of the elderly have meaning. Yet it was so hard for them to shape meaning during the advanced years of their lives. I think that's what Roy's dilemma was during the workshop. Having been the artist and the writer, he couldn't become the common man capturing a moment in time – his mother canning. His poetry and other writings were in the library at the facility – I should have made time to sit down and read that work. How very well I understood his question lurking behind the simple writing activity, his fear of reduction: Is this what my life has meant? To be in this room, capturing three sentences about a summer day sixty years ago?

Honey Nut Cheerios

The shot I settled on after asking people for suggestions throughout the month was Honey Nut Cheerios, part honey whiskey and part rum chatta. Connor wanted me to take it as a shot, rather than on the rocks, so I ate up the spinach artichoke dip and drank two huge glasses of water in preparation for midnight. No bells or gongs or lighted balls marked the hour, but shortly after our watches and cell phones reminded us of the time, Connor and Tim raised their glasses full of Harp Lager, and I raised my Honey Nut Cheerios, clinked glasses with Tim and Connor and downed my shot.

In the other room, the female singer had just finished with a set featuring Katy Perry, and without her voice in the background, the Claddaugh felt calmer, mellower. At midnight, few people filled the seats at the bar or at the table.

I needed the quiet after the emotional turbulence earlier in the day. Although Connor had said months in advance that he wanted to have a drink with his mom and dad on his twenty-first birthday, the details had remained murky until the day just before the occasion. Connor's idea to go out just with me and Tim had morphed into Tim and Rachel and me, and maybe a cousin. Tim and I didn't want to exclude Nathaniel, so we'd added him to the list. But Connor had told me that afternoon that Nathaniel's coming to the bar seemed silly. Like Connor was taking his family to the bar for his birthday. What was that about? That was weird, he said.

I reacted to his comments about family, wondering aloud what was so wrong with family. But I knew I focused too much on family, and I hated myself for wanting to argue with him and convince him I was right. Why did I have to make my point all of the time? Why couldn't I just honor what he wanted? The dilemma I'd created made me critical of myself. On the one hand, I felt that I knew what was best for all of my children; on the other hand, I thought I was being an emotional jerk. But I didn't know which part of me to believe or honor. I knew our children needed their individual time with us. Maybe I was just pushing family too much.

When I went up to take my shower to prepare for the evening, the tears wouldn't stop. I hated my crying jags. Sometimes it seemed like I could go for weeks or months, and even with the depression lurking in the background, my face stayed dry. But then something would happen, and I would have to retreat to the bedroom and give in to whatever had been unblocked.

I didn't want to exclude Nathaniel and leave him home alone. It felt wrong for him to be alone on the night of his brother's birthday.

I knew I was fatigued. On the previous night, Rachel had had her final benefit concert in the Lansing area with her friend Rachel. I was proud of all Rachel and Rachel, Rachel Squared, had done with the concert series and proud of myself as well for doing the bucket-list item she and I had talked about for several years – singing a duet with her in public. I was so happy to share the stage with her, happy not to have flatted my notes, happy not to have tripped over the microphone cord, happy to have remembered the nod to the accompanist, happy not to have broken down in nervous sobs of overwrought emotion.

But when we all split up after the concert, Rachel went off with Ryan and her musical theater friends, and Tim, Connor, and Nathaniel went off to take my mother-in-law back to her house. When I got home, Clover was waiting for me, a huge consolation, but I was still alone. I don't know what I expected. I'd done one of the things I'd set out to do – I'd sung a duet with my daughter in public. Yet what had prompted our musical number at this point in time was her upcoming move to Philadelphia, and the dwindling time I had left with her in my house before she moved away.

I wanted Connor to have whatever he wanted for that first legal drink in a bar, but I didn't want Nathaniel to be left alone at home. Connor argued that Nathaniel was a minor and didn't belong in a bar that late at night – that the other four of us by virtue of our ages had earned the right to drink. He explained this to me standing at the edge of my bed, or maybe sitting on it. I'd had so many conversations there on the king-size bed with each of my children, most of the time with a positive feeling ending the conversations and a hug before their departure but sometimes with one of them storming out.

I thought I realized then the truth about my reaction and why I wanted Nathaniel to go. In spite of my constant battle with depression and *the voice*, I had tried to maintain a realistic view of life and death issues, keeping a focus on what I thought I could do with the time I had left. I was pretty sure I could make it through the fall and to Paris for Christmas. I was pretty sure I wouldn't die while Connor was on his study abroad, which was one of my original worries when I was first diagnosed. I was pretty sure I would last through Connor's graduation from college and through the next June, when Nathaniel would graduate from high school. These were goals I was fairly certain I could achieve based on what Dr. Gadgeel had told me and on what I'd read about my disease and treatment.

But I knew the odds were not good for making it to Nathaniel's 21st birthday. I wouldn't go to a bar and hear Katy Perry and speculate about the age of the books on the shelves in the side room and swallow down a Honey Nut Cheerios for my youngest child's 21st birthday. That would be like a miracle, and I didn't believe in miracles.

After Connor left the room, and I lay back against the pillows, burying my face once again in the pillowcase, I knew I couldn't forsake the moment I'd have with my second child for the moment I'd never have with my third.

Connor was the child rolling in my belly when both of my parents died, when I started drinking coffee to keep myself awake on my trips from Lansing to Pontiac after work to visit them in the hospital, even though I'd read caffeine wasn't good for fetuses. He was the child I felt most guilty about because after he was born, I was still torn up by the grief of my parents' deaths and overwhelmed by raising my spirited daughter. I nursed him as long as I could but when I was nearly curled up in a ball with grief and depression, I had to give up the nursing to take antidepressants so I could be a better mother to both of my children. But of my three children, he had a temperament most like mine—usually outwardly sunny but often inwardly brooding. He wanted to keep the quirky sense of humor he'd inherited from me, but he was afraid of inheriting my depression gene.

In the end, Rachel stayed home with Nathaniel, while Connor, Tim, and I went out for a drink just before Connor's birthday on June 28, 2014. I ate some dip, we listened to a woman sing Katy Perry songs, and we drank to Connor at midnight.

We went home when the glasses were empty, and Rachel got in the car to take Connor back out to another bar, one where they had hundreds of beers on tap, something I knew nothing about.

Nathaniel stayed home, but he wasn't alone.

Decision

I asked Nathaniel to come and hang out with me in the bedroom so I could talk to him. I sat atop the comforter as I waited. After twenty years, the colors of the fabric were still bright, the contrast of black, marine blue, magenta, and jade squiggles and geometric patterns still lively enough to keep me awake. It was the comforter my mother had paid for as a present for that last Christmas we'd spent with her. I'd had to cash the check when she was in the hospital with the near-fatal heart attack that January of 1993, an act that made me feel avaricious, though I didn't select the comforter until after she'd passed away.

As a school-aged child and young teenager, I'd spent hours reading in my bedroom, rarely sitting upright in a chair. Like the passenger seat of my van, my side of the bed was an extension of my office. But back then there was little cooking and only a short list of cleaning chores that took me away from my bedside activities.

I told Nathaniel that I was thinking of leaving my teaching job at Oakland. That I'd found a way to replace my income for a bit, and I thought I'd like to just stay in town instead of commuting. Focus on him instead of all of my students and their stories. I asked him if he would think any less of me if I wasn't an instructor at Oakland University any more.

He told me he wouldn't think any differently but he wanted me to do what was most important for me to do. That he would only be disappointed if I didn't do what was important to me. He understood that I found my teaching rewarding, but he knew that the work and the drive made me really tired. And yes, maybe if I stopped working there, we could spend more time together and he wouldn't need to take the bus home. Maybe I could work on my writing.

I started to cry, my voice quivering a bit, and he scooted next to me on the bed and grabbed my hand. "Is this about Jeremy?" he said. "You feel you should go back to college because that's what Jeremy did when he had cancer? He just kept on going and you think you're supposed to do that, too? Because it's not the same thing. You already went to school and did that. You don't have to go anymore if you don't want. It's good that Jeremy did because that's what he wanted for his life. I'm okay with whatever you do if it's what you want."

I told him, as I had before, that he was a very good boy, a good man. "I'm not good at comforting people," he said. "That's twice today, and I didn't do a great job either time."

"Who else did you comfort today?"

"Mrs. Freeman. She was crying on our driver's training drive."

"Crying because it was your last drive? Because she'll miss you?" Mrs. Freeman had taught Driver's Ed to all three of my children. "Because you're the last Dalton?"

"No. About something else. She had tears in her eyes, and I didn't know what to say."

"Two women in one day," I said.

"Yeah. It was pretty hard."

"I appreciate it, and I'm sure she appreciates it."

"Are we done?" he said, starting to scoot back to the foot of the bed. "Sure."

In the car on the way to the Lugnuts game back on July 4, I told Rachel and Connor what I'd already told Nathaniel – that I'd decided not to go back to work in the fall, that I found it too exhausting with my cancer and too stressful, though I would really miss my students. I wanted to tell them because we would be seeing our friends and the subject of my resuming teaching after the summer off would likely come up. I wanted to be honest.

"Why can't you just say 'No comment'?" one of the kids said from the back seat.

"Have you ever said that to a friend when you're in the middle of a deep personal or emotional discussion?"

"Well, I've said things just like that, about not wanting to go there," one of them said.

"How are you going to replace your income?" Rachel asked.

"No comment."

"She's going to sell her body," someone said.

"She's going to do a Walter, like in Breaking Bad." It wasn't the end of the conversation, but it was a good start.

I didn't want to tell anyone the answer to the questions, my children in particular, until after the extended family reunion. I didn't want to talk about it in a large group of people. There was a stigma associated with "disability." I engaged in the stigma myself when I clarified for the few people I did tell that I would be receiving regular Social Security Disability, the kind based on money put into the system over the course of my life, not the other kind, the supplemental disability based on income. The man who'd opened my case file and taken my original claim at the Social Security office had emphasized to me that it was MY retirement. What I'd paid into the system over my years of working. I had earned it myself.

But I worried about what people would say if they knew I was planning a trip to France with family in December. I'd wanted to go for most of my adult life after studying French in college. Didn't I deserve to go to France? The voice said, "Of course not." It was a class thing.

I didn't belong to the right class to travel abroad. Not if I was on disability. Maybe my children did. They were the next generation, more global than my generation and more entitled. Tim was of an appropriate class and had already gone abroad a year or so after he graduated from college, after saving money from roofing for his dad's business to afford the trip.

Yet I was not entitled, or at least I didn't feel entitled. I thought the trip I was planning was a sinful indulgence, especially if I lived any longer than five years from my diagnosis. I had established in my code of right and wrong and truth and what's fair that I only deserved the trip, deserved disability, even, if I knew I'd be gone soon.

I prepared notes for my meeting with my Department Chairperson, Kathy Pfeiffer, before the date we'd planned to meet. To give myself courage, I kept my planner with the page of notes open in my lap while we talked.

I began by telling her that at the end of the semester, I was exhausted mentally and physically, so I applied to the Social Security Administration after researching disability online and learning that there was something called a "Compassionate Allowance," a provision that allowed individuals suffering from certain diseases to have an expedited application process. I told her that for people like me on specialty drugs such as Tarceva, it was hard for the oncologists to predict when I was going to die. But I was going to die, in spite of the drug's miraculous qualities. A cure for stage IV lung cancer did not exist. Yet, meanwhile, I had to live while a war was being waged in my body. (I would learn a year or so later when listening to a radio show while driving that some cancer patients struggled with the war and battle analogy, but at that point, I used it pretty automatically.)

She knew that my youngest son was still in high school. I explained that I wanted to have energy to see my youngest son through as much of high school as time permitted instead of being exhausted from my commute and always reading student manuscripts. As a result, I needed to give up all of the upcoming academic year's classes on my schedule. I needed to "step away" from teaching. That was the language I used.

Making that decision was tough. I'd worked my way up from one class per semester to two and just that year I'd completed my first full year with the golden number of six adjunct sections, three per semester. When I'd started, another woman had been chair, and I'd worked with her to craft my commuting schedule. It felt sad and ironic that I had to give it up after only a year. But it wasn't just my health and my son I worried about. I questioned whether I was giving students the level of education they deserved.

Yet I was desperate with a sadness about how much I would miss them. I'd communicated with a few from Nebraska, telling them about Jeremy's memorial service.

I knew that I was classified as a special lecturer with few benefits but that I was still basically an adjunct. So, I asked her, was there any way I could hang out on some roster somewhere, in case I could come back in some way? For Social Security purposes, I needed to not be working. Where there any options for me?

She told me to think about the possibility of doing just one class. I told her that I couldn't in order to quality for Social Security Disability. She promised to connect with a human resource person and encouraged me to follow up with that person in a few days. She supported my decision and said she would miss me. She said there would always be a place for me in the Department. We talked about our writing and she encouraged me to look into books by Meg Wolitzer and Stephen Pressfield.

She gave me a hug goodbye, and we promised to keep in touch. I tried not to make comparisons between my leaving Oakland and my leaving the Writing Program at LCC, but viewing the two decisions through the same lens felt inevitable. In both cases, I felt like a failure. At LCC, I was flattened by the weight of paper-grading and a destructive depression that made me feel ill-equipped to succeed at teaching, writing, or family life. At Oakland, where my adjunct load was lighter, with much less pay, I still felt ill-equipped. I struggled to make things work before the cancer arrived. With the cancer and the commute, I felt doomed.

I went to the basement office in O'Dowd Hall where most of the adjuncts kept their office hours posted next to the door, even if they never showed up there. I'd made the decision a few years earlier to keep my office hours and student meetings in a more accessible spot – in Café O'Bear, housed within the student union building known as the Oakland Center, or right outside my classroom, in the hall of the boring but efficiently laid out South Foundation Hall. Earlier, as the year ended, I'd taken out most of what remained in that office. But there were still a few items – a few textbooks and a lamp. I looked around at the four walls, the cubicles which revealed so little of the adjunct teachers' personalities, all of us reluctant to claim too much of the room, reluctant to lose any item we might leave there. It wasn't a bad place, this dungeon room without windows. But it didn't fit into my life anymore. I grabbed the textbooks in one hand. I wrapped the fingers of my other hand around the neck of the lamp, pulled open the door, and left.

Beside the Pool in Utah (July 20, 2014)

I reclined under an orange umbrella so I wouldn't get skin cancer. Luxury's lap supported me as I sat beside the pool at the Montage Deer Valley Resort in Park City, Utah. The Empire Mountain (Guardsman Pass/Daly Mine) rose in the distance. I had accompanied Tim on one of his summer work trips; his organization's generous policy allowed him to cover the economy air fare of one guest. Before our family had expanded, I'd accompanied him several times. A few times we'd even rented a car and driven to whatever destination with all the kids in tow. But in recent years, with my work schedule and the kids' busy lives, I'd just sent one of the kids with him. Until now, when I reclaimed the marital privilege.

The water gulped gently at the brick brown edges of the pool, overflowing. Outside the bar, next to the pool, a guitarist sang a fast version of Cat Stevens' "Moonshadow." And then "Heart of Stone," the strummed chords louder than the shush of water or the flutter of poplar leaves against the white barks of the trees lining the fenced-in area. Women's voices nearby talked fast and giddy, and a man and his daughter tossed a blue ball into the pool basketball hoop. A breeze picked up the edges of the terrycloth chair cover the waitress brought me, and the leaves became louder.

New arrivals entered the gate for the pool area – a young woman carrying a single diaper and a bag, a dark-haired man, and a toddler with blonde hair. The blue ball rose up, caught by the wind, and escaped from the water. The father followed and captured it, but it escaped again, and I, the woman wearing not a swimming suit but black cropped pants and a fuchsia tank top, followed the ball and returned it to the water, where it bobbed, forgotten by the man and his daughter, gently travelling the edge of the pool, the overflowing water, until the toddler, whose diaper waited in the bag, spied the ball and captured it, before immediately released it.

Letting go. When I thought of how it might be to die, I imagined it would be like releasing the ball, not caring so much where it went. Letting the water take it.

If there was something that I didn't face, it was the moment of death. I needed to learn to sit with it. Here. Now. Under the orange umbrella.

The Allergy Office

The clock in the allergy office was large, and I imagined the doctors had decided on the size because people constantly checked it to see if they'd met the thirty-minute waiting requirement after getting their allergy shots. But it was old-fashioned, the numbers in Roman numeral type, so far removed from the digital age as to be almost unreasonable given that so many allergy patients were children. The finish had an antiqued look, stressed, and bronze-gold in color, but worn through. From time to time, the microphone system came on, and a nurse announced a first name and a cubicle number, the announcement followed by a clunk. I envisioned a performer, new to the stage, trying to get a microphone back in the stand. Then I thought of other clunks, like the clunk the gas nozzle made after you put it back in its place.

The young man across from me was knitting, and I wanted to ask him what he was making. If he were a woman, I would ask him, but since he wasn't, I felt awkward, like I was calling attention to what he was doing. It was on a circle, whatever it was. Maybe a cap? A sock? He wore a shirt that said "Michigan State Horticulture." When the office door opened, a rush of arctic air moved in, even though the door didn't lead to the outside, just to a hallway.

A woman brought a wheelchair in, and as she unwrapped layers of cloth, the person in the chair emerged, a woman in a red fleece jacket, hands bent down at the wrist in clenched fists, maybe of a palsy or arthritis. Another blast of air came in with a mother and a son. The woman in the wheelchair turned on a small, hand-held television. Canned audience noise of a game show environment floated up from her chair, interspersed with small, electronic beeps. The clock brand was Harrison Gray, established 1823. Another mom, son, and blast of cold air.

I was also a mother with her son. My son wore Skull Candy headphones, so if I were to say anything at that moment, he wouldn't hear me. He taught me headphone etiquette for summoning him when he got this pair for his birthday from his sister. "Tap me on the shoulder," he said. But when he was in another room of the house, I didn't always know to tap. I called out and got no answer. When I investigated, he would be somewhere, ears covered in black muffs, head tilted in hands, staring at his iPhone.

What he heard through his ear phones blocked out what I heard now. The television static from the wheelchair, the rumble of allergy patients' voices behind me, the tramp of snow boots on the carpet just outside the door. A few throat clearings. Aggressive flipping of magazine pages.

Her Skin

Dots of skin speckled the waistband of my knit pants like fine grains. Beneath the cloth, on the folds of my black underwear, the speckling was patternless, yet uniform, as if someone had spilled salt that should have been dashed elsewhere.

The oncologists called it the Tarceva rash, though it looked more like acne than any eczema or pruritic disorder I had ever seen. In those first few weeks after I started the drug, I wondered if the doctors used the term "rash" because they wanted to spare the sufferers the indignity of returning to adolescence and a vocabulary that referenced pimples, pustules, and craters. But I learned over time that the rash could come differently to each Tarceva taker and in many different iterations for the same person. The dry, flaking skin. The cracks. The eruptions and cysts like acne. Red, scaly patches. And beyond the rash – darkening pigmentation and an idiosyncratic hirsutism, especially on the face.

Tarceva, the trade name for the drug erlotinib, was a targeted therapy that addressed cancer in individuals whose cancer had an epidermal growth factor receptor (EGFR) mutation. Lung cancer often developed unrecognized, sometimes advancing to stage IV with no external manifestation. For those who had an EGFR mutation of their cancer, Tarceva kept cancer at bay – for days, weeks, and months. The lucky few even got years. The drug didn't provide a cure or remission but an inexplicable suspension of cancer that differed for each patient, depending on how early in treatment the patient's cancer developed resistance to the medication.

A suspension. An abeyance. I struggled with what to call the action the drug took on my cancer. My oncologist said the cancer was controlled, yet I didn't feel that I was the one who controlled it.

The epidermal growth factor receptor earned its name because it dealt with the epidermis layer of skin. As a result, one of the primary side effects of the drug was the rash in its many iterations. My first Tarceva lesson was about the way the drug desiccated the skin. The specialty pharmacy nurses who monitored patients' first few months on the drug counseled them to drink more water than they imagined possible and apply moisturizer at every opportunity; my pharmacy included a bottle of lotion with the first shipment. In those first winter months, my husband rubbed lotion on the skin of my back each night. Various-sized containers littered the counters and tables throughout our house. Some heavily perfumed. Sweet Pea. Peppermint. Cloying scents. A pump dispenser of Sarna, with camphor and menthol. A new kind of Aveeno, with a hint of lavender. When I forgot to moisturize my arms, fine white cracks formed across the pigment.

The welts appeared suddenly, sometimes as thick lumps distorting the surface of the skin, sometimes as puffy, fluid-filled pouches that rested atop it. The comments on the boards referred to Grade 4 rashes and weeping sores.

Dry skin was only one aspect of the changes. For many who take the drug, the most troubling skin problem was the continuous development of acne-like cysts on the face or trunk. I'd lived with this side effect for over two years, and I still thought of it as a blight that had taken over my cheeks, my nose, and particularly my chin. I thought of the biblical leprosy I'd read about as a child — faces disfigured by a disease akin to rot, people marked by their deformities, stigmatized and marginalized by fear. And I remembered meeting Lucy Grealy when we both taught at the gifted and talented writing camp. Lucy's face had been ravaged by Ewing's sarcoma, the reconstructive surgeries a slow process; at times there were still missing chunks of her facial structure the observer had to fill in.

Dr. Gadgeel didn't even bother to hide his delight when I talked about the persistence of the rash. To him, and to so many of the oncologists, the presence of a rash signified that the tyrosine-kinase inhibitor (TKI) in Tarceva was at work, blocking or inhibiting the mutant proliferation of the protein enzyme, kinase. As long as the rash kept blossoming, kept rising in bumps and inflamed cysts on my chin, each papulopustular pore generating a small, fine hair, the Tarceva was accomplishing its goal. In leaving marks on my face, it was announcing success. I knew that researchers had found correlations between the existence of the rash and positive treatment outcomes, leading some oncologists to adopt a policy of "treating to rash" – maintaining the dosage of Tarceva at a high enough level to keep the rash ever-present, the cancer presumably controlled.

Patches of dark brown mottled the surface, like flecks of cinnamon shaken onto a chai latte, skating the liquid and meeting the oil of the milk to join the flecks in a pooling shadow on the cream-colored foam. The pigmentation darkened as the sun interacted with the drug and the external layers of skin. Every few months I purchased a new, darker shade of foundation to camouflage the patches and the blemishes, but the shading on my skin was never even.

The cysts of my Tarceva rash were of the acneiform variety – the same type of cysts from *acne vulgaris*. When I was an adolescent, my mother taught me that vulgar meant "uncouth," but I learned later that it actually meant "common." My rash was common, yet the medical websites noted that those who suffered from *acne vulgaris* sometimes had self-esteem issues and depression as a result of their skin malformations. At first, Dr. Gadgeel prescribed the oral medication minocycline and the topical antibiotic clindamycin. I used the drugs routinely, but after a while, the minocycline seemed to affect my stomach, and I reduced my daily dosage, eventually stopping the antibiotic altogether near the end of the second year.

But I continued to experiment with topical applications. Each day I palpated my chin, navigating with my fingers what felt like a topographical map of the Rockies. I contemplated what product to put on my face. Clindamycin antibiotic gel. Hydrocortisone cream. Adapalene gel from years ago, stuck in the back of a bathroom drawer. Neosporin. I shouldn't touch my face at all. In moments of stress or anxiety, my fingers crept up to my face to palpate. Anyone who has been to a dermatologist for acne knows that you're not supposed to touch your face. I knew I should stop. In the car, when I drove home at night after visiting my son at college, my hand left the steering wheel and found my chin in the dark.

I returned to the dermatologist I'd dispensed with when I'd received my original diagnosis and assumed the worst. The dermatologist who'd said "Holy fuck," when she learned about the diagnosis and then immediately covered her mouth. I told the dermatologist that my oncologist had given me the go-ahead to experiment with other medications. I'd read an article on PubMed that talked about the use of adapalene, which I knew would be hard on my skin. The dermatologist gave me two samples to experiment with, one of them a stronger adapalene, the other a drug known as dapsone, or Aczone. When I determined, almost a month later, that the Aczone might work slightly better than the adapalene, I read online that an oral version of the drug was originally approved for the treatment of leprosy.

As a Tarceva taker with over two years under my belt, I still hadn't come to terms with welts that came and went on the visage I presented to the world each day. Yet I knew that when the rash receded, if it receded, the absence of blemishes would be filled with portent. I found myself in the contradictory position of wanting the rash to fade but not disappear. To abate but persist in a more contained version. A clear, unblemished face meant the drug was failing.

Heavy, thick eyebrows — Brooke Shields eyebrows, they told me to make me feel better during puberty — traveled through a cycle of inflammation, infection, and regrowth. Scabs formed around short bristles of coarse, emerging brow, which poked the finger I raised to touch the snips, barbed-wire sharp.

For my back-to-school photo in Mr. Predmore's fifth grade class, I wore a green corduroy jumper and a white print blouse with a bow at the collar. If you looked closely at the photo, you could see reddish, scaly patches rising up from my neck underneath the blouse. Eczema. The rash was out of control for most of my elementary school days, erupting in patches behind my knees, on my inner arms at the elbow crook, and on my neck. When I looked at other kids, the skin at their elbows and knee junctures was clear — the bend in their limbs a joint, nothing more, not a surface of dry, fingernail-etched skin and small red sores. I always had splotchy oval patches on each arm and behind my knees, a ring encircling my neck, the borders of each patch red and irregular, signifying my allergies. With each new topical prescription from my pediatrician I hoped to erase a bit of the border. Salves, unguents, ointments, creams. Thick, tar-like, and smelly. Thin and odorless. Thirty-five years later, the location of my eczema moved. Now my shins were covered. Clover licked the patch on the right one.

A forest populated the skin between my nostrils and my upper lip. For years, a slight moustache resided at the corners of my mouth, two thin copses of wispy trees, divided by a clearing, a pair of sentries. Now most of the hairs grew in thick and black. The aesthetician smoothed the green wax on the skin in sections and tugged. Cold stones dissolved the pain. Afterwards, in the car, I stared into the rear-view mirror at my face, the small area of skin above my lip smooth, hairless.

The truth was that long before I ever took a single dose of Tarceva, I had skin issues. In those elementary school days, my eczema was part of a larger constellation of problems also – chronic allergies and acute and chronic asthma. I was the only one in my elementary school who stayed in for recess to avoid exercise and the Michigan cold. Exposure to either could trigger an asthma attack immediately. Dusts, molds, and pollens wreaked havoc with my airways and lungs, so I stayed in and read books or waited for Mr. Grimes, the music teacher, to come and serenade me with his guitar. Yet there appeared to be no connection between the chronic and often acute asthma from my childhood and my diagnosis of lung cancer at age fifty-three.

The tiny slits in my fingers widened with the cold. Fingertip fissures. Juice from the garlic and onion crept into the fissures, burning. I spackled them with Neosporin and wrapped them in Band-Aids. Stopped chopping.

On the basement floor of Sparrow Hospital where the surgeons operated, it was cold that evening when I had surgery for pericardial and pleural effusion, the condition that eventually alerted me to the advanced lung cancer in my body. Everyone in the room wore a bouffant head cap like the kind I'd worn as a young girl when my mother wrapped my hair in colored rods and squeezed the Lilt permanent solution onto my scalp. We were waiting for the cardiac surgeon, Dr. Pridjian, to come into the room to mark me for the surgery. First, I had to make my own mark, and then he had to make one, on the side where the surgery was to be done.

"What surgery are we going to do on you tonight?" the nurse asked.

"Left thoracotomy and pericardial window," I said.

"Nice. You've got it. Now just make a mark, anywhere on your chest, on the left side of your body."

When Dr. Pridjian later scrawled his signature under my left breast, he sighed. It was Halloween in 2012, almost midnight. He'd had an evening packed with emergency surgeries, mine one of the few he could afford to delay for a couple of hours. Later he told my husband that when he cut into me, he emptied out more bloody fluid than he'd ever seen in a chest.

But in those moments after Dr. Pridjian signed, I thought of my shock when I first saw the movie *Hospital* as a teenager and realized, along with everyone else watching, that the surgeons had performed a hysterectomy on the wrong woman. In the cold of Sparrow's basement before surgery, the staff members did routine checks, making sure that I was the correct patient, making sure that they were cutting into the correct side of my body. I wouldn't learn until weeks later that the cause of my tamponade and pleural and pericardial effusion was adenocarcinoma of the left lung with metastases. On that Halloween night, as I entered the fog of anesthesia, I wondered how long it would take the ink marks on my skin to wash away.

I didn't like to tell strangers who learned about my cancer that I was a nonsmoker. Dealing with strangers was always tricky. I withheld as long as I could, especially if revealing a detail to the parent of my youngest son's new friend; I didn't know how prolonged the contact would be. But then sometimes the fact of the cancer came out in a rush, at the wrong time. So much for withholding.

And the surprise people expressed at the severity of the diagnosis was followed by questions, sometimes subtle, sometimes not, about causes. Only medical personnel would ask outright about the smoking. Strangers skirted the smoking issue. I wanted to believe that there was one kind of lung cancer from which we all suffered. That I didn't have to judge someone else's lifestyle decision to smoke cigarettes – my dead mother had smoked – just as those other people didn't need to judge my decision to gain weight to the point of obesity.

I wanted to take a Silly Putty imprint of the surface of my face and arms to preserve the mottling, knowing that, unlike newspaper, my skin had no petroleum-based product to foster the transfer of images. When the hair fell out, my arms were smooth, like a swimmer's before a meet. The non-hairy wrinkled skin on the inside of my elbows appeared to be a mesh of double

139

helixes crowded together, any pressure creating a ripple of puckers, an expanse
of human crepe the texture of cancer.

But I was marked by my non-smoking privilege. My cancer had the non-smoking mutation, and the drug controlling it clearly marked my face. I rose each morning, and before I even formulated a thought, often before I even peed, I twisted open the Tarceva bottle, shook out a tablet, and filled a Dixie cup with water. I swallowed the 100 milligram tablet, knowing I belonged to a privileged class of patients whose cancer had a mutation and another privileged class of cancer patients with health insurance to cover the drug that retailed at $6,959 per thirty-day supply. I told strangers in whom I did confide that I was privileged also because I'd never had to sit in a chair, wrapped in a blanket and listening to music or reading a book to distract myself from chemicals dripping into my body through a traditional chemotherapy infusion.

I did not want to obliterate the marks on my face that separated me, for now, from the others. I reached for my face, my skin.

Walking Clover

Before we even made it out of the house for the walk, I was anxious. There were two worst-case scenarios, one that involved her and one that involved me. Both stemmed from what we had come to know about her strength. At fifty-three pounds, she was svelte and lean. Perfect, the vet said on her last visit. But not dainty. Strong. Strong enough to knock me over when jumping up on me, and while I wasn't an Amazon woman, I was tall and big-boned with a solid center of gravity in spite of my puny arm strength. Occasionally, when I put her on the leash outside our back door, she became distracted by a chipmunk scuttling under the porch, and as I reached down to clip the hook to her collar, she tugged unexpectedly. I held on, but I nearly lost my balance as the full tilt of her body angled away from me.

I was afraid that I would gain a false sense of security during our walks and one day she would become so distracted that she would tug me in that same manner. I wouldn't be ready for her. I was afraid she would tug my hand so hard that I'd fall and break one of my cancer-stressed bones. I received Xgeva injections quarterly to strengthen those bones, but I didn't know what would happen if I broke one. Would the cancer hidden there be more likely to invade again?

What if she tugged me so hard that she surprised me and instead of falling, I accidentally released her? And what if just then a car came through the neighborhood, and she raced in front of it in her excitement to be free? Or if she seized a moment of freedom to explore and bounded away with me in pursuit, until she her wound her way to The Main Road, where I would run after her, gasping for air but unable to catch her? And she would frolic into traffic on The Main Road, and I'd see her cream-colored body struck by a bumper, hear her howl, just once, before she lay down to die across the entrance from the golf course on The Main Road, just hundreds of yards away from our front yard, which was forbidden territory?

Those were the two scenarios I held in my head each time we walked.

I should have learned to walk her when she was younger. The vet had said not to take her on the main sidewalks or to parks where other dogs roamed, because her immune system wasn't ready yet for the germs of the other dogs that she would sniff out. By the time I'd read about loose leash walking and how to establish control, it was too late to walk her just in the back yard. By then I learned how incredibly strong she was. I thought it was just me, but then others commented on it – the assistants at the vet's office, the teacher of the dog training class.

We bought the Gentle Leader and Rachel began to take her for walks based on what she'd learned from her boyfriend. But when Rachel left for Philly, and Connor left for France, I knew that with Nathaniel's busy schedule, it would be up to me to walk her.

I watched the Gentle Leader video and sorted out the loops and clasps and locks of the contraption which was neither as innocuous as a thong nor as menacing as a cannibal's face restraint, but somewhere in between.

The Gentle Leader video, helpful as it was, increased my anxiety. *Make sure the clasp around the head is tight. You should be able to fit one finger underneath. Make sure the nose loop is loose enough to give the dog's mouth room to move but not loose enough to fall off.* Like all of the helpful suggestions I'd read as a parent, the instructions came from a voice of authority; I was looking for an authority of my own, and sometimes hearing other people speak with such conviction weakened rather than empowered me. I was afraid of losing control.

And so, on the days when my mind and my body met in a zen unity of confidence and strength, I placed the Gentle Leader on Clover. Eager as she was to be out and about, she waited patiently as I put the device on her, even though later she would rub her face along the patches of grass in an effort to tear the loop off her nose, and I would bite my lip to keep from saying, "It's okay, Clover," in a comforting voice, worrying all the while that she would keep up her rubbing when we got to the pavement of the sidewalk and would skin her nose from the intensity.

We walked out the back door, skirting the slight hill where she pooped, the hill she had pulled me down before, when she was just a puppy, spraining my ankle. We left the back yard through a small gate. I tried to remember what I'd learned from the video and the trainer without hearing the *don't* voice, another voice that often paralyzed me.

She sniffed at the black fence behind which two dogs lived, though they were inside today. She sniffed the brown mulch. Such a smelling dog, Rachel and I said. The neighborhood behind our house was large, but our walk was a short one, once we got out the back walkway to the neighborhood road. Right. Down one block. We met a dog named Sam, whom we passed at a distance, owner and dog on each side of the street. Another dog, one with an invisible fence, lived at the house at the end of the block, and we crossed there. I tightened my grip on the two parts of the leash I held exactly as the video instructed. After we crossed the street, Clover inspected the base of the streetlight; all streetlight bases had remnants of birds' nests.

Five minutes later, we passed what turned out to be Sam's house. For once, Clover didn't bark or tug. She just sniffed. Sam's owner called him back to the garage after asking my dog's name. "You are too old, Sam," the man said. I told him Clover was a year and a half old, but I was still learning how to walk her on a loose leash.

You are supposed to vary your puppy's walk to make the journey more interesting, but I needed routine and control, so whenever we walked, it was the same walk, a square, the square being the geometrical shape recommended in the dog training book by the Monks of New Skete because it allowed you to change direction. We entered the last leg of our square when behind us there was a loud engine rumble, and a school bus pulled up next to us on the side street. I'd selected a bad time for our adventure. Bodies would step off the bus. Calamity might ensue.

One passenger, a young woman with a musical instrument case, descended from the bus. She watched us cautiously and edged around us as Clover barked. The young woman reached a mailbox, opened it up, retrieved some paper, and headed down the driveway toward the house. Clover was alert but not manic. I seized the moment as an opportunity to loosen the hold of one of my hands on the leash, and I reached down to sweep up three leaves I'd been eyeing on the grass next to the mailbox, two reds and an amber, some form of maple and then another leaf whose tree name I couldn't remember from childhood. I was taking a risk, letting a hand off the leash, so I replaced it quickly, shocked but secretly thrilled by my own daring.

The young woman entered her house. The bus which dropped her off started up again and reached the corner, its brakes groaning a metal stop before the vehicle turned right to head out of the subdivision and onto The Main Road we lived on, the road Clover could see from our front window. The road onto which she must never venture.

We crossed the street in the neighborhood, headed down the sidewalk, and walked through our neighbor's yard to our gate. Once we were inside and I'd latched the gate closed, the vigil departed from my body. I held onto the leash, but I gave myself a moment to look down at the three leaves I'd collected. Negligible in weight, the leaves were hefty with the past. My mother taught us to iron the leaves between wax paper. I did such waxings with my own children. I should pull out the iron and memorialize the autumnal day, the successful walk.

Then I remembered how dangerous a hot iron could be, poised on the edge of an unstable ironing board. Ironing leaves was not a suitable pastime for the owner of a strong, adventurous dog. I decided to trace them in my journal instead, saving the wax paper for another time.

Immunology

October 29, 2014

We sat in the beige chairs in the allergist's office, waiting for Nathaniel's name to be called. Today he would have his milk, egg, and peanut allergies retested. We were hoping that he would lose one of the allergies – that at least one of them would have lessened to the point that he would be able to try small quantities of food that he had avoided for sixteen years of his life. That he might be able – if he had lost his milk allergy – to have pizza with real mozzarella cheese or a cone with real ice cream. That he might be able to eat cheese with his bread when we went to France in December. Or crêpes made with real eggs.

I brought a small blanket because the weather turned colder yesterday, moving from a high of seventy-five degrees on Monday to a high of forty-five degrees when we visited the cider mill last night, where he did not eat the doughnuts, which, of course, were made with milk and egg. I remembered the skin prick tests (SPT) that I myself had to undergo when I was a young child and later an adolescent. The prongs of the skin prick testing device and the intradermal hypodermics were one thing; the cold air of the examination room on your bare back and your shirtless arms was quite another. Yet the cold could be ameliorated much more easily than the prick from a needle or scratch from a prong.

A nurse came in with questions about Nathaniel's symptoms and family history. She asked us if the resident working with Dr. Hennessey could meet with us before the allergist did, but she assured us that seeing the resident wasn't a requirement. Nathaniel agreed, happy to play a role in someone else's educational process.

Dr. Chang entered the room. He reviewed the material on the computers and asked more questions about Nathaniel's allergies. He left.

"He says 'okay' a lot," Nathaniel remarked, after the resident left. I told him that the residents had to practice how they responded to people. It didn't come naturally to all of them, no matter how well they knew their biology or their medicine. Dr. Hennessey was a natural conversationalist, known by many in our community by his major non-medical achievement – winning many consecutive days in a row on *Jeopardy* because of his wide range of knowledge and probably also his ability to hit the buzzer and keep his composure long enough to formulate the answer in a question rather than just blurting it out, like I would.

Dr. Hennessey entered and said we would test for all three allergens. The nurse told him about our upcoming trip to France and our hope that Nathaniel might be able to eat some of the notable French cuisine. Dr. Hennessey shared that when his son was in college, he did a year-long study abroad in France, so the doctor and his wife were able to visit twice. "I've been to Paris in April, and it's everything they say it is," Dr. Hennessey remarked. I didn't expect it to be warm when we were in Paris, but I did have high expectations for the trip. I'd wanted to go to Paris since I'd read French novels in high school in translation and then studied French for three years in college. I loved the language and the literature, and going to Paris with my family seemed to be the most perfect vacation I could ask for.

When the nurse prepared Nathaniel for the tests, she swabbed his forearms with alcohol.

As she flicked the prongs against his arms, he said, "These are the gross ones." But then we realized that these tests were scratch, not intradermal, and the nurse told us something that we didn't remember – that they didn't do intradermal for food allergies – only for environmental.

Nathaniel was relieved. The intradermal injections hurt more, kind of like a TB test.

The right arm had three antigens labelled with ink the nurse penned on his arms. E, M, P.

146

From the crook of his elbow down to his wrist. Employer, I thought. Empathy. I didn't play scrabble regularly, but my brain worked in patterns when it came to letters. There was a fourth mark for the control.

She offered him a pillow to prop his arm up, but I declined it, giving him the blanket I'd brought instead. Then I hated myself for speaking for him, denying him the chance to have the pillow if he wanted it. He was plenty old enough to speak for himself. In addition, one of my goals for him since my diagnosis was that he develop independence and maturity at a young age.

In the first few minutes, the skin by the "M" stayed smooth and beige-white innocuous in its Caucasian uniformity with the rest of his skin. But after five minutes, the red began to set in, first as a faint pink tinge, then as red streaks, and finally as a hive with dime-sized center, red inflammation surrounding it. The "E" was unremarkable ("unremarkable" being the operative medical term) so the plan we've followed for the past year of allowing him to eat baked goods with eggs cooked for twenty-five minutes or more had worked. The "P," too, was fairly tame, given what we've heard about the lasting nature of peanut allergies. But the milk was still a major culprit, and I risked encountering data charges on my cell phone as I Googled common recipes for crêpes to see if milk was usually required. When the allergist finally came back in, he assigned the Egg a 2, the Milk a 4, and the Peanut a 3. The results of the test could range from 0 to 4+. In the past, Nathaniel had taken this same test and had scored higher numbers for the egg. His highest reaction had always been to milk, even though the peanut allergy tended to be viewed as the most deadly. Dr. Hennessey had also told us that sometimes these skin tests could still present a "reaction" or a sort of "false positive" when the body had already become immune to the allergen. Therefore, the "2" was a promising reading, because even though it was reactive, the reaction wasn't too strong.

When Nathaniel was a toddler, shortly after he'd begun to have some odd reactions to baby food and the scrambled eggs his siblings had loved to have plopped on their high chair trays, he had been with his dad at his grandma's house and had crawled up on a dining room chair and reached for a piece of pizza on the table. He only got a slice of pepperoni, from which, someone recalled later, a string of cheese had dangled.

I'd been off writing somewhere that Sunday afternoon, and when I came home that evening shortly after my husband returned with the kids, we noticed that Nathaniel was acting lethargic. Soon, his face had gone white and his breathing became labored. And then the white began to look bluish, and I called 911.

When the EMTs came to the house, they told me to climb on the stretcher. They instructed Tim to put Nathaniel on my chest. They strapped me in, and wheeled me to the ambulance, where they loaded us up quickly.

But then they didn't move their vehicle from the street in front of our driveway. They stayed there, calling in to their dispatch, requesting permission to administer epinephrine. I held Nathaniel close so he could bury his face in my neck, and I grasped his thigh firmly so they could inject the drug. And only after the drug was administered did they start up the truck and drive to St. Lawrence Hospital, where we were wheeled to the emergency department. Nathaniel was observed for quite a long time at the emergency department and then transferred to the main Sparrow hospital for an overnight stay. Each new doctor who met him and heard the details of his case was amazed at the severity of his reaction to such a minute bit of milk product.

At the allergist's office a few weeks later, during an appointment we'd made before the pizza incident even took place, the doctor confirmed that Nathaniel had a severe allergy to milk, as well as egg and peanut. As an infant, he'd almost fallen into a failure-to-thrive classification a few months after he was born because he wasn't gaining weight, in spite of the fact that he was a happier baby than his two siblings and rarely vomited like his older sister had as a child. I understood then, at the allergist's office, that I'd been poisoning my child with my breast milk; I was a heavy milk consumer myself. I'd been told to watch onions and broccoli while nursing, but it hadn't occurred to me to cut out milk. No wonder he didn't like to nurse much.

The incident that had signaled to us just how dangerous eating could be for our youngest son had taken place more than fifteen years earlier. Now we were at the allergist's office again. He'd spent the intervening years learning about how to manage his food allergies. He'd become diligent about reading labels, indifferent and unconcerned when he had to turn down treats at friends' houses or during class at school. Now the allergist was telling him that while he still had to be vigilant about the milk, he might be able to eat eggs. "But we need to do a food challenge. You need to come back with an EpiPen and some scrambled eggs. We heat them up in the microwave and then let you eat them little by little."

We signed up for an appointment in November. On my third cancer birthday, Nathaniel would eat scrambled eggs under the close supervision of the allergist to see if he had outgrown his egg allergy. Not only would he be shedding his braces that fall; he would likely be shedding his life-long allergy to eggs.

Immunology is the branch of biomedicine that examines the immune system. In humans, immunology often refers to the study of how the body's response to foreign invaders contributes to health and/or disease. Immunotherapy uses knowledge about the body's response to invaders by developing ways to boost the body's resistance to those same invaders. While the field originally developed around the classic area of diseases and disease prevention of threats like polio, measles, and mumps, a natural extension of the field occurred with the recognition of allergic responses. In 1943, the American Academy of Allergy, Asthma, and Immunology was created as the beginning of the specialty for the field.

When I was a child, the field of allergy and immunology was in its infancy. Yet the pediatrician in the town next to the one where I grew up in Waterford, Michigan, James A. O'Neill, had expanded a practice of allergy as part of his work as a generalist treating children from birth to age eighteen. I was a child with both chronic asthma and chronic allergies. I'd spent my childhood learning as much as I could about how my allergies and my asthma worked. After Nathaniel was diagnosed with food allergies, I travelled a similar path of education, connecting with the Food Allergy and Anaphylaxis Network and learning as much about cooking with substitutes as I could. Early on, my friend Beth had given me the "Wacky Cake" recipe made with cocoa, vinegar, and baking soda that we used as our standard birthday cake for years. Then, I learned that our local health food store carried Ener-G Egg Replacer, which expanded Nathaniel's food preparation and consumption horizons significantly. And now, in 2014, finding a milk substitute was never a problem with the soy, almond, and rice varieties on the market. But we were still elated at the idea of freedom from the egg allergy and looked forward to the oral food challenge that awaited Nathaniel in November.

November 26, 2014

We arrived shortly before 3:00 PM. This time, Tim had gotten off work to be present for the festivities. I'd brought an EpiPen and the liquid Benadryl, the dynamic duo he was supposed to carry with him at all times. And a Tupperware container full of scrambled eggs.

Dr. Hennessey came in to check on Nathaniel and make sure there was nothing about his health on this day that would suggest a reason for postponing the challenge — the Oral Food Challenge (OFC).

They would be giving Nathaniel one teaspoonful of eggs at a time, waiting thirty minutes, and checking him for reactions such as hives, swelling, and shortness of breath.

Throughout the procedure, the nurses morphed into waitresses, concerned about making sure that the eggs Nathaniel tasted for the first time since infancy would be heated to just the right temperature. He took a bite, less than a teaspoonful, and drank from a Dixie cup of water that the nurse gave him. I took a short video with my iPhone, explaining to the nurse that I didn't originally want an iPhone but had been convinced of its merit and now needed to learn how to use the various features. I enjoyed capturing Nathaniel's face as he tasted the eggs and smiled his pleasure. I used lots of soy margarine in the preparation. I loved my own scrambled eggs quite buttery. When Tim asked him how they tasted, Nathaniel says, "Good."

And later, "Really good."

I don't remember how many "doses" of eggs he ate. But within a couple of hours, Dr. Hennessey was able to say, with final certainty, that Nathaniel had beaten the egg allergy. He could now eat eggs, prepared in any fashion, as long as none of the other ingredients contained one of the other foods to which he was allergic.

We discussed crepes and my Google research revealed that most crêpes were, in fact, made with milk, and Dr. Hennessey mentioned that there was now a special blood test we could have done that would determine if Nathaniel's milk allergy had a component that would allow him to introduce small quantities of milk into his diet with products containing milk that had been cooked for twenty-five minutes or more. It was a test that only two labs in the area processed. He would get the information.

A week later, I would drive Nathaniel to the lab, where they would take a vial of blood and ship it out. The test was called "ImmunoCAP Allergen Components." We'd get a report telling us Nathaniel had high levels of both alpha-lactalbumin and beta-lactoglobulin, but that the highest level his test revealed was for casein, at 3.96 kU/L. According to the ImmunoCAP brochure, the casein proteins were heat-stable and did not break down when they were heated; therefore, Nathaniel did not have the option of cooking milk in baked goods to lessen the potential effect of the allergen.

Later still, I would replay the video from the allergist's office on my iPhone, pleased at how polite Nathaniel was when the nurse handed him each spoonful of egg and cupful of water.

His father's voice in the background talked about the consistency of the egg and its texture, how satisfying scrambled eggs were. But when Nathaniel took his first bite and his father asked him how it was, he said, "You know it's good! And there's more than a half teaspoon here." And then his smile emerged. I saw my youngest child on the tall rectangle of my phone, so poised, so adult, so charming, his face chiseled at the cheekbones and the dimples. I couldn't believe this person was the child I'd clasped so tightly to me on the stretcher in that ambulance in front of the driveway of our Cumberland house so many years ago. And now, with the passage of time, I could extract the peril from that moment and think only of the two of us that day, his toddler body contoured to mine on the stretcher, physical comfort for both of us. In the allergist's office, he was across the room. Long and lean, hunched over at the shoulders. "You can stop now," he said to the video camera.

He could eat eggs, any way he wanted. Except with milk or cheese, of course. "But don't go crazy or anything," Dr. Hennessey said. "Wait until tomorrow to have a heaping plate."

We'd talked about running out to a breakfast restaurant for dinner to celebrate his food challenge and my birthday, but we still had to figure out the butter issue with eating eggs out, and it was getting late. Many guests would be arriving the next day for our combined Thanksgiving and Christmas celebration, including Rachel, who would be flying into Metro from Philadelphia to see the relatives she wouldn't see at Christmas because she would be in France with the rest of us.

I needed to begin food preparation for the next day's feast. Nathaniel begged for eggs for dinner, and I wanted to be prudent, and say, "No, wait." Tim said he'd make them. And they looked to me as if I were the final arbiter. It wasn't what the doctor ordered, but I gave the go ahead, knowing that in the future he'd continue to make most of these decisions on his own. For now, the EpiPen and the Benadryl were close at hand. For now, I was here to watch over him.

Paris Lodgings

Our apartment in Paris was located in Montparnesse between the sixth and seventh arrondissments on the seventh floor of an apartment building on the rue de Sèvres. From what I could determine based on our email exchanges, our hostess, Valérie, was a sweet, accommodating sort. Jeremy's mom told me to check out VRBO when she learned I was planning a trip to France. The first time I saw Valérie's place on VRBO, I was captured by the abundance of light. I would not be in Paris in April, so I would need the light. I also fell in love with the piano, which would be in the bedroom I called Rachel's room.

Even though the number of beds was limited and one of the boys would be on the couch and another on an inflatable on the floor, the place was large. We would be able to eat at the same table and look out the window at rue de Sèvres below.

At 1012 square feet, the apartment was larger than the house I grew up in, so we wouldn't be cramped. My family of five grew up in a house of only 800 square feet. Two bedrooms and one bath. My father added a patio, which we never called a family room or a T.V. room, although the only thing we did in that room was watch T.V. My mother didn't add the half bathroom in the basement until after my parents divorced and we three girls had left for good.

When I woke in my bedroom next to the bathroom on school day mornings before going to elementary and middle school, I would hear the water of my father's bath through the walls and know that I would have to hold my urine until he got out. Later, when my older sister and I were in first middle and then high school together, we developed an elaborate routine of bathroom usage. We each rose and washed our hair in the kitchen sink (although there was a shower head in our tub, the full-sized window in the shower prevented functional usage). Then we each took a bath. We accomplished all of this before my father rose, bathed, ate the breakfast my mother prepared for him, and walked to the corner where our neighborhood was bordered by Williams Lake Road, one of the major thoroughfares that wound through Waterford around the lakes. His co-worker, Bill Caswell, picked him up each day at the entrance to the subdivision, which was framed by two stone pillars on each side. He and Bill Caswell, whom we always referred to by both names, would ride together to the experimental division of Pontiac Motors, on Joslyn Road in Pontiac.

Our bathroom schedule was about water usage and temperature – how we could get through our baths and hair washings before the water got cold, so we could all leave the house on time. I don't even know when my younger sister or mother bathed, how they got out the door or if they had warm water for their daily ablutions. What went on after I left was not my affair.

Now, during this week of researching Paris lodgings, my stomach roiled. Perhaps it was the worry about finances for the trip or for Connor's apartment in Kalamazoo once he returned to school from his study abroad. But more likely, it was the Tarceva. I was experiencing more Tarceva moments, so on the night after I booked the Paris lodging, I woke up realizing that I'd counted bathrooms but not toilets. I snuck back to the VRBO website, almost afraid to look, afraid that this apartment I'd lobbied the family for might have two tubs and showers but not toilets. Water closets.

I clicked on the VRBO photos to find the proof I needed. There were two pictures. The beige toilet was in the bathroom with rose-colored towels, a white wallpaper with columns of a blue design moving vertically up and down on the paper. A rose molding near the top. But the other bathroom had white fixtures, although I couldn't see the toilet itself, just the lip of the tub.

Yet the listing said the toilet was there. Two baths. Two toilets. Luxury. I could go back to sleep.

III. The Truth About Paris

December 21, 2014 – January 3, 2015

Groceries on Rue de Sèvres

Just inside the door to the right, the baguettes rose from the floor like umbrellas in a stand, except not so neat, more like thick, gnarled walking sticks. At least that's how I remembered seeing them for the first time. Or perhaps instead of standing in vertical position, they emerged horizontally from woven baskets just inside the door of Carrefour down the street from our Paris rental. Maybe they rested heavy, like layered bricks or stones from an Egyptian pyramid, stacked neatly on top of each other. Or maybe they lay stiff, piled like pretzel rods.

Fresh, maybe even warm at some points during the day, but not that afternoon, when we dragged ourselves to Carrefour that Sunday after our post-flight naps. Jet-lagged, our bodies heavy and cumbersome, our brains still fogged, we began the short walk to the market, each step a sluice in our faces. Passersby speaking French to their companions. A shop door opening and closing with a bell's ding. An entrance. An exit. Commonplace transitions made potent by foreign observation. Bodies bustling because even though Parisian Christmas didn't flash as garishly in its commercialism as its American counterpart, it still propelled, electrified.

Outdoor stands extended from the storefronts. A large bone wrapped in beef stood under a light, encased in clear glass, a jewel. A hand with a knife sliced, removing pink layers. Images bounced against our bleary, wakeful eyes.

The baguettes wore paper sleeves with blue printing for their Sunday duty. Grabbing one, we looked for a grocery cart in which to place it. The two-part cart system became apparent as we searched. Plastic baskets nested inside one another by the door. Wheeled carts, less plentiful, appeared scattered throughout the store; the baskets latched onto the carts.

We stayed together as a family only for the first two aisles, and then I realized we no longer needed to travel in a clump like a family of grapes. We spread out to explore. Pleasure arrived in the smells and staccato bursts of French that exploded here and there, pleasure in the distinct packaging which sheathed the items, similar to yet different from American packaging. But the words on the labels provided the most delight for me – delight because I could pick up an item, read the words, and comprehend much of what I read, just as when I'd stepped off the plane, entered the airport, and understood so many of the signs.

After all those years, long forgotten French words returned to me. When the French spoke, I couldn't understand more than a phrase or two, the words coming so fast, like American words, many of them mumbled, like most American speech. But when my eyes could absorb the written language, slowly, taking in the letters one by one, in their syntactical French beauty, I found meaning, enough meaning that I knew, just by reading the labels, which foods my allergic son could consume without fear.

In a corner of the refrigerated items, I discovered rows of sauces in small boxes. Packaged like American juice boxes, several came together, bundled with shrink wrap. Béchamel. Hollandaise. I wanted to buy a head of cauliflower and experiment, tasting each one. How clever that they made it so easy to cook like the French in France.

The next day we would return with Connor, who had more experience and would steer us toward the packaged gnocchi, which he would cook along with spaghetti sauce, ladling the sauce onto the gnocchi. But he wouldn't arrive until the next morning, and we sought to become successful shoppers on our own.

I wandered to another corner on the opposite side of the store from the sauces, where bottles of milk stood on the floor, shrink-wrapped in sets of four or six. Not refrigerated. I was astounded to discover that the French drank largely non-perishable milk. Later, while researching milk on the Internet in Valérie's apartment, I found an explanation in the information about ultra-high-temperature (UHT) pasteurized milk, something much more common in Europe. It wasn't like the cartons of almond, rice, or soy we could buy off the shelf in the states. France's UHT milk was regular cow's milk but treated so that it didn't require refrigeration. I could buy some for the rest of the family's use, but I still needed to find something non-dairy that Nathaniel could drink. I kept picking up different brands on the edges of the pile which rose like a wall of bottled water in the states. I couldn't find non-dairy milk. Later, as we joined back together in the center aisles, I learned that Tim had located some soy milk elsewhere in the store, and we decided we would go with that and search harder the next day for almond, which Nathaniel preferred to rice or soy when he had options. But he seemed eager to try some soy puddings we'd found in the dairy case by the yogurt. Sans milk. We had enough Nathaniel-friendly food in our cart that we knew we'd make it to the next day without difficulties – he wouldn't go hungry.

We rolled our cart tentatively toward the check-out lanes – two small lines near the front of the market. The thought of speaking with the cashiers conjured up for me a faint sense of dread. Rachel had already expressed her feelings of intimidation about communicating in France. While I had disembarked from the plane thrilled to see French words in front of me, and hear the spoken language, indecipherable yet slightly familiar to my ear, Rachel admitted to being stunned by a feeling of otherness and isolation. She'd travelled abroad to Scotland just after high school to perform in the Edinburgh Festival Fringe and had been undaunted by the variety of brogues she heard. But here, in France, the language barrier took her by surprise, and she felt out of place, no longer the confident adventurer leading her younger siblings.

We'd done fine without Connor at the airport when buying our museum passes; those people often dealt with travelling Americans. And Valérie, our landlady/host, had been so gracious and welcoming when we'd met her at the apartment, speaking to us in mostly English but a bit of French as well, to help us acclimate. Nathaniel had studied French for over three years, now. But speaking another language in the real world came with more pressure to perform than in the classroom.

As we put our items on the line, I inhaled, preparing to speak. The cashier said something. I couldn't understand. "Pardon?" I said.

"I think she wants to know if you want bags," Nathaniel said.

"Yes!" I said. And smiled. Smiling seemed important. "Oui, I mean." The clerk responded.

I asked her to repeat her response.

"The bags cost money." Tim and Nathaniel had deciphered the French at the same time.

"Oh. Well, Valérie says we use bags for the garbage chute. We'll ask for three."

We managed to pronounce "trois."

The cashier gave us the total, including the price of the bags. I held up our money, demonstrating that we had enough but needed to figure it out. The clerk made a gesture with her head, asking for permission, and then selected the bills out of my hand.

As we moved past the check-out line to return our cart and basket, I grinned at the rest of the family, and they smiled back. In triumph, I thought. I was already fatigued from travel and overwhelmed by the stimuli, but I felt competent as well. We had purchased groceries in our neighborhood on the rue de Sèvres without offending or feeling offended ourselves.

Awakened and unmuted, we could engage the city.

Père Lachaise

According to Rick Steves, Bus 69 provided the best way to see Paris and get a feel for its structure. The bus transported individuals from east to west and back again. On the day after we arrived in the city, we walked from our apartment on the rue de Sèvres to the Avenue Joseph Bouvard and found seats in the rear of the bus by windows, just as Steves suggested in his book. As the bus travelled across the Champs de Mare Park by the Eiffel Tower, we noticed that the street on which we travelled changed names to rue St. Dominique, and the bus then began its trek across town to the 20th arrondissement, home to Père Lachaise Cemetery. The kids teased us about turning Rick Steves into a God, so that on only our second day in Paris, we avoided mentioning his name, calling him he-who-shall-not-be-named in Harry Potter fashion.

Few could admit aloud that Rick Steves knew his business, yet the Bus 69 tour did provide a grounding orientation to the city. But our family had left much too late in the day, between jet lag and our typical family way of moving slowly. It was dusk when we debarked from the bus near the cemetery's closing time. We made an impromptu decision to hop on another bus and return to our apartment, planning to visit the cemetery the next day. We needed to re-learn our rhythms for being together as a family, re-learn how long it took for us to settle on plans and prepare for an outing. We all knew Rachel liked a schedule so she had a clear sense of when things would start and what would happen next. She and Tim loved history, and they wanted to see so many historical attractions. But Tim was also slow to move in the morning, and Tarceva made me a very cautious traveler in the first few hours of the day. Already faint grumbling resonated in the apartment, mumbles about who had moved too slowly, who needed to be more chill. I needed to become again the mother of toddlers and teenagers, saying in a too-bright, breezy voice, "We know how to be flexible, right, guys?" We'd deviated from the carefully laid-out game plan Tim and I had created for using our museum passes.

On the second day we arrived near Père Lachaise via the Métro, walking down Boulevard de Ménilmontant until the burial ground appeared, not quite majestic – just another area of Paris fenced off with black wrought iron pickets and crumbling gray stone. We entered at Porte Principale and strolled along Avenue Principale.

It was December 24. Christmas Eve Day. Gray, with rain threatening. The atmosphere crept around us, wrapping our limbs, and I felt that we'd been planted in a set for a black-and-white film, the director of which had dictated that not only the medium but the props themselves must be black-and-white. A tinge of gray brushed onto the backdrop, so that the grave markers appeared charcoaled into a pastel drawing, some maker still smudging the edges.

I thought of one of the last illustrated children's books I'd purchased for Nathaniel – a dark Addams-family version of "The Spider and the Fly" poem, almost like a Tim Burton movie in its cartoonish horror. But Père Lachaise felt more *Schindler's List* than a Tim Burton film. Maybe not on a sunny summer day, but today, when the clouds hung so low and the sky spit out small gobs of spatter from time to time. We worried about whether we might face a deluge from a dark sky both menacing and striking in its beauty.

We should have printed off a map ahead of time in order to locate the graves of famous people. If we'd read the Steves guide more carefully, we would have known to stop at a nearby florist shop for a map. But I hadn't read that part. In fact, I learned later that the Rick Steves book even presented a clearly labelled map of key points in the cemetery, ironic because we always had the guide with us – either in my purse or in Tim's backpack.

A sign near the entrance provided plot numbers, but there were no pamphlets so we moved in the general direction of where we might want to finish our tour. With Oscar Wilde. Edith Piaf. Jim Morrison.

Connor said he'd never seen so many large graves at a cemetery. I knew my child self would have been fascinated by the house-like tombs, with the cemetery as the larger village in which the dead resided. The tombs rose in layers as the cemetery's terrain changed, so that sometimes, as a visitor, I climbed hills and looked down to survey the layers of graves, while at other times, I stood on a flat plain peering up. My adult self recognized the houses as crypts and mausoleums, crypts with bodies buried below ground, mausoleums with bodies buried above.

The gray kept spreading into the landscape. Age transformed the white into gray; age produced streaks of a blackish soot at the edges of the stone and inside the lettering. Baron Haussmann's grave appeared on our left, one of the first few graves. Haussmann was the man responsible for changing the shape of the city, Tim had told me. On rue Principale, we stayed together for the first few graves, but after talking and walking for a few minutes I sensed the kids' desire to branch out. Nathaniel strode up the lane and off to the left. I watched as he disappeared behind a section of graves, worried that he would become separated from the rest of the family. Yet I myself lagged, studying some of the dilapidated mausoleums and crypts, doors off hinges, piles of leaves and bits of trash inside.

How does a city bury its dead? Père Lachaise was a municipal museum. And who takes care of the dead, once their relatives have expired along with them? I wondered whose job it was to take care of the non-famous dead in this powerful place, where the atmosphere was made more powerful with the side-by-side placement of the old and worn and the carefully preserved.

I knew that I found cemeteries interesting not primarily because of the architecture but because of the atmosphere and the commemoration of the lives lived by individuals I would never know and about whom I might not ever learn the history. Thus, in this foreign land, where I couldn't possibly know a plebian soul buried, I visited to honor the lives of the dead, not just the lives of the great artists and personalities. The lives of the unknown. Yet it would be the flashier graves that we would most likely take note of and remember.

Back at home in Michigan, my parents lay buried in Christian Memorial Garden in Rochester. They'd chosen the site before divorce had rent them apart. The Memorial Gardens allowed no rising markers, headstones, or sculptures. The flat surfaces created a uniformity powerful in its own right. I'd heard and observed that headstones sometimes fell over time, as soil eroded, ruining the planes of perfection that existed when the stones were erected.

I felt guilty that I hadn't been to visit my parents' graves in a while. After my sisters and I had selected their markers, we'd been diligent, often bringing flowers and ordering grave blankets in the winters. The graves were in a town an hour and a half away from where I lived, so more recently I'd visited only when I made a point of seeing my sisters or when I was down in Rochester teaching. Earlier, though, in those years after they died, I would sometimes come and sit there, next to their graves, talking and singing to them. I loved the idea that my mother's bones were underneath me – that if I really wanted to, I could dig up the dirt, crack into the coffin, and wrap myself in my mother's embrace, and the same two arms that had held me for so much of my childhood, albeit bony now, would hold me again.

Tim wasn't sure he even wanted to be buried. Early in our marriage, I'd told him that he didn't have a choice. Funerals and death were for the living, and however disgusting and fake embalming could be, I would need to see his real dead body in order to bury him. He'd conceded that I had a point about the ceremony and the need for closure belonging to the living. Yet when I was diagnosed with cancer, I realized that however much I wanted to have access to my mother's body and know, factually, that I could reach her skeleton, I myself no longer wanted to be buried underground. I was afraid of the dark in the depths of the soil. Perhaps I should be cremated. But what if my children needed my bones in the same way I needed my mother's?

As I stood in Paris and snapped the picture of the dilapidated graves that weren't being taken care of, I worried about my parents' graves. How much had the grass grown up over the edges of the markers embedded in the ground? Had red ants created nests around the marble?

I wanted to see Edith Piaf's grave more than any others. Oscar Wilde's would be meaningful, because he was a writer and I'd known about him ever since I'd seen *The Picture of Dorian Gray* on television as a teenager. But Edith Piaf was a singer. Before we left for Paris, Tim and I had watched some French movies to remind ourselves of what the language sounded like when spoken quickly. We'd watched *Paris, Je t'aime*. *Séraphine. Amélie. La Vie en Rose.*

Each movie was playful or stunning in its own way, but the Edith Piaf movie with Marion Cotillard wrenched my heart with its depiction of the urchin child who grew up in the street and transformed herself into the Parisian Sparrow.

"La Vie en Rose" was that familiar melody I'd never quite known the name of until hearing it featured on a show that all three of my children had loved at some point in their adolescence or early adulthood – *How I Met Your Mother*. But the videos I'd seen of Edith Piaf singing the song struck a more poignant note than the footage of the mother of Ted's children singing the legendary Piaf song in the sitcom episode. Piaf was the Sparrow, her eyes wide open, full of pain, warbling through the French vowels and consonants, bringing the beauty and pain of living to the musical line of the song.

In the week after I saw the movie, I looked up some of the songs on YouTube to see the real Edith sing them. "Non, je ne regrette rien" with its knell of repetition, the trumpets keeping a steady rhythm of utterance, the echoing words like a confession. My husband had told me he didn't want me to regret anything when I died. But I already had regrets. Perhaps I needed to make Edith Piaf's song a mantra I could live by.

In a letter my mother had written from Germany in the early 50's as a civilian with the Air Force, she mentioned hoping to see Edith Piaf in concert. Yet none of the subsequent letters discussed any performance she might have attended. My desire wasn't logical, but I wanted to see the grave of a singer my mother may not have even heard in song during her time in France.

It was a connection, however tenuous, and the connection is what helped to bring the dead alive for me, to help me honor them.

I found the rest of my family members in another part of the cemetery containing memorials to the veterans from the world wars. Someone had found Oscar Wilde's grave, one that we recognized easily from the vignette in *Paris, je t'aime*. We surrounded it, trying to do justice with our iPhones, trying to capture the large structure, the parts of the human visage emerging from the sides of the stone. I tried to snap the words of the narrative on the side of the monument in the frame of my iPhone. The kids had just taught me how to narrow or expand the frame of the picture by swiping two fingers together or apart across the screen.

I needed to find a restroom, but I was determined to find Edith Piaf's grave.

We walked in a direction that led to one of the many exits of the cemetery. I told them that while we walked toward the exit, I would keep looking for Edith. It helped to follow others in the cemetery who seemed to know where they were going, and now there were more of them, moving off in a direction of graves gently terraced down a hill, these graves not the older mausoleums-like houses with their Victorian spires but more like what I was accustomed to seeing in America. We hurried now, but I spotted a large grave with a mountain of flowers and felt sure it must belong to Edith Piaf.

When I arrived, I could barely take the scene in. Others stood by the grave, making it difficult to snap a picture, but I aimed and snapped a couple to look at later, turning back to my family. We needed to leave the cemetery soon. The sky had grown even darker, small splotches of rain marking the cobblestones underneath our feet. A crowd gathered at a memorial across the way, Jim Morrison's grave. I told the kids that I didn't like The Doors, but an old friend and roommate had fallen in love with and married a man who was convinced of their brilliance. I needed to take a picture of the grave to honor my friend with whom I was no longer in touch. A tree grew in the circumference of the grave, its bark obscured by large stilts of what looked like bamboo encasing the diameter. A weaving of souvenirs in the bamboo created a second skin around the tree. Condoms. Chewed bits of gum. Métro tickets. Locks. Hairbands. I searched in my pockets for something I could leave.

The Bandaids I carried for my finger splits! I wove one into the larger nexus. "To help him heal," I whispered to Nathaniel. We both grinned at the silliness of the ritual, but I still felt proud that I'd honored the dead. Splatters fell harder on the cobblestones underneath our feet. Pigeons congregated, and I tried to capture them as well. Pigeons in a graveyard. In Paris, France. It felt so ordinary and extraordinary at the same time.

The cemetery would be closing soon, and we needed to figure out our evening plan. Earlier we had discussed heading straight from Père Lachaise to Nôtre Dame. According to the schedule I'd looked at that morning, Christmas Eve masses occurred almost hourly throughout the evening with variations on the central celebration. We left Père Lachaise uncertain about whether we would catch the next mass but knowing we must escape the impending rain. We walked to the Métro.

Ten days later we would leave Paris. Four days after that, on Wednesday, January 7, 2015, after we returned to Michigan and Connor returned to Strasbourg, terrorists attacked the offices of Charlie Hebdo on Rue Nicolas-Appert in the 11th arrondissement, just blocks from where we'd honored the French dead. By virtue of our trip to France, by virtue of our Christmas Eve visit to the 20th arrondissement, we had a new proximity to the dead. We mourned.

Je suis Charlie.

Paris Christmas

When we talked that morning over breakfast, Tim expressed doubt that we'd be able to gain entry to Christmas Eve mass at Nôtre Dame. The kids voiced lukewarm opinions about going. Tim had been baptized a Catholic but no longer practiced the faith. My parents had baptized me in the Lutheran church, and I'd endured three years of confirmation to prove myself worthy. I'd argued for the kids to be raised Lutheran as well. Over time I'd grown proud of my religion, which I felt was less judgmental and more progressive than the Catholic faith.

Out of respect for Tim's family's faith, however, especially his mother's, I'd trained myself to say "mass" when talking about Catholic church services. I'd always attended some church service or mass on Christmas Eve, usually singing "Silent Night" with a candle. I hoped to continue the tradition, even if it meant worshipping in a Catholic church and being denied the body of Christ during communion, since Lutherans weren't allowed to take communion in Catholic churches.

If the church had to be Catholic this year, la Cathédrale de Nôtre Dame de Paris struck me as the best possible concession prize, no small peanuts, offering a decent chance for affirmation, albeit reluctant, from my former-altar-boy, lapsed-Catholic husband, my history-loving daughter, and my two French-speaking sons. Nôtre Dame would offer a richer experience than some obscure Lutheran church. If Paris even harbored any Lutheran churches.

I'd pulled up the website on the computer that morning, scrutinizing the list of masses, noting the most plausible times, given our plans for the day.

When we came around the corner of la Cathédrale that evening as dusk began to fall, a long line wove around the building and through the plaza, yet we all noted that the line did, in fact, appear to creep forward.

"We need to get in line," I said.

"But is this the right line? Or is it just a line for a tour?" one of the kids said.

"I think it's the line for the service," I said. "Mass, I mean."

We fell into the queue and kept moving forward.

"This can't be right," Tim said.

"But the website mentioned several different masses throughout the day," I said. When we finally entered the doors of the building, other bodies pressed against us, creating throngs. Official-looking men redirected people to different areas, gesturing for silence and trying to keep pathways clear. The faces of the men didn't encourage question-asking, although they didn't appear unkind. In America, Fire Marshalls served this role. I felt giddy, even though I still couldn't tell if our plan had worked, couldn't tell if we were being herded with the other sheep to the right place. Perhaps anyone allowed entrance would be permitted to observe silently a mass in progress and would then be led to an exit?

Our five bodies edged up a bit in the crowds; I kept my eyes on Rachel's olive coat and Tim's hair. Now rows of pews came into view, clerics stationed at various points, a priest at the front in full, elaborate robes, speaking into the mike, although I couldn't quite hear the words. French vowels and consonants? And suddenly the people at the back of the church rose as if to leave. Were they leaving? Or were they just moving forward for communion?

I couldn't tell if we had arrived at the end of something or in the middle of something, and as I examined my family's faces and the faces of some of the other tourists around me, they all wore expressions of confusion – could we take the seats? Would we be interlopers if we sat down? Would we be jerky Americans stealing the seats of the good citizens of Paris?

But in another few moments, it was clear that the movement into seats appeared to be part of the plan; people rose, went to communion, and then left. The priest still spoke but other faces from our throng had pressed forward at the same time as we did and were finding seats in the rows ahead of them. We whispered at one another and surged forward, taking seats. In front of us an extended family had settled in. Gray-haired, nicely dressed adults with young grandchildren next to them. A young girl with a velvet skirt. The parents of the children flanking either side of the grandparents. I imagined that they'd journeyed in from their arrondissements to enjoy Christmas Eve mass. I remembered dressing up for Christmas as a child and then years later, selecting dresses for Rachel, my only daughter. Red prints with holly, white tights, and black patent leather shoes.

The priest spoke in French, and though his words came out too quickly for me to comprehend, he sounded wise. The previous seat owners had left programs outlining the details of the masses throughout the day, both in French and English. Now the choir and lay people began to sing "O Come, All Ye Faithful," but in the Latin version, "Adeste Fideles."

I sat in Paris with my family, simultaneously united with my dead mother who'd taught me the Latin version of the song when I was merely a child. As if discerning back then that I might one day need to sing the older lyrics.

Once outside, we took photos with our phones by the large tree with blue lights that illuminated the plaza in front of la Cathédrale.

Back at Valérie's apartment, we drank wine, ate cheese and baguettes – soy pudding and baguettes for Nathaniel – and peered out the window at the Christmas lights on rue de Sèvres. We surprised the kids with a CD version of *The Polar Express* I'd had made back in East Lansing from the cassette tape we'd purchased years ago with a hardback copy of the children's book. Once I observed that the VRBO site listed a CD player as one of its amenities, I determined that we'd be able to maintain another Christmas tradition of listening to William Hurt read *The Polar Express* while turning the pages of our own copy. Over the years we'd all memorized the inflections of Hurt's voice, especially when he spoke as the voice of Santa from the note under the tree on Christmas morning: "Fix that hole in your pocket."

When the kids were younger, the three of them would have gone to bed right away after *The Polar Express*, crowding onto Rachel's bed to feign sleep until Santa arrived. Tim and I would have begun the work of assiduous and commercial Christmas parents, Tim taking joy in listening to the Pope say Midnight Mass in Rome as he assembled a ping-pong table. I'd nibble cookies and carrots, gnawing the carrot ends to create convincing deer teeth marks, responding to the kids' note for Santa with left-hand printing to confuse even Rachel, the oldest.

But since the kids had grown older, I'd begun retiring earlier, and now, in Paris, I kissed them goodnight and went down the hall from the living room where we all gathered during the day. Our time during the Christmas Eve day had been magical, exhilarating, even, yet I felt weary and couldn't shrug off a sense that I was marching through the days, not unlike I did at home in Michigan during the holidays. Preserving so many traditions was stressful, especially while trying to plan sight-seeing and enjoy the moments all at the same time. And we still juggled family dynamics a bit awkwardly. Connor had arrived in Paris a day later than planned, euphoric because of a new relationship he'd begun. Rachel was happy to be with all of us but seemed bent on being the ultimate whirl-wind tourist while simultaneously acting a bit withdrawn.

The day after we'd arrived, she'd woken up with an odd swelling in one of her finger joints near her palm. She'd always been a child unfazed by routine aches and pains but conversely terrified by what she couldn't understand or explain. Connor told her about his struggles with ganglion cysts during his high school tennis career. But I sensed that Rachel was troubled also by adjustments in her new life in Philly. I wondered also if she worried at some buried level that her two brothers, with their shared knowledge of French, might be more likely to bond without her on this trip — one more factor contributing to an increased isolation. I knew from my own life with my sisters, one older and one younger, that in a family of three siblings, it was not uncommon for one to be standing on the outside, whether for a moment or an era.

I tried to purge the thoughts from my brain as I sat on my side of our Paris bed and wrote out the notes I'd planned. The trip to Paris and opportunity to spend Christmas with Connor in France served as the major gift this year. Back in the states, as I'd fretted about money, concerned that the bulk of the trip's cost would end up on our already bloated credit card balance, I'd known that I wanted to give the kids some other small thing in addition to the trip at Christmas.

Each of them struggled with money issues. Rachel had just landed the job in Philly a few months earlier and was paying rent money back to Ryan in small installments. Connor attended a small, expensive liberal arts school where it seemed to him that everyone else had more money than his family did; he lived and breathed on whatever dime we gave him, and even with the parent loans from the government, day-to-day expenses felt tight. Nathaniel could probably claim the title of most privileged of the three because he lived under our roof. Because I didn't want his adolescence infected with cancer, I pretended money issues didn't exist, although I now admitted more frequently, "No more money left until pay day."

When my mother died, my sisters and I had split up our mother's special coin and bill collection. Originally it consisted of silver quarters, half dollars, and dollar coins from the fifties and sixties, but later, she'd added two-dollar bills and Susan B. Anthony coins. One third of that currency sat at the bottom of a grocery bag in East Lansing in the closet of the master bedroom. During the fall, I'd taken some of the coins and exchanged them for euros. Now I sat in Valérie's bedroom and wrote individual notes to Tim and each child, telling each of them that my dead mother and I wanted to give them 50 euros to buy something meaningful for themselves in Paris. Something that they could keep indefinitely, provided by Dawn and Esther.

I sat on the bed with the notes and the euros and a few other Christmas gifts I'd brought from home, along with stockings, and began the annual job of filling them up, finding a good angle at which to slide the bright silicone spatulas into each stocking, and then the oven mitt, the hand lotion, and the note about how I'd transformed my mother's money into euros.

As I worked, hunched forward, I occasionally leaned back and looked through the row of windows on the wall to the right. Valérie had told us we could leave the window open slightly to provide a balance to the steam heat rolling out of the registers. A low noise rumbled from the streets below, but I focused on the visual that rose in front of me -- the golden dome of Les Invalides – the Army National Museum. For me, the Dome signified that I'd accomplished a major goal. I'd lived long enough to join my son in Paris. I sat on a bed, filling Christmas stockings for my children.

Tim came in and said the kids had gone to sleep while he wrote an email to his mother. I rose from my spot on the bed and carried the stockings, hidden under a blanket, to the ottoman that rested in the hallway next to a small asymmetrical stand of tiny white lights. The light stand became the tree; the ottoman, a mantle. I arranged the stockings and placed a towel over them, keeping them hidden from the prying eyes of anyone who might rise in the night to use the bathroom. I liked to maintain secrecy, even with mostly grown children. I was still a mother, alive, with Connor returning home from his study abroad in less than a month.

We woke up in Paris on Christmas morning, the kids delighted to have their stockings from home, though everyone teased me for carting silicone spatulas onto two planes and through customs just to fill stockings.

Connor had planned his own surprise. He'd brought to Paris the souvenirs he'd purchased on his travels since late August. He pulled the items out of the bags he'd brought along, one by one. Candy he'd purchased for me in Italy. He also gave me a copy of a Jane Smiley book, *Some Luck*, which he'd purchased at Shakespeare and Company, the bookstore down by Nôtre Dame, which he would take us to in a few days. Also for me, a calendar from Italy, where he and his friends had stayed next to the Mediterranean Sea. For his father, a fleece zip-up from Uniqlo, since Tim lived in fleece jackets during the wintertime.

As he pulled out his gifts for Rachel and Nathaniel, I reminded him that as I'd carried him in the womb into the second trimester, I'd read Smiley's *A Thousand Acres*. It kept me company while my parents lay dying in Pontiac Osteopathic Hospital's intensive care unit. I sometimes told students the story to illustrate how one could read and even enjoy a novel without capturing any deeper meaning or any significant allusions. I'd liked the book and remembered reading it, though I'd had to coax my brain to re-enter the novel each time I left my mother's hospital room and returned to the waiting room. Years later, when I learned that Smiley had based *A Thousand Acres* on Shakespeare's *King Lear*, I laughed and told people that while I enjoyed the book, I hadn't been a discerning reader at that moment in my life. I didn't catch any of the *King Lear* shadow.

The sun from the window highlighted Connor's dimple as he smiled and explained each item before handing it off. For Rachel, a shot glass and a small bottle of limoncello. For Nathaniel, another small bottle of limoncello and a Paris St. Germain soccer shirt, red and navy. Such joy Connor radiated as he presented the gifts along with stories about his travels. Such exuberance at that table in the living room overlooking rue de Sèvres.

We welcomed the slower pace of the day. Though I'd enjoyed our morning, fatigue had set in and I felt dragged down suddenly, in spite of our sparkling surroundings. The push to get out of the apartment each day proved challenging with our five personalities and individual agendas. I wanted to keep pace with them, but I was growing weary after almost a week of daily activities. Rachel seemed less focused on the ganglion cyst in her finger, and the swelling had, in fact, subsided a bit. But people had demonstrated some impatience, and I worried about keeping the peace and civility. As if they knew my thoughts, Connor and

Nathaniel happily dove into their respective blanket lumps to get more sleep.

After morning became afternoon, Connor and I stood side by side in the kitchen making crêpes. He'd learned how from Madame Torreilles and his friends in the study abroad program. I followed the measurements on the web recipe I'd looked up and asked Connor for his guidance as I added the liquid ingredients to both batches so we could make sure the consistency was accurate. Valérie's kitchen had a set of pans with removable handles, another novelty, and we found the right size frying pan for the crêpe-making effort. We'd decided to make several types – sweet crêpes for brunch and savory for dinner after the movie. And of course, a whole batch of Nathaniel-friendly crêpes. Connor and I made as many as we could and then stacked and stored them in the refrigerator.

Back in the states, we usually went to a movie together as a family over the holiday break. In Paris, we'd planned to see *The Hobbit: The Battle of the Five Armies*, the third of the movies made by director Peter Jackson about the Tolkien book that preceded *The Lord of the Rings*. We'd spent the last two Christmases watching the first two parts of the *The Hobbit* trilogy as a family. Rachel had introduced us to Martin Freeman, passing on her fascination with *Sherlock*, starring Freeman and Benedict Cumberbatch.

Connor looked up theatres and found one showing an English-speaking version with French subtitles. After we entered the Métro tunnels at our nearby stop, we boarded the train, eager to see who else might be riding around Paris on Christmas.

A band of musicians at the other end of the car we entered began to sing Christmas carols, infusing the atmosphere with a festive mood. The musicians spread out in the car, encouraging people to join in with the singing, and I began to sing the English lyrics. But my family members made faces at me, frowning. I realized then, that I'd forgotten the lesson Tim and I had tried to instill in them from Steves: to be wary of strangers who engaged them in conversation or offered them things. They might demand money next.

I put away my voice and sank into a seat, lowering my head. A song, I chided myself, counted as a thing offered. I tried not to feel hurt by the experience of being silenced.

At the movie theatre, I tried to read the subtitles to improve my French. I enjoyed all the scenes except the battles. I preferred to focus on family dynamics, love interests, and historical bits. Years earlier, Rachel had swooned her way through all *The Lord of the Rings* and *The Pirates of the Caribbean* movies, plastering Orlando Bloom posters on the walls of her room. We'd teased her for that, but it was nice to see Orlando again.

On the way home from our Métro Stop at Duroc, in the dusk of the Christmas nightfall, a man stumbled into us just a block from Valérie's apartment, muttering a few words of French.

"Pardon?" Nathaniel said, his response polite and automatic.

The man repeated himself, his voice rising. We froze for an agonizing moment, but then he moved away, mumbling again, now to himself.

As we entered our building and stepped onto the elevator, the kids began talking about the day and how silly I had been to attempt to interact with the singers on the Métro, how no one should have spoken to the man on the street we'd just encountered. I said I was relieved not to be the only one who screwed up the rules of behavior for travelling in other countries.

Nathaniel said, "Don't compare me to you. If I ever fall that far, I'll kill myself."

The elevator jolted as it stopped at our floor. We were silent. The remark had perhaps started as a teasing comment in line with the bantering throughout the day, but it fell flat.

I closed my eyes and clenched them tight. "What did you say?" I croaked out.

But I didn't wait for an answer. I pushed past them and used my keys to enter the apartment. I felt my heart pounding as I hurried toward the back bedroom, feeling that I was falling fast. I closed the door and threw myself on the bed, wondering why my son would say that to me, why now, today of all days? Did he hate me so much? How could I not have known? *Fall that far?*

Later, Tim came in and told me everyone had apologized. The comment had been intended as a joke, one of those jokes the kids sometimes made at my expense because even though they knew I could be sensitive, they knew I also tried to be a good sport. As a result, they didn't always choose their words carefully. I listened to what he said, the wisdom and care in his voice as he tried to comfort me and told me how awful they all felt. He said they hoped I would come out for the crêpes Connor had finished. They looked so delicious, so savory.

I knew I should try. For the family. But I felt so drained. And slammed. I needed solitude. Interacting with people exhausted me. Even my family. My brain kept creeping back to my youngest son's words earlier, the inflection in his voice. I searched for an explanation for the exact word choice, "fall that far." I needed to listen to my mindfulness CD or look out the window at the light cast by the Eiffel Tower onto our corner of Paris. But a voice in my head told me that my children merely tolerated me, and what my son had said in that moment of frustration in the elevator indicated the truth of how he viewed me. I was a buffoon, and he would never fall that far.

Red

On the morning after the incident, I slipped out of the apartment into the still darkened streets and wandered the neighborhood before finding the Bar de la Croix Rouge. No one sat outside at the tables under the awning. As I approached the entrance, scraps of dawn began to color the streets. Five people stood inside at the bar, four of them men, two of them departing just after I entered. The voices murmured low, but as I stood waiting, a few odd rumbles thrust themselves into the air above the clatter of cups and hiss of the espresso machine.

The waiter stared at me as I spoke halting French, and then, when he realized I wanted to sit for a while, his arm grew large with gesture, imploring me to find a table.

I sat. And he brought the café and croissant on a plate. Two men wearing ties and business suits entered, business as usual on the day after Christmas. A young man followed them and greeted an older man at the bar. The younger waiter smiled at them.

The older waiter who'd served me walked briskly around the small café while the younger waiter remained stationary. Both wore black bow-ties and white shirts. I thought of the workers who greeted me when I stopped at the Tim Horton's drive-through window sometimes back at home, their hoodies protecting them from the cold air rushing in when they reached their hands out for the money and offered a tall cup of coffee out the window in return.

The lines next to the older waiter's eyes showed experience, though his dark hair belied his advanced years, his slender hips encased in the black trousers. Unlike the younger waiter, he wore a vest over the white shirt. A row of black shiny buttons led from the top of the "v" to where the vest fell just over his waist.

American music drifted down from the speakers, though it took me a moment to realize I understood the words and knew the song. Linda Ronstadt and the Nelson Riddle Orchestra, an album I'd once owned on cassette tape, until it melted in the car one summer day in the Virginia heat. Followed by Michael Bublé. *You're just too good to be true.* Contemporary torch.

I'd eaten the croissant in seven large bites and now pressed my right index finger against the papery brown skin fragments, attempting to bring them to my mouth before they dropped off. A tapping sound accompanied the scent of orange as the younger waiter turned his hand to maneuver a juicing device, tapping to dislodge the pulp.

If I possessed any talent for visual representation, I would have sketched the chair across from me, with its rattan frame and weaving of what looked like vinyl lacing, a pattern of white woven with bits of red flecks, like perfect beads of blood strung together in vertical lines. Shiny red beads glistening under the lights of the café as the morning rays filtered in the front window near my seat.

I rose and walked to the end of the bar with my bill, asking the waiter for another. Another café. Another croissant. He took the 20 Euro bill I held out and gave me a few coins, gesturing for me to sit again.

When he came back to the table, I tried to memorize the front of his vest and count, longing to know how many buttons his fingers travelled each morning before he came to work.

But he turned too quickly after I said, "Merci," his trousers walking away.

Abandoning Versailles

As I stood in the serpentine line at Versailles, I realized that I lacked the temperament and the energy to be one of the people who did Paris in a flurry, even with a Museum Pass that lasted four days. Not only did my bones revolt as I moved my limbs each day over miles of cobblestones, up and down Métro stairs, carrying my purse with the guidebook and the Epipens and the carnets. I also battled with the implication that one must see everything or risk losing out. I would not see everything, but I would not lose out. I must process things at a slower pace.

I wanted to live in the moment, even if the traces of that moment disappeared like ash wisping away from a fire. Louis the XIV built a palace that allowed people to remember him forever, hordes of people, in interminable winding lines, and yet I wanted to preserve in my memory not the spectacle of the Palace and its Hall of Mirrors but the view of the man and son in front of me in the line with their quiet and determined steps forward. I wanted to preserve the faces of the trio of workers who bustled behind the small coffee bar that I found after leaving the line, workers who dealt with their own interminable line of Versailles visitors at the Starbucks up the street from the Palace. The workers' faces welcomed, so patient as they asked each person who made it to the front of the line what she wanted.

I did not regret leaving the line at Versailles. I understood, finally, that it didn't matter if my body presently showed no evidence of cancer. Pain still resided there – at the bottom of my feet, in my right hip, down my right leg, across my shoulders, regardless of the origin. Perhaps something other than cancer caused the pain. Yet as I'd stood in the line earlier with my family trying to justify leaving, I realized that I must grant myself permission to stop merely watching the cobblestones under my feet to make sure I didn't trip. I must say "no" to the Sun King and decide on this day in December I didn't want or need to embrace his version of light.

Light transplended elsewhere. On a bench in Starbucks next to a silent young man on his computer. Four Brits on a holiday to the right who'd thanked me for moving closer to the young man, creating space. The sun's rays penetrating the window glass behind me, warming my back.

Teasing out the shadows from above the espresso machine. Illuminating the profiles of the Starbucks baristas who greeted each visitor seeking a respite from the brilliance of Versailles.

Le Petit Lutetia

We decided on Le Petit Lutetia because our moments at Versailles had enervated us.

Valérie had listed the place on her information sheet as a local spot just up the street on rue de Sèvres. The early hour and nearby location made the choice unanimous, and the elegance of the restaurant's exterior won me over. As we stepped into the foyer, I focused on the waiter, who smiled, asking how many. Off to the left, the bar sported a few customers on stools.

The waiter gestured, and our party of five entered the main room of the restaurant where we were seated in an alcove, part booth, part table. I took one of the booth seats, relieved to position my back against the wall to help with hearing.

Connor's face wore a bursting-with-information intensity. "Did you see him?"

I'd apparently missed something. Tim smiled, nodded. I watched the other two kids for their reactions. "See who?" I said.

"Gérard Depardieu! At the bar!" Nathaniel had not watched "Paris, je t'aime" with us, nor did he possess Connor's extensive film knowledge. Connor tried to explain Depardieu's popularity as both a French and American actor and reeled off a list of his movies.

I hadn't seen him. I tried to think of a glimpse I could claim. I remembered a waiter's mischievous smile and someone with dreadlocks. A man. In the Paris movie, Gérard Depardieu played a waiter.

We discussed ordering wine. I asked if we could get something sweet. The rest of them had such sophisticated tastes. I generally preferred eating dessert rather than wasting my calories on alcohol. And with alcoholism in Tim's family and in my own father, I often abstained.

But with the diagnosis, I often found myself drinking Riesling, one of my mother's old favorites. Or Moscato, the wine Rachel had introduced me to. And for my older sister's birthday, I'd figured out how to make mojitos, learning the art of muddling.

The waitress came to our table. With short hair slicked back, she wore an impish grin.

Connor began speaking in French but switched to English when he heard the waitress speak it comfortably. "Does he come here often?" He leaned forward, nodding at the other room. "Gérard Depardieu?" The study abroad stint must have made him more confident.

"All the time," the waitress said. She tilted her head and smiled. "He drinks a lot!"

Connor explained that when we entered, he spotted the actor right away. "I looked closely to make sure, and that's when the waiters started laughing because of my double-take."

After the waitress left, we talked about her voice, the guys commenting on her cute French accent, especially when she said the "t" in "a lot."

We'd never been to Hollywood but had discovered a star in our own arrondissement in Paris. In addition to sharing glee about our discovery, we celebrated the food and wine. We decided on a rose, Côtes de Provence Sainte-Victoire 2013 by Chateau Coussin; the bottle sat wrapped in swaddling in a stand next to me. Rachel and Connor both ordered chicken in a pot, the pots delivered right to the table. Everything gleamed with a hint of gold luster, as if specks of metal had clung to us all from our time in Versailles, hitchhiking back to Paris.

The others spent the meal telling me that I hadn't missed anything by walking away from the line at Versailles. I felt that our time in the restaurant served as proof that I hadn't made a mistake by leaving, hadn't committed some impetuous act of omission I would later regret. We'd picked the best restaurant at which to dine, and two of us had seen Depardieu.

Tim and Nathaniel went to the marché to get groceries, and Rachel, Connor, and I stayed to share the large bowl of chocolate mousse the waitress brought. We kept dipping our spoons into the common bowl, licking them and then dipping them again, quietly listening to the next table where a large group spoke a mixture of French and English.

Later, when I emailed Valérie, thanking her for the suggestion and mentioning the Depardieu sighting, Valérie explained that he lived in a house up the street from the restaurant. He often drove his motorcycle around and was well-known in the neighborhood.

That night, after we returned to our apartment, I researched him on the Internet to remind myself of his movie credits in addition to *Green Card*. I thought I remembered him in *Jean de Florette*. I enjoyed the way the waitress had cocked her head and rolled her eyes when saying "a lot," but I felt bad that I knew such personal information about Depardieu. The IMDB entry online said he'd lost a son. Losing a son would cause a lot of drinking, I imagined.

I thought of the first Hemingway story I'd ever read," A Clean, Well-Lighted Place," imagining Gérard Depardieu at the bar in the story. Would he play the role of the patron or the guest? The character Georges in *Green Card* delighted with humor and sincerity. Who knew if Depardieu could claim light-heartedness as a trait or if he dwelled in a cache of sorrow?

The *Green Card* character was light-hearted, but the bar guest in Hemingway's story suffered from sleeplessness and a graying perspective. And the waiter who served him recognized it. Some people kept so much agony sewn into their daytime selves, allowing the darkness of their stuffing to escape only as the light dimmed. Outside of Valérie's window a banner of red lights spelling out Christmas greetings hung just below, stretching across rue de Sèvres. I wondered if Depardieu roamed on other nearby streets with darker corners.

Bir-Hakeim

We headed toward the Métro stop not far from Champs de Mars. I had been unable to stop the tears since we'd left the Eiffel Tower, even as the five of us wandered on the pathway bordered by booths with scarves, food, and postcards. Tim moved forward to talk to Rachel, and I watched as her body stiffened, shoulders hunching in the olive-green coat I'd bought for her one Christmas when she was still in college. It was a coat I knew she had grown to love, and I loved seeing her wear it, even though we now kept our distance from one another. I'd been difficult, warped by some alien thoughts that kept nagging at me, telling me I was doing Paris wrong, telling me I was ruining everything. She'd been difficult, too, frustrated with our delays, wrapped in some gauze of impenetrable sadness.

We descended slowly the steps to the outdoor plaza adjoining the Métro Station at Bir-Hakeim, one of the few Métro stops that was above ground. Although we had passed the kebob and crêpe stands, and the crowd began to wither, the smell of foods still lingered, beef and sugar and vanilla captured in the air above the plaza. By the Métro station, the scent of bread joined the other remnants; in Paris, there was always bread.

The open plaza, recessed at the base of three sets of steps, felt like the stage of an amphitheater. If we remained in our positions at the bottom of the three sets of steps, we might all be actors. Rachel's face began to wobble, her shoulders rose, and a deep blast of air came out. And when we reached the bottom of the steps, I heard a small sob roll from my daughter's chest to the top of her scarf near her throat, ready to spill out of her mouth.

The coat. I needed to focus on the coat. I'd purchased the long olive-green garment on a whim that Christmas, knowing that Rachel might not like it. She needed a new coat but would probably want to pick it out herself. Still, I made the purchase, and instead of wrapping it, I left it on a hanger and hung it from a hook off the mantel early Christmas morning. When the family came downstairs to open their presents, I watched Rachel's face to see when she first perceived the coat. I wanted to assess her reaction, to measure somehow, if she truly liked it. In the end, I'd had to bring it to her attention, and in those first seconds of discovery I heard the strand of reservation in her voice, a strand that was nonetheless braided with excitement and gratitude. That was how mothers listened and watched when they gave gifts. They looked for that wisp of enthusiasm. When Rachel took it back to college, the roommates said it brought out the green of her eyes, and I imagined her swaddled in the coat, warm and protected in the fierce cold of a Michigan winter on a college campus.

That Christmas was a few years back. Yet Rachel had always been so good about using things well, not replacing them until the wear and tear was evident. Not just because of frugality but because of attachment. We all became too attached to things, couldn't let them go. Now the olive-green knee-length coat stood in the plaza, paired with a worn, cheap multi-colored scarf, its frayed fibers pilling. Textured weaving still strong enough to pull up in front of a face to hide tears. My daughter was the dramatic one, yet I cried more often. Not in front of people, usually, but face down on a bed, sounds muffled in sheets. When I was hurt. Or so sad that I didn't want to be alive anymore. I'd cried at the tower, looking out at the wet, gray city on a day of post-New Year's rain. The city was stunning from each of the four tower's sides. I tried to absorb the images, but the tears kept streaming down the sides of my face.

We were leaving Paris the next day. Connor would go back to Strasbourg, and the rest of us would travel back to the U.S., leaving Rachel in Newark to take a train back to Philadelphia. We were leaving Paris, and all I could do was be angry. Angry at Rachel because her drama had infected the trip – her swollen finger, her unhappiness at her new job in Philadelphia, her struggles living for the first time with a boyfriend. Angry that my husband hadn't thought to plan one evening or afternoon for just the two of us. Angry that I had to intervene when someone's stubbornness prevented us all from moving forward. Angry that I had to be the one in charge of compromises. Angry that they were all so willing to let me cook and clean Valérie's kitchen, and deal with the clogged sink, and load the washing machine.

Across the street from the plaza was a parfumerie. I needed to escape. My husband spoke softly to Rachel. I should be consoling Rachel myself, but I couldn't handle anyone else's sadness. I took a step closer to them, but looked off to the side, focusing on the "f" of the parfumerie sign.

"I have to go," I said to Tim, without looking at Rachel.

"What?" He squinted at me.

"I have to go. I'll see you back at the apartment. I know how to get there."

I had the Métro map in my pocket, folded in half, sandwiched between soggy tissues. We stood at the juncture of two sides of the plaza steps. Tim looked like he wanted to say more, to ask more questions, maybe tell me something but I just repeated, "I have to go."

And I walked away. Away from my family.

I tried to breathe in deeply when I walked inside the perfume store.

Colorful rectangular boxes lined the shelves, sheathed in plastic, many of the names familiar from the states. Red and pink and black impressed onto the cardboard containers, atomizers with testing samples positioned neatly on each shelf. Liquid in my eyes made the bottles and the cartons blurry.

Perfume reminded me of my mother. Not real perfume, which was much too expensive. Cologne. My mother loved cologne. Arpège by Lanvin. For so much of my childhood, the bottle stood on my mother's dresser. Gold liquid in a tall rectangular vessel with a black top. I had the idea that I would buy a bottle of cologne to take home to remind myself of my time in Paris. The prices, although discounted, were daunting. I wasn't sure I could bring myself to spend that many euros, which translated to nearly twice the amount of American dollars for an ounce of Tommy. I didn't want Tommy. I could buy something French, a bouquet of crushed petals like the floral notes that hung in the air above my mother's dresser. Create an apparition of my mother here, in this shop. I could test only a few perfumes on my wrist; I didn't know where the strips were in this discount parfumerie. And I didn't want to ask because my lashes still felt wet with the endless tears, and I didn't know where my voice would be.

I fled again, this time from the parfumerie back to the Métro station. I tried to use the machine to buy my ticket, but I didn't know how. We'd been using the carnets that I purchased at the tabac each day. I'd tried so hard to make travelling easy for all of us, and now, I didn't know enough to figure out how to work the machines. Behind me, they approached. I heard their voices. I couldn't prevent myself from looking back to see their faces. But I couldn't stand the idea of speaking to them, so I gave them a stone face and walked past because I didn't know how to be available in that moment like I'd been when my daughter was two and a half and rolling on the floor in some oppositional temper tantrum. Sometimes I could talk her calmly through the moment, but after my own mother died, I often needed to walk into another room.

When I saw my daughter begin to sob, my daughter who cried so rarely as an adult, I should have enfolded her green-clad shoulders into my arms and told her it would be okay. I was her mother. Comforting was what I was supposed to do. And I had often done it well in the past, but on that wet, gray day before we left Paris, I couldn't move from the steps where I stood to the steps where my daughter stood. I had to walk away.

I knew that I'd entered a dark fog of depression, and it had inked the day darker. What I didn't know, what I wouldn't know until some months later, and what I wouldn't find a name for until years down the road, was that as thoughts squirmed through my brain, painting my world black and ash, my daughter had trauma from the past whirling through her brain as well, trauma we would find a simple shorthand for in the years to come. *Me, too.*

I had only contempt for the mother who walked away at Bir-Hakeim. I dreamed of embracing my daughter in her dark time, crawling with her onto that breaking bough, rocking her, being the mother for her that my own mother had been for me most of my life. Touching my face to my daughter's silvery brown hair, inhaling the perfume buried in its strands.

Au Sauvignon Café

We had words, then hugs, even laughter, the latter coming when I made the pitch for Au Sauvignon Café, featured in the Rick Steves guide. I'd invoked Steves again. This time I read them a description of the café and how its location allowed for people-watching on the Sèvres-Babylone. According to Steves, the café had a zinc bar. I wasn't sure what a zinc bar was, but I was eager to find out. Like Le Petit Lutetia, the establishment was located just a few blocks from Valérie's apartment. We could walk our neighborhood streets one last time. We could sit and observe, not hurrying to reach another landmark.

We made a plan. Rachel and I would visit the chocolate store across the way and buy some last-minute souvenirs. Tim, Connor, and Nathaniel would hang back a bit to finish packing but would join us later at the café. To get there, we just needed to turn left out of Valérie's apartment and walk a few blocks up rue de Sèvres, past the construction, past the Bon Marché, past the large intersection where the road shifted from Sèvres to Babylone.

When Rachel and I arrived at Au Sauvignon, we discovered that the café offered limited seating, the area much smaller than we had imagined. With only two of us to hold a table, we risked refusal, but we boldly requested a table for five. We didn't know whether to order anything beyond beverages because we were still trying to eat cheaply on our last day in Paris. When the waitress came back, we ordered a cheese/charcuterie board and checked our iPhones regularly for texts from the guys. At last a text arrived. They were just a few blocks down the street. On their way.

Once the others came in and sat down, we tried to explain what we'd learned. Rick Steves definitely deserved credit for his accurate description of the authenticity of the place, because the older woman waitress did not seem to understand my broken French or Rachel's English. It was clear that the menu was limited. But they did have les huitres. When we had first arrived in Paris and met up with Valérie at the rue de Sèvres apartment, we'd told her that we planned to cook at the apartment quite a bit because of Nathaniel's allergies. He ate a lot of chicken, which we could cook safely at the apartment, but he'd also discovered recently that he liked mussels, which he hoped to eat while in Paris.

As I sat with my family, I appreciated everyone's attempts to be careful with each other after the day of emotions. The horizon would bring another turbulent day. The next morning four of us would fly out. Connor would take a train back to Strasbourg, returning to the home of Madame Torreilles, his host, to finish out his study abroad.

Someone finally said, "Are we eating dinner here, or what?"

The menu disappointed. The older siblings had grown tired of taking Nathaniel's food restrictions into consideration. I had grown weary of cooking in the apartment, although Connor often helped. I wanted a final dinner, but I felt reluctant to seek out another place, reluctant to admit that Steves had failed us, or, more accurately, that I had misread Steves. I'd focused on his description of the people-watching aspect and not so much on the food.

"They have mussels," I said. "We should at least get Nathaniel mussels."

We called the waitress over, and Tim and Connor placed a drink order. We requested the mussels, pointing at the menu to indicate the quantity we wanted. Then the conversation turned mundane as we discussed packing and straightening up the apartment for Valérie.

When les huitres arrived, we all stared at the tray and then at Nathaniel's face. He looked uncomfortable. The mussels were not what any of us had expected. One of us looked at the menu again and gained a glimmer of understanding. Somehow, we'd thought "les huitres" was a term for mussels. We'd ordered les huitres earlier in the trip, and the waitress at that previous restaurant had clearly understood what we meant, if not our poorly chosen French words. Les huitres were oysters, not mussels.

In this case, raw oysters.

None of us but Tim had eaten raw oysters before. The only raw things I ate were vegetables – crudites. Tim would ingest rare beef happily, but he didn't feel moved to eat the oysters.

Nathaniel picked one of the oysters up and brought it to his lips. We watched. He finally shook his head and put it down.

When the waitress brought the check, she looked with surprise and confusion at the platter, still full of oysters. "Vous mangez?" She repeated the phrase several times.

"Merci. Non."

Well, she asked, did we want to take the oysters home? On our last night in Paris, we needed to clean out Valérie's refrigerator, and we didn't have time to learn how to cook raw oysters before we left. "Merci. Non." I said.

She placed the bill on the table and shook her head, carrying the platter away.

We stepped out into the fresh January air and began a leisurely pace back toward the apartment. Rachel, Tim, and Nathaniel walked ahead, and Connor fell back to walk with me. I wanted to apologize for my teary silence on the Eiffel Tower, my unwillingness to speak aloud for fear of hurting Rachel's or Tim's feelings. I told him that part of me wished I'd stuck with the original bucket list dream I'd had – meeting him in France and leaving the others home.

"Yes!" he said. "We would have had so much fun, just the two of us."

"We have gone too fast, seen too much," I said. "I should have planned to just sit in cafés a bit more." I paused. We were walking on the evening streets of Paris for the last time. We needed to look up, look around. "My sadness wasn't about you, originally, but now I feel like you're frustrated with me and I've ruined our relationship."

"No," he said. "You couldn't do that so easily. It's just that you're so emotional whenever I see you, and I don't know what to say. I'm learning how to have emotional conversations, and I'm not sure I'm very good at it."

I thought I'd been doing a pretty good job of staying steady and even on the outside, keeping the tempest internal. Staying cheerful. I knew that it wasn't just about me; he referenced his new relationship as well. Learning about that relationship and its development had been one of the high points of the trip. Seeing the young woman's face on Skype. "I didn't realize I'd been so emotional before Paris," I said. He seemed relieved to address it.

"Or it seems that way to me. Living away from home."

I tried to trace back through the time I'd spent with him since my diagnosis. I realized that I couldn't fault his perceptions, based on the scenes I remembered. The talk we'd had as a family the previous year when I'd felt hurt after my birthday. His birthday, when I'd been so emotional about Nathaniel being included. And now. He'd spent two summers home since the diagnosis, so there must have been other times as well. Suddenly I felt heavier in my boots on the cobblestones. "Sometimes I think I ask for too much," I said finally.

Once I said the words, I regretted speaking them aloud. I'd voiced a secret fear, this fear that I wanted too much, akin somehow to the fear that I was privileged, entitled. I wanted him to say, "No, of course not." Or, "You don't ask for enough!"

But I didn't know then what I wanted, only that I didn't want to ruin for both of us the last day we had together in Paris. I didn't remember what he said on that night we walked the rue de Sèvres for the last time, only that his words didn't provide the reassurance I needed.

So I shrank, my brain withdrawing. On the outside, I laughed and cajoled and stopped to comment on the mechanical Christmas displays that still operated in the windows at Bon Marché. As we walked west, the lights from the Tower danced in the sky, blending with the illuminated golden dome of Les Invalides, not far from our apartment. Napoleon rested peacefully in his tomb there. I walked with my adventurous son on a street in Paris, and I should savor the moment. But inside my brain, I despised myself. The curtain had ripped at the temple, and the truth would not set me free but would trap me forever.

The Plane Ride Home

I sat across the aisle from Tim, with Nathaniel on my right. He'd taken an interior seat so I could be on the outside with easier access to the aisles and the trek to the bathroom. Before we'd come to Paris in December, I hadn't flown in a while and didn't know how much the seat back in front of each passenger now played a role in his or her entertainment. Because I liked to read and write, I usually did a good job of keeping myself occupied when I flew, and I didn't fly often enough to dread the monotony of the cramped feeling, although I was happy to have a family member next to me so that some of my extra fat could fit into the space occupied by a loved one rather than by a stranger.

On the way to Paris, I'd kept myself busy with paperwork and reading, but on the way back home, I wanted to distract myself with movies and forget about the shell of sadness that shrink-wrapped my soul. I'd made significant mistakes; I was sure of it. Had I enjoyed myself? I assumed that I must have, to some extent, yet I felt like I'd been tiptoeing through some region of land mines, and I wasn't sure I'd avoided them. What felt odd was not knowing. In tripping *through* the land mines, had I tripped *off* a land mine? Were some of my relationships with my family members dead?

The four of us had packed up our belongings and completed last minute cleaning, leaving notes for Valérie. We'd wheeled our suitcases out into the rain, and Connor walked with us to the block where we would pick up our Roissy Bus to get to De Gaulle Airport. I hugged him goodbye, knowing he would return to the States in just over a week, after he finished his semester in Strasbourg. But in that wet mist, as I looked at his face, I worried that we'd all been irrevocably damaged by the trip, that maybe we'd reached the limit of how well or how long we could be together as a family.

I'd been so very wrong to push for the family trip to France. We'd wasted so much money if it was all a big mistake.

I tried not to punch too hard at the touch screen in front of me as I searched for a movie to distract me from dissecting the mistakes I'd made handling family dynamics. I'd allowed my emotions to bubble over the pot that always simmered on the stove in my brain, letting the voice of doom, the voice of criticism begin its chant in my head, reminding me of all my failings. I needed to escape from the voice's negative messages.

The Hundred Foot Journey. The movie looked like it would be about India and cooking. Plus, it had Helen Mirren in it. Then I realized that it was about India and Paris and cooking. I selected the movie. I'd listened to Jhumpa Lahiri's novel *The Lowlands* on CD, mesmerized by the Indian childhood story of the two brothers, frightened by the violence of the Naxalite movement. Now, on the screen, I saw that violence mixed with the heart-warming shots of the mother cooking with the family spices, passing on her knowledge of how to season the food to her son Hassan, who was eager to learn her talent, followed by the dark shots of the violence in their part of the country, the attack on the family's Indian restaurant and the son's mad, heroic dash to save the family's spice satchel.

The screen lit up again with images of the French countryside, a car, a woman on a bicycle. My brain created screen shots, even as the movie continued – the heap of spices in the middle of the pan, sizzling, so that I could almost smell the ginger, the cumin, the turmeric, and the cardamom, juxtaposed to the flash of the woman on the bicycle looking for fresh items with which to cook, the verdant French countryside, leaves on trees. The vivid colors in front of me on the back of someone's plane seat created such a sense of longing; I wanted to enter into the richness of the world in front of me, the world of France that I had just left, and perform a better version of what I'd done, experience it all more acutely but more perfectly without the flawed human emotion I'd brought to the first journey.

I looked across the aisle and saw my husband smile faintly at his phone. He was texting. Throughout the whole trip, I'd had confusion about when I could text – when it was free versus when it cost money; we'd decided we should only send texts to another iPhone user if we were lost or needed to reconnect with the family. I wondered who he was texting.

"Connor," he said.

I'd checked my phone, but I hadn't received anything. I'd sent him a message, wishing him luck as he navigated back to Valérie's apartment and then back to Strasbourg. I noticed that Rachel, a few seats ahead of me, texted as well; Nathaniel glanced at his cell phone, too.

I wanted Connor to text me a message telling me that he forgave me for the Eiffel Tower tears and for my departure at Bir-Hakeim. He must be so sick of us all, happy to return to Strasbourg. Yet he seemed to be texting all of them. Why not me?

What I wouldn't understand until a few days later was that even though my name was listed in the phone group to which my son texted, the messages weren't coming to my phone. He hadn't meant to exclude me; a technical glitch we discovered days later kept me out of the group discussion the four of them had during the long flight back to America.

It's funny. As crazy as we all drive each other, as nasty as we can be to each other, as wonderful as we can be to each other, I still really missed you guys when I walked back to Valérie's empty flat. Families are funny like that. I loved every minute of Paris with all of you.

But I didn't read those words on the flight. I stared at the screen in front of me, watching the Indian family and the French restaurant owner learn how to walk the hundred-foot journey. I sat in my airplane seat, the belt across my lap, keeping me secure, my eyes hot with tears.

IV. The Brain and The Breath

January 4, 2015 – November 22, 2015

The Truth

My psychologist said that the voice went to Paris with me. It stowed away somewhere on board the plane and then dogged me every step of the way on those Paris cobblestones.

I'd pushed myself for days before our departure, wrapping up Christmas stateside with our relatives, which had included an unplanned excoriation of my alcoholic younger brother-in-law, just a few days before we left town. We'd encountered him, plastered, at my mother-in-law's house when we brought Nathaniel over to put up her creche. I'd learned Terry was driving again, without a license. Nathaniel, his godson, had recently earned a learning permit and travelled the roads now.

Apparently along with his drunk uncle, who couldn't be trusted to stay away from a driver's seat, licensed or not.

I didn't say anything that night but came back the next day and let him have it as my mother-in-law waited in another room, afraid to witness my vitriol. When I left for Paris a few days later, I still reeled with the disgust I felt, which was originally directed at him but had changed directions and was now directed at myself and my impassioned, judgmental, and uncensored reaction.

I saw events; I reacted to events; I came to conclusions about events. But my perception? My perspective? Could I be sure of its accuracy? If you knew me, you'd know that I'm transparent to a fault. Friends might describe me as lacking in guile, with no capacity for duplicity. My children would say I'm too honest.

Yet I feared that when emotions, mine or those belonging to others, began swirling around me in vortices out of my control, I couldn't read a situation accurately. I failed to discern or know the truth. Or even the most rudimentary of facts or possible solutions. And beyond the obvious maxims – that everyone has a perspective, that truth is not knowable, yada yada yada – each element of my experience, not just those moments occurring since my diagnosis, but throughout my whole life, defied certainty, knowability. A stamp certifying veracity. I didn't know wherein lay the truth.

The voice would tell you that most of the time I'm the bad guy. I was fat, lazy, and stupid. Too slow at commenting on student writing, too demanding of my children, too hard on my husband. Overly sensitive to teasing. Cruel to Kirby Vacuum Cleaner and Cutco Knife sales-people, even when the latter labor only to earn money for college tuition, something I know quite a bit about. Cruel to my addicted salesman of a brother-in-law.

I wanted to be right, *in the right*, morally correct with my actions and reactions while simultaneously as empathetic as possible, yet once time passed, I always felt wrong.

Take the Paris trip, for example. What did I expect? That I would travel to Paris with my whole family, and we'd all occupy our best, wildly happy selves, forget our individual struggles, forget that the reason for the trip to Paris, the reason for using a couple thousand dollars of retirement money from a few years of teaching had to do with my impending demise, although the "impending" part was murky? I wanted the chance to see a place I'd dreamed about during three years of college French. I wanted to see it before I died. Which would be when? Soon?

Did I expect an absence of conflict? In *my* family? With my daughter joining us from a new life in Philadelphia, where she faced challenges of living with a new significant other in a new town, while adjusting to a new job? With my middle son tasting the life of pure freedom during a study abroad, something that never would have been a possibility in my own college experience? With my youngest merely trying to earn the respect of his older siblings by peppering his remarks with clever sarcasm? With my husband trying to stay in touch with an ailing mother back in the states?

I generally described myself as a realist, yet I'd studied the French Romantic writers as well. And somehow, I'd imagined our time in Paris with the romantic hues of a French film, an idyllic vision of a family trip to a paradise. Yet if we entered the realm of the idyllic, then didn't the four of them deserve to go to Paris with a woman who didn't have cancer, who continued to nurture them as the mother and wife with whom they'd spent decades?

Wasn't part of the truth that my family members, as ill-equipped as I to deal with a stark diagnosis that didn't take my life immediately but rather allowed me to linger in a seemingly healthy enough state, would begin to view my calamity and the accompanying illness as having run its course, thereby releasing them from the need to see me as compromised, suffering, or in need of caretaking? I was a transmogrified Chicken Little squawking about the sky falling; when would my listeners grow deaf and weary?

Each of them dealt with anxiety, a genetic tainting of perspective that sometimes caused them to avoid, turn inward, or shut out external distractions. Perhaps they shut me out at times, but did I expect them to also treat me as an invalid, fuss over me, take charge of my life?

In truth, I suspected that providing support for someone who walked with the Sword of Damocles hanging over her head felt exhausting. Especially when that someone found it challenging to claim her own right to existence, whatever the cost.

Maybe the voice did stow away, but I felt I should take responsibility for the cloud I created with that sword suspended over my head. I wanted to figure out the truth, but I didn't know if I had any confidence in its existence. Cicero talked about the Sword of Damocles with respect to concepts like "Virtue" and "Happiness." The American political scene conjured up the idea of "false narratives" and "fake truths." The prospect of confronting any such principles of certainty or undeniable truth filled me with fear and dread.

I shared one version of my story, and the voice told another. I'm not sure either of us told the truth.

Old College Hall

I noticed the pea coat first. It appeared in French class and then a few days later in Modern European Intellectual History. The year was 1979, the time during the month of April at the beginning of spring term, just weeks after Magic Johnson had led the Michigan State Men's Basketball team to an NCAA title.

After watching the coat for a few days, I finally approached the owner before history class and asked if he happened to be the same pea coat wearer as the one in French. Yes, he said. But I had known that all along. And after French one day, when we parted on the Wells Hall Bridge, he told me he studied at the Student Union between French and history, and I could come if I wanted to do so. He commuted to campus, so he remained all day until his classes finished up. As we walked, he lit up a cigarette, a Now, not as strong as my mother's Tareyton 100s; I wondered why I had to be attracted to a smoker.

Even before the lilac trees started blooming on campus, I stopped going back to the dorm after French for lunch on history days, instead walking with him to the Union where he would join the cafeteria line to purchase coffee and I would go to Old College Hall, the small room to the side of the grill. The sun boomeranged into the room through the high windows on the north side of the building facing Grand River, illuminating the shellacked large wood tables carved with words and initials. The room offered only a dozen or so of the tables, each with a few chairs. Most days the two of us were fortunate to have our own table. On the walls around us the same wood tables, detached from their bases, hung as decorations, carved circles of polished graffiti, mostly names and plus marks. Who went with whom. Who loved whom forever – TLA, true love always. Sometimes quotes. Dates and years. Preserved wood table-tops, rustic and western. I wondered how many people it took to raise each one, hang it on the wall.

Waiting for him became the thing that I most looked forward to in my day, and I went to Old College Hall whenever I could, not just on the days we had history after French, but every day, even earlier in the day, every spare moment that I didn't have to be in class or working at the library or eating a late dinner with my roommate or sleeping.

I would take a seat at one of the wooden tables, often facing away from the doors, and attempt to concentrate on what I was reading. Stefan Zweig. The construction of the passé compose in French. I waited for the sound I'd come to associate with him: the scuff of his shoes against the floor. His body, so thin and angular, could have glided across the linoleum, but he settled into his shoes in a way, I later learned, that he couldn't always settle into life. Or love. Yet when I perceived the muffled scrape of his arriving feet echoing in the small room with the large high windows overlooking Grand River, I settled in, my hands resting on the table, fingers reading the grooves of someone else's recorded love history. I watched him take off his pea coat and roll up the sleeves of his shirt. Watched him pour the packets of Coffee-mate and sugar into his coffee, twirl the liquid with a stir stick, and clamp the stick in the corner of his mouth between his lips.

Watched him and waited.

Red Dress Exhibit

On the day Tim and Nathaniel left for Tim's business trip to Hawaii, I told them to leave the car in the city lot across from the bus pick up at the East Lansing Marriott. Connor and I would pick it up later.

But Connor decided not to come home for the weekend, so I needed to get the car myself.

I made a radical plan to drive my van to the parking lot of the Wellness Center, about a mile away, where I would need it later. I would then walk to the city lot to pick up Tim's car and finally drive to my friend's art exhibit opening, enjoying a bit of social connection before returning home to Clover and a dinner in solitude.

Later that afternoon, I put the first part of the plan into motion; I drove from our house to the Wellness Center, parking my van there. I would return much later in the evening for an oncology massage using an old gift certificate.

After locking up my van, I began my walk to the East Lansing City Parking Lot. I'd just gotten out of the office complex and onto a sidewalk, when I passed an elderly gentleman. "Be careful," he said. "It's slippery." We smiled and then bowed our heads against the snow. The air, white and heavy, padded my lungs with a soft energy, not frigid or brutal but comforting. I arrived at the lot and found Tim's car without incident.

I'd always been comfortable driving my van through the snow, balking only near the end of my commuting days to Oakland University during winter storms because of the van's age and my Tarceva fatigue. Tim's car handled well, but it wore a dozen or more years also, and I couldn't always adapt to its lighter weight. I recognized that the snow had indeed picked up its pace, and I needed to make it from East Lansing to

Katalyst Art Gallery in Old Town of Lansing, back near our old Lansing neighborhood. The Red Dress Exhibit was opening, featuring my friend Barb's seemingly whimsical exhibit. In the car, I turned up the heat, enjoying the warmth, traveling a work-horse pace on largely empty roads.

In Old Town, a parking space sat vacant right in front of the gallery. I bustled in from the cold outside, feeling large and athletic but soft, too, with the flakes on my hat.

They'd hung the exhibit on one long wall, linear fashion. As I transitioned from the quiet car and the excitement of the snow, I realized I didn't like my art to be linear; I wanted to start in the middle. I decided to absorb Barb's work both ways – first by examining the pieces that called out to my senses and then by starting over at the very beginning and moving down the wall.

Near the cash register at the back of the gallery, a small group of women, most of them Barb's friends, stood talking. I wanted their voices to come into my head as sounds, not words, so that I wouldn't attach language to the paintings in front of me: the women in red dresses.

When I had taken in what I could, I approached the group, greeting my friend Barb and smiling at the others, many of whom I didn't know. Someone asked what I did, if I painted, sculpted, or just loved art. I admitted I was a writer but often didn't call myself one; I hadn't garnered traditional success. "Congratulations on being a writer today," a young woman said.

After I arrived home from the exhibit to the quiet, I had enough time for dinner and a brief rest. The extent of the snowstorm manifested itself in decreasing traffic on the main artery in front of my house, the last segment of my plan seeming more radical as the inches mounted.

Dusk had fallen, the air crisp now with the dropping temperatures and the increased precipitation. Tim's car was safe in the garage, but I knew that the snow coated my van in a nearly vacant parking lot at the Wellness Center. I had my oncology massage appointment there at 8:00 PM. When I'd booked it, the idea of getting a massage just before bed had sounded relaxing. I hadn't thought about weather forecasts. Yet I could envision no other option; I felt adamant about not asking for help. I'd anticipated that massage as a treat while Tim and Nathaniel were away. An indulgence, although a gift certificate had rendered it cost-free. Except for the transportation. On this wintry evening, television stations encouraged people to stay off the roads. Why should I ask anyone to come out for a hair-brained scheme to pick up a car?

I can't remember how many inches had fallen on top of the existing snow when I walked out my front door, but I entered a hushed world of dusk-shadowed white. The streetlight at the end of our driveway lit up a patch of flakes. Although we lived on a major east-west artery that ran on the north side of Lansing and East Lansing, there were no sidewalks in front of our house; the snow on the sidewalk across the street bore no signs of foot traffic. I would need to walk in the road up to the corner light just past the school, where sidewalks lined both sides of the street.

I'd dug out an odd ski mask I'd purchased a few years earlier, advertised as a balaclava, so the air I breathed was warmed by fleece. Even as a college student, I'd struggled with cold-induced asthma on top of my environmental allergies, so I'd wrap scarves around my face to warm my breathing space. My breaths came naturally, yet I hadn't realized how the labor of walking would be intensified by tramping through the snow. When I reached the deserted intersection, it occurred to me that on a Sunday evening, no plows would make it a priority to clear the sidewalks until the next day. And if school were cancelled, the sidewalks would wait.

I'd made it to the intersection, I told myself. An accomplishment. The plows had come through already, and in the distance I could hear beeping and the drag of plow blade against the snow already packed on the pavement. I had a straight path, a major curve, and another short jaunt to the next intersection. Then one more curve and a straight path to the next intersection; the complex in which the Wellness Center resided was just past that third intersection. I trudged slowly down the edge of the plowed but snow-covered road, hoping that any cars venturing out would see my human shape and stick to the narrow, plowed path in the center of the road.

Each step became its own single movement, with a beginning, a moment of peril, and an end. I fell over, my balance difficult to maintain in the drifts. When I made it to the second intersection, I fell again. It took me three tries to regain my footing. Nearby, the stoplight continued its snow-glazed pattern of green and yellow and red, despite the lack of traffic. My thighs covered in snow, I looked down the snow-fogged street to the next intersection, beyond which I'd reach the Wellness Center. It was such a short distance. But I was exhausted, my breathing labored, the ice crystals from my breaths coating the fleece by my mouth and nose.

When I reached the Wellness Center parking lot, my van sat there, right next to the entrance, where light spilled from the windows. As I entered the building, I pulled the balaclava, half-soggy, half-frozen, from my face. The woman at the reception desk greeted me warmly and told me my massage therapist would be with me shortly. I looked around the waiting room, its lighting soft, comforting, the air tinged faintly with eucalyptus, rosemary, and lavender.

At Barb's Red Dress Exhibit, I'd been struck by the angles of the elbows and chins of the women wearing red. A neck turned to the right, chin raised. Elbows attached to arms and hands wrestling with a back zipper. All those women. Their powerful angles.

I was a writer from Michigan, a woman with stage IV lung cancer, a mother on Tarceva who could still walk through snow.

How a Chuckit! Ball Launcher, a Sheet of Insulation, and a Carafe Changed My Life

A Chuckit! Ball Launcher

Tarceva often made my feet icy cold, so most winter days were two-pair days, even inside. And luckily, two pairs of the right kind of socks often served to insulate my feet from the cold just fine when I went outside to throw the ball to Clover.

When Clover saw the Chuckit! device in my hand, she lifted her shoulders, raised her nose, and began panting in anticipation, as only a ball-loving dog can.

More than six months earlier, after I'd purchased the first Chuckit!, Tim had made a face, as he often did when it came to spending money on new, untried things. He failed to grasp the necessity of the device. "Can't we just throw tennis balls?" he said. "We have plenty of those."

He made a valid point. Tennis balls did work fine. For him. Clover loved the lime green, and if she could see it, she could retrieve it. He took the Chuckit! back for a refund. It wasn't the tennis ball size, at any rate, he said – they were out of that model. And if we were going to buy the device, we should at least make sure it was compatible with the balls around the house.

But I had healing, sclerotic spots in my spine where the original metastases from my lung had developed. And arthritis. Some days, bending over challenged my achy, creaky body.

I waited a few months and then went back to the pet store to buy the tennis-ball size of the Chuckit! Device, but I buried it in the hallway closet and left it there. Tim began throwing regular tennis balls in the back yard every day. One day he threw fifty before Clover begged to stop, coming inside and collapsing next to the bowl of water, slurping greedily. I told myself we were doing a good job as pet owners, providing exercise opportunities for our dog.

But the cold weather descended. Tim got busy again at work. Our family took the trip-of-a-lifetime journey to Paris, and Clover vacationed at an animal resort where the staff provided three walks a day, three more than she enjoyed at home. When we returned home from France, we discovered ice patches on the deck outside our back door like mixtures of clear and opaque solids, something Nathaniel might study in chemistry class. Or like egg white drying with sugar crystallizing in the albumen on the Nisu bread my friend Ann used to make.

Because winter had returned and I had grown accustomed to Tarceva-invigorated cold, I put two pair of socks on my feet before lacing up my boots. I added a sweater layer and pulled on long underwear before donning my corduroys. I took the Chuckit! out of the back closet, unwrapped it from the plastic wrap, and unearthed the special watermelon-colored Chuckit! Balls from where I'd hidden them in the back corner.

I reached outside the back door, grabbing the tie off to connect Clover. Then I stepped onto the ice-coated deck. Cold air entered my nose and mouth, travelling to my lungs.

An impatient Clover jumped on her hind feet, her nails tapping on the ice. She pawed at my body, trying to reach the device.

I loaded a watermelon red ball into the cupped end of the Ball Launcher. I crunched my way off the deck and onto the snow. Then, holding the launching device in my right hand, I extended my arm and pulled it off to the right side, as if preparing to send out a fishing line.

I snapped my wrist.

The watermelon-colored ball flew. Not high, in a lovely arc, like Tim's balls flew, landing with a convincing bounce, but with a low, steady

209

parallel hum about four feet above the snow. When the ball dropped, Clover pounced on it, digging in the snow with her nose to grasp it securely in her mouth before racing back to me and depositing it at my feet. I reached down to capture the ball in the cupped end of the device, raised the Chuckit! wand, pulled it back to the right, and launched the ball again.

I realized finally that because my husband didn't live in my body, he didn't know where my wandering pains – metastatic, arthritic, or age-related – might move from day to day. He couldn't understand that the launching device, however simple and unnecessary it might seem, reduced the energy it took my arm to launch the ball and reduced the strain on my knees and hips. I didn't need to bend so far down to pick up a lime green ball in my hand; the device simply reached for the ball and cupped it. Like a man might cup a woman's breast.

A Sheet of Insulation

In the parking lot at Home Depot, I felt the wind resisting against the 4 x 8 sheet of Styrofoam I held, and just at that moment, I realized that I'd forgotten to put "Schedule appointment with the dealership to get key fob remote for car door lock fixed" on my to-do list. The omission troubled me as I walked the board on the top of my shuffling boots. I took many short steps to the driver's door to unlock it, reach inside, and hit the lock-opening button, which was the only way to open the van's trunk.

I shuffled the oversized Styrofoam back to the van's rear and held the board steady as a car slowed behind me. "Need a hand?" a man offered, his face friendly, not patronizing, not shaded with ulterior motive. I thanked him profusely, saying "No, thanks," in as breezy a voice as I could manage.

My first job, other than babysitting – child care, as I now tried to pc it – was working as a cashier at a lumber store and sometimes stocking the shelves. As a visitor to Home Depot, I did know, in fact, quite a bit about caulking guns, copper fittings, switch plates, and machine screws. But I'd never worked in a yard, lumber or otherwise. I'd never carried a 4 x 8 piece of anything or fit it into anyone's car trunk or van. I was skilled at the money thing, earning praise by the main office for always balancing the day's receipts, but I fell short with the physical labor thing.

I gripped the Styrofoam board by the short side, holding it like a slice of pumpernickel toast, and fed it into the back of the van at an angle. It went in three quarters of the way and then stopped. Two feet of lilac extended from the back of the van.

It was Styrofoam, for chrissakes. That was my dad talking. Not to me, to himself, whenever he hit a handyman problem. But I heard him. Clearly, I needed not only to angle it but to get it pushed up above the seats, even the front ones, even if I would need to duck a little while driving. The van's interior could accommodate the width; I just needed to work the Styrofoam past the seat belt dispensers that jutted out from the van's ceiling. I knew I didn't have a physics gene with which to calibrate my eyeball and create the perfect angle, but beyond that, I wondered if I had enough strength in my upper arms to wiggle-wave the bottom part of the eight-foot piece past the obstacles. Owens Corning Foamular 150 R-75 11/2. That would be the stock book description.

I'd selected this thickness because it would be sturdy enough to keep Clover out of the living room but light enough to cart through Home Depot's parking lot to the van. Tim didn't like the dog in the living room, and I needed to work at the table in the dining room. There were no doors between the two rooms, and child gates were too narrow to block the space. I knew that Clover's hairs proliferated throughout the main floor; keeping those hairs out of the living room would maintain a more appealing environment there. But where could I work?

Now, in the parking lot, I realized that even with a lightweight board, I didn't have enough strength in my upper arms to do the necessary jiggling into the back of the van.

If I could bend my head down, like a bull, I could use the space between my neck and my shoulder to gain purchase and shove the board in. I would lose a sight line for the task of working the board past the

211

seat belt dispensers, but I needed a new approach. Lowering my head, I inhaled, abandoning strategy and precision, going for brute strength.

During my days at Pine Lumber, we had sold a lot of rolled Owens Corning Fiber Glass Insulation, which we stored in the upper loft of the barn shed that held all of the plywood and 2 x 4's and clear white pine; the guys who worked in the yard, agile and strong, could scramble up the rungs to the loft and pick up the insulation roll with gloved hands, hold it away from their bodies and toss it to a waiting truck or pallet below. Years later, when my kids ate fruit roll ups, I would think of those rolls of fiberglass insulation, the shiny aluminum wrappers, the pink cotton candy layer swirled inside, the guys coming in from the yard after loading up enough rolls for a whole construction site, their sweat making lines in the dust on their upper arms.

Sweat. Dust. With determination, I wrestled the sheet beyond the seat belt dispensers and maneuvered it into place just over the headrests in the front seat.

Once I arrived home, the purple slab slid easily out of the van, and I walked it through the back door, angled it around corners, and positioned it neatly between the living room and the dining room. The lilac shade of the Styrofoam picked up on the plum color in the wild floral wall paper we'd inherited along with the forest green carpet from the previous owners who had golfed. I made sure that the writing on the board faced into the dining room, so people who entered our house would see the oddity from the front door as they peered into the living room but would not necessarily identify it so clearly as a piece of foam insulation.

When Tim saw it, he said, "Lovely."

Carafe

I planned to use a coupon from Bed, Bath, and Beyond to buy the carafe. When Nathaniel asked me in the car on the way there why so many people went gaga over Bed, Bath, and Beyond, I told him that it was because people could almost always find a 20% off coupon.

He laughed, stopped me in the middle of my response, and made me repeat the word "coupon" as he held up his phone and took a video.

I assumed he was going to send it to friends to make fun of my speech or my habit of finding coupons to reduce the price of things I bought.

But he said that he needed the video as proof to show a friend who said that there was only one way to say the word "coupon" and that people who pronounced it with a "kyoo" sound at the beginning were wrong. That meant he took the video to defend me, in a way. I felt mollified, pleased, and a bit sad that I had immediately jumped to the conclusion that he would be making fun of me. Later, I went online and looked up the word "coupon" in a dictionary, showing him the two different pronunciations.

The carafe involved one more favor I wanted to ask of Tim. I wanted hot coffee in our bedroom in the morning.

It seemed like a lot to ask, especially since I was perfectly capable of making coffee myself. He had taken over transporting Nathaniel to school in the morning, so I no longer had to rise early, if I chose not to, and it was so easy to choose not to. My body craved the extra sleep, and I imagined the extra morning rest my body received for the first time in years became one more layer of insulation protecting me from the invading cancer.

But if I slept in, the minute I awoke, I felt compelled to go downstairs and tend to Clover. Guilt compelled me. Tim and Nathaniel had taken over feeding Clover weekday mornings and letting her out as well. Lingering upstairs for another hour to write and do my mindfulness meditation would have worked well. But I hated leaving Clover crated in the morning, and I knew that if there were errands to run later or if I wanted to go to a coffee shop to work, the time Clover spent in the crate might later translate to something chewed. A hand towel on the counter. A hot pad, retrieved from a drawer left slightly ajar.

And in truth, I was afraid. I was afraid to put pen to paper, afraid to fail at writing. And afraid to listen to my mindfulness tracks on the old Walkman, afraid to fail at mindfulness, even though Jon Kabat-Zinn's voice in my earphones steadfastly assured me that failure was not a possibility. I wanted to awake and drink my coffee, and without even thinking, pick up my pen to write or cue up my Walkman with the Kabat-Zinn CD as coffee surged through my body.

Intention. Legitimacy. Schedule. Routine. The morning light fractured through the blinds on the south window. The wallpaper, a pale salmon, maybe rose, with a pattern of small, dime-sized blue bouquets in alternating vertical lines. I sipped coffee from the cup next to my bed. When the cup was empty, I walked to the bureau where the Oggi carafe I'd purchased the day before held warm coffee that I imagined my husband had brought up to me.

My psychologist told me that one of the most important aspects of beginning a routine was intention. I must have sincere intention to move through the items in my morning schedule. The difficulty for me – for anyone trying to change a routine – was finding and maintaining the intention. I found it far easier to sleep in, pull the covers over my head when my husband awoke, and go back to sleep. Who could say what was healthier? Perhaps my cancer benefited most from the extra rest. Yet perhaps my brain benefited from creating intentions for my day, my life. The famous quote said that "the road to hell [was] paved with good intentions." Cancer didn't factor into the equation. Or the quotation. And I'd never been the type who memorized and recited old quotes.

I poured myself another cup, tiptoeing on the bedroom floor to keep Clover from hearing my footfall. From the front of the house next to the main road, the loud hum of a truck reverberated against the banks of snow the plows had piled off to the sides. The walls around me displayed foam-cored museum prints of our favorite art – Winslow Homer's *East Hampton Beach*, Monet's *The Magpie*. Cheap but artistic, I told myself. *Artistic*.

I didn't think the issue centered solely on intention; it also involved legitimacy. If entering the world meant stepping into a muck of fear and self-loathing, then I needed to begin the day arming myself in this room with its faded wallpaper, dusty surfaces, and stacks of books. The room served as an arsenal. My coffee, my pen and paper, the quilt around my shoulders – all armaments. The Dickinson slant of light from the window, but light from the morning, not the afternoon. Here is where I shored up. Shored up, so I could step out and become legitimate. Whether the time in this safe place involved rest or mental exertion was irrelevant.

In the future, I would explain to my husband the significance of the carafe, the beauty of its insulation feature, and the many associations I created in my head surrounding this morning routine. When he understood how these aspects fit together, he would realize that this simple morning task could be the one great thing he could do for me each morning, even if it delayed his departure to work. He would embrace the carafe and make the coffee – at least on weekdays. With notes, wishing me luck on my intentions for the day. I would be eternally thankful for Oggi carafes and husbands prepared to make use of them.

Quail [Under Glass]

I am writing to thank you for the
lovely piece of art you sent back
with my son when he visited your
home in Portland.

He tells us you're an artist, working in glass. The
tableau imbedded in the rectangle of fused glass
captures motion before our eyes.
[I never met your daughter. My son

describes her with a single word: selfless.] The
family of quails travels east, ready to move
forward and slip off the right side of the glass
world, mother leading her brood

into our world, into being. Three small quails,
her babies, step after her, their heads at different
angles in the plane so they become vital, blown
into life from the dust in someone's hand.

The last baby quail tilts forward, a
wayward toddler seeking footing,
unsteady, maybe willful in teetering
from art into life, a clean escape.

Bird books explain that the California
quail alone wears the plume atop
its head. This party of four
a quartet of dancers from the gay 90's,

the roaring 20's. Each quail wearing a ruffle
of feathers like the flounce of a skirt, artist
crafting ruffle with the absence of color
in clear glass. [I found an old photo of your

daughter online, her eyes a warm, Facebook blue.]
Peppering of dots creates earth below dancing
quails; above them a milky swirl
in the firmament suggests clouds,

perhaps a materialization from a dream, or
from a rubbed brass lamp [I am sorry your
daughter broke up with my son on the last day
of his visit to your home.]

My fingertips graze smooth concavity near the
top edge of the rectangle, bottom edge a more
finely pebbled texture. [I know that she
struggles with her skin.

Hates it, my son says.] I wonder if you intended
to create bubbles in the glass or if they grew on
their own, imperfections. No matter.
They remind me of water, the pain of breathing.

Dead White Men

I hadn't set out to spend nearly four months reading the works of two dead white men. Events just evolved that way. I'd always wanted to read *The Education of Henry Adams*. The autobiography, written in the third person, told the story of Henry Adams, grandson of John Quincy Adams, the sixth President of the United States; and great-grandson of John Adams, the second president of the United States. The book topped the Modern Library's list of one hundred most important non-fiction books written in the English language from the twentieth century. It was one of Tim's favorite books.

I knew a portion of the Henry Adams story – the sensational part. His wife, Marian Adams, who went by the nickname of Clover, was a brilliant woman who entertained in her home and maintained close relationships with leading artists, thinkers, and politicians of the day. But at some point, she found her life wanting and swallowed potassium cyanide, the photographic fluid she used to develop the photographs she took. Tim and I had visited Rock Creek Cemetery in Washington, D.C. where Adams had commissioned a memorial for Clover, one crafted by Augustus Saint-Gaudens. I'd read *Clover Adams, a Gilded and Heartbreaking Life,* by Natalie Dykstra at Hope College, one of the Michigan colleges which Connor had almost attended to play college tennis. I'd always wanted to write a historical novel about Clover Adams, before writing novels became a pointless exercise because of the difficulty of publishing them once they were written. We'd named our dog Clover; Rachel suggested the name, probably because of our Irish roots, but I'd latched onto it. I felt affinity for Clover Adams. I felt affinity for anyone who committed suicide.

I expected to view Henry Adams as a stuffed shirt, white privileged chauvinist.

I'd come to the Vermont Studio Center in Johnson, Vermont, to work on writing of my own. As I retired each night to my bed in Bevins House, one of the homes within the art residency complex, slipping between the sheets with my heating pad to relax my back muscles, I joined Henry Adams in time, trying to picture his Quincy, the bustling New England community in which he'd been born and raised, a preeminent descendant of a famous founding father family. Quincy was a small town when he was born in the early 1800's. The suburb of Boston into which it had evolved was a community vastly different from the one that Adams had known.

I found it difficult to enter into the book and immerse myself in the historic period it described. Years earlier, I'd purchased a copy and mailed it to my friend Penny, thinking I'd read the book as I imagined her to read it. Yet I didn't. I got busy with some other book, and then another, and another. I suspected that my reticence was related not only to the investment I'd have to make in tackling the older prose style. If truth be told, I was angry with Henry Adams. I was angry with him for not recognizing Clover's loneliness and constant struggle to create meaning in her life, especially after her father died. I had told Tim how shabby I thought it was that Adams never talked about Clover in *The Education*. His decision to leave her out of the book, capturing their entire relationship and the death with only a chapter title – "Twenty Years After" – struck me as cowardly and ego-centric.

I knew I'd be a defensive reader as well because of the sheer volume of history the book contained. Tim knew the context behind all of the political and historical events in the book. I would read along, trying to understand as best as I could, realizing I would miss the significance of so many exchanges, quandaries, and debates that Adams reported and explored.

But as the quiet of my Bevins-2 room was interrupted from time to time by the sound of the furnace and a soft snore from the artist on the other side of the wall, I began to feel empathy for the man who'd written about himself from the third-person point of view not as a clever rhetorical trick – he'd planned to produce only enough copies of the book to give to friends – but because his self-effacing nature probably couldn't face the grandiosity of the first-person narration. He needed to present his description and analysis of events more obliquely.

In a chapter on the Great Exposition of 1900 in Paris entitled "The Dynamo and The Virgin," Henry Adams lays out a metaphor, comparing two different perspectives and periods of time. The dynamo, an industrial revolution creation in the world of energy and motion, is a symbol of power, just as the Virgin is a symbol of power. In a previous book, Adams had presented his fascination and captivation with the cathedrals at Chartres and Mont St. Michel. The cathedrals, which deified the virgin for the observer, perhaps even regardless of his religion, demonstrated a force that was, to Adams, a force related to the power of sex. Yet Adams believed that America – or Americans, more precisely – didn't feel that power or attraction in the way he did, or in the way Europeans did. The Virgin, as a symbol, lacked a divine essence or mysticism in the eyes of most Americans. For them, the dynamo, exhibited in intense permutations at the Great Exposition, represented the tremendous power and attraction of the era; beside it, the Virgin was meaningless.

Yet Adams also viewed the Virgin not only as a symbol of power, but also as a symbol of infinity. Infinity, attraction, powerful force. This is the trinity that Adams discerns in the Virgin, and it is a trinity that he applies to the American women he knows – his feminine compatriots. They are superior to the men of his generation, he feels. And thus he reveres them. And he mourns the fact that other men don't recognize their value, steeped in this triad of traits.

As I trudged each day to the cafeteria at the Vermont Studio Center, discussing art and writing with my fellow residents over lunch before heading to my writing studio, I wondered if Henry Adams could be viewed as an early feminist. Or was his worship of the Virgin, his non-Catholic worship, it must be noted, for he was raised as a Boston Unitarian Universalist, sublimated mourning for his beloved Clover, whom he failed to appreciate as much as he might have, as much as she needed? She was known to be a spirited and witty conversationalist, a woman of letters, a lover of family, an artist needing to be recognized by the world around her.

I knew from early on in our marriage how much Tim loved the Chapter on the Virgin and the Dynamo; I knew too that he found it nearly impenetrable in spots.

I felt empathy for Henry Adams, in spite of my frustration with him for failing Clover. I saw in him some of my worst traits. He had the need, at times, to see things in black-and-white terms, to make evaluations of people in a consistently moral sort of way. He tried to acknowledge the complexities, the shades of gray, but sometimes he failed. Yet he lived during a period of which I had no understanding, in a world steeped with the kind of politics that I could view only with cynicism when looking at any statesman other than Abraham Lincoln. Adams expressed himself, most of the time, in such self-deprecating terms that I felt the need to come to his defense, if only in the conversation I had with myself in my brain.

And while he might be avoiding a confrontation with his past and even his culpability by deleting the portion of his life that he shared with Clover, it was a thoughtful avoidance, a painful skirting. His offering of his education was, in most ways, humble: *Here. Make of it what you will. I learned a few things, but I was a slow learner who was lucky enough to be born into a family that could afford to support its slow learners.*

He reminded me a bit of Tim.

II.

If Henry Adams's voice was the quiet voice of observation and thoughtful humility, Herman Melville's voice, the voice of Ishmael in *Moby Dick* as delivered through the voice of Anthony Heald on my audio CD, was raucous and crotchety. I first heard the voice when Rachel was required to read the book for a class at Oakland University. Even though she'd been an intense and constant reader since the age of five, I worried that she might find the novel daunting. I was well acquainted with the book but had never read it myself. Rachel liked and admired her teacher, Professor Jeff Insko, saying she'd drag herself to class even when she lay at death's door; she couldn't bear to miss any of the entertaining and thought-provoking lectures he provided. But I wondered, would she read the whole book with its peculiarities? Enough to pass a midterm or a final?

To insure her education, I bought the book on CD. She returned it to me at the end of the semester, having passed the class without incident. The cellophane had been removed from the box, which had clearly been opened, but the CDs still glistened silver and luminous, without scratches or mars. I opened the first disc and tried to listen to the story.

I hated the voice. The narration seemed rough in execution, the CD poor in quality. The prose presented was elliptical in sense.

For years Rachel had listened to books on tape, telling me that she was able to clean her room only if she had an audiobook to which she could listen. My own first audio book was Michael Chabon's *The Yiddish Policemen's Union*, narrated by Peter Riggert, star of the movies *Local Hero* and *Crossing Delancey*. Peter Riggert's voice was husky yet smooth. By the end of my time with that book, during my early commuting days to Oakland, I was in love with Peter Riggert, in love with Michael Chabon, in love with Meyer Landsman, Chabon's main character. A character who also reminded me of my husband.

I wanted to be in love with *Moby Dick*. At the end of the children's movie based on Roald Dahl's *Matilda*, the heroic Matilda has been freed from all the cruel adults in her life and has been united with Miss Honey, her beloved teacher; she uses her magical powers to pull *Moby Dick* off her shelves and begins reading: "Call me Ishmael." It is a moment of delight.

But I was not delighted with Herman Melville, or Ishmael, or Anthony Heald. The box of CDs languished in my car. At one point, the CDs scattered out of their packaging and rode about loosely in a small basket, rubbing up against other CDs, Kleenex, hand sanitizer, and coupons. One day, I pulled the disks out of the basket, took them inside the house, and washed them with warm water and dish detergent in the same gentle way I washed the PlayStation disks Nathaniel occasionally brought to me. I taped up the box with heavy-duty clear packaging tape and reassembled the disks in order. I placed the box in our family room bookcase, where it sat for another few years among dusty oddities – the coiled clay snake Nathaniel or Connor had fashioned in elementary school, Tim's container of ever-ready dental floss, and a Korean plaque my old student Heashin gave me one of those years I tutored her and her brothers.

Not long before my drive to the Vermont Studio Center, I pulled the box of CDs off the family room bookshelf. I'd be on the road for a long time, and though I'd checked out of the library some other books on tape, I was determined to finish the audio version of *Moby Dick* one way or another. I had a print copy that I could reference in the evenings to ensure that I didn't miss anything if traffic got dicey and the road required my undivided attention.

III.

During my time at Vermont Studio Center, Henry Adams and Amy Bloom, contemporary author of *Lucky Us*, *Away*, and *Where the God of Love Hangs Out*, among other works of fiction, were my evening companions. I wanted to finish the Adams book, but at times, with a brain tortured by my own prose trials of the writing day, I found it difficult to engage in Henry's world; I needed to sneak into the era of the 1940's that Bloom created in *Lucky Us*. Yet when I left Johnson, Vermont, on a bright, travel-worthy day so unlike the stormy Valentine's night on which I'd arrived, *Moby Dick* – Anthony Heald's *Moby Dick* – became my escort.

With my Bevins room and my writing studio room in Maverick emptied, my belongings repacked into my van, I headed for our friend Ann's house in South Berwick, Maine. Ann had been our closest friend when we lived in Virginia. She studied history with Tim, at Mister Jefferson's University, in the graduate master's program. When I'd moved to Charlottesville the year after Tim began his program, the three of us became fast friends, and Ann turned out to be my last roommate before Tim and I got married. Until she left Charlottesville, Virginia, in 1988, she was our major social activity. We ate dinners together frequently, at our dinky upstairs-of-a-house apartment or at her sloping-floored apartment in downtown Charlottesville, where her lop-eared rabbit chewed the phone cord and lots of other objects in her apartment, keeping us all amused. If Ann called us, whoever answered the phone would talk to her; we shared her equally; she knew us equally. Three anxiety-ridden, deep-thinking introverts, we found that our communion made us laugh, freed us from our more brooding solitary selves.

We'd kept in touch over the years, visiting Ann and her family in Maine a few times.

She was Nathaniel's godmother, the only non-family member we chose to sponsor the kids in their Lutheran faith. She'd come to Michigan shortly after I received the lung cancer diagnosis. She had her own health struggles with multiple myeloma.

Though the sun warmed the windshield of my van on that day I travelled to South Berwick, I knew that Maine, like Boston, had been pummeled by the snow that winter. Several residents at the Vermont Studio Center were dreading their return to New England after their two- or four-week residencies. I drove south from Johnson through the state, and the temperature rose as I drove. The snow which had collected on my car in its parking spot at the Vermont Studio Center began to melt, chunks of ice and sections of snow sliding from the top of my van and thunking onto the ground in those first few hours on the road. I put on the *Moby Dick* CD, ready for a break from my diet of Adams with occasional Bloom pilferings. And with the rays of the sun pulsating against the windshield, I made my way south and east, so I could pick up I-95 heading from Massachusetts into Maine, not far from the Nantucket whaling area Melville had described early in the book. I listened to Anthony Heald as Ishmael, and learned about Queequeg's developing fever, his request for a coffin, and his subsequent outfitting of the coffin to serve as his final resting place.

When I finally reached the outskirts of South Berwick, Maine, I wound around the roads leading to Ann's house, marveling at the neat stacks of snow. I pulled up to a home that looked vaguely familiar and saw a three-sided wall of snow framing her family's driveway. Zach, Ann's husband, loved all things outdoors. Snow, for him, provided the opportunity for skiing, though his free time was limited since he commuted two hours both to and from Boston each weekday to teach at Boston Latin.

But I was visiting on a snowy weekend, and Ann and I did warm indoor activities. One night we watched *A Beautiful Mind* on Netflix. Ann had seen the movie once but wanted to see it again and knew I would appreciate it. I found nearly all films about mental illness meaningful, but I was afraid to watch, afraid of the darkness. Yet I found I was captivated by John Nash's story, the brilliance of his intelligence revealed alongside the chaos and fragmentation of his schizophrenia. Ann and I were both taken with his solution to his problem – to learn how to live with the voices. Of course, he couldn't have done it without the help of his wife, and look at what she had given up, to allow him to pursue his brilliance. But still. I knew this "living with the voice" solution was the one my own psychologist was helping me to work through. The voice would always be there, in my head, in spite of my anti-depressant medication, and it would always say harsh things to me. And even though I wasn't a schizophrenic and didn't face the dangers that someone with that diagnosis faced, even though the voice in my head was a different sort of voice, I still had to learn to live with it.

Ann and I talked about our mindfulness practices and how we worked on quieting our mean and judgmental voices and embraced gratitude and empathy without beating ourselves up for our occasional mean thoughts. Ann was one of my few friends who came from a solid and traditional Christian religious tradition but embraced as well many of the tenets of Buddhism, making her the most liberal and ecumenical of believers.

Before I left Maine, we visited Portsmouth, New Hampshire, and ate soup and popovers. We enjoyed lobster and shrimp one night, with Zach performing the lobster immersion duties. On a frozen beach next to the ocean, where large piles of snow rose indistinguishable from ice flows beside them, Ann gave me a New England beach pebble for good luck.

IV.

When I left Maine, I was headed for Philadelphia, where I planned to have dinner with Rachel and Ryan, spend the night at the inexpensive hotel near Swarthmore I'd stayed at when I moved Rachel down, and then drive back to Michigan. Like the trip to Maine, the trip to Philly was uneventful, though long. In *Moby Dick* land, Queequeg had survived his fever, thereby earning himself a canoe casket. Anthony Heald moved me through the intensification of Ahab's troubles and the final series of ships the Pequod met with on its way to meet the white whale -- the Bachelor, the Rachel, and the Delight.

Tim had argued that it was crazy for me to drive all the way down to Philly for a few hours with my own Rachel and her boyfriend, but I'd asserted that if I had to spend the night somewhere, anyway, to break up the trip, it might as well be Philadelphia, where I could see my daughter. And I knew the drive from Philly to home.

Before I'd left the Vermont Studio Center, Arista, the resident school artist, had shown me how to work the Siri map and direction feature on my iPhone so that I could follow Siri's voice instead of trying to decipher the instructions on my cell phone screen. I preferred driving with paper maps anyway, and I wasn't averse to pulling over to the side of the road to examine my path as it appeared in red and black lines on an accordion-folded rectangle that I draped over my lap, its paper edges flicking against the steering wheel each time I made a right or left turn.

After my visit with Rachel and Ryan and a night of rest at the Day's Inn, I began my trip back home, tracing the route I knew from Philadelphia to Lansing. About an hour into the drive, a sign on the road announced that I might need to take an alternate route, and that I should call the number listed on the sign to get recorded instructions. Meanwhile, Siri told me where to go.

It became apparent after a while that my route was not, in fact, the path I was accustomed to following on the Pennsylvania Turnpike, but a combination of other state roads. I had no clue where I was on a map. My van's reliable compass told me that I was headed generally west and generally north.

And then, the weather intensified. I felt as though I'd been teleported back in time to the hours two and a half weeks earlier, retracing the snowy path I'd taken from Michigan to Vermont through Canada. The heat rolled out of the dashboard vents, keeping me warm but drying my eyes, making them feel gritty as I tried to maintain a bug-eyed alertness. Shoulders hunched, I gripped the wheel and listened to the snow ice ticking against my tires on the road and the roof of my van. I'd dubbed myself a road warrior after I'd made it to Vermont Studio Center on Valentine's Day, but in truth, I was exhausted. My time at the Vermont Studio Center and then at Ann's was rejuvenating and relaxing. But I'd pushed myself way beyond the limits that my Tarceva-fatigued body usually went.

Yet I seized on an idea. I hit the play button.

I'd last checked in with Herman Melville, Anthony Heald, and Ishmael a few days earlier on my route through the northeastern states south to Philly. Now I needed to stay awake.

Anthony Heald would project his voice, Melville's characters' voices, into all the crevices of my van, filling it with his interpretation of Ishmael's revelations about the events on the Pequod.

227

On the passenger seat next to me was a large bag of the molasses cookies Ann had made for me to bring home for Nathaniel. I had her permission to eat as many as I wanted, but I was trying to leave the bulk for Nathaniel. When she'd come to visit us shortly after my diagnosis, back before Nathaniel had lost his egg allergy, she'd made Nathaniel her famous cookies with an egg replacer. But the cookies next to me were made with real eggs, which he could now eat. I promised myself that I would be judicious, nibbling slowly, keeping my hands on the wheel, raising each cookie I chose to eat up to my lips for a small bite, followed by many chews.

The water was surrounding the passengers on the Pequod chasing *Moby Dick* just as the weather was engulfing my blue car in a sea of white ice flakes. My daughter cleaned her room to audio narratives – now I would drive to them, keeping the narrative as a pleasant diversion, not something to be absorbed, analyzed, or thoroughly comprehended. I needed to find a way to keep my listening brain active enough that it stayed awake but not so active that it began to turn over events in a manner so analytical and contemplative that the narrative became a distraction rather than an accompaniment to my driving.

Earlier in my listening experience with *Moby Dick*, I'd begun to feel an increasing admiration for Melville's exhaustive way with details. When my brain attempted to catalogue the many world places he referenced in his discussion of Nantucket whaling, I was astounded by the sheer volume of specific geographical facts he alluded to in the novel, never mind the knot-tying and sperm and white whale characteristics he described for the reader. I didn't have a PhD in literature; I'd never taken a class about *Moby Dick*. I found myself craving a classroom, wanting to analyze and discuss, wanting to raise my white hand tentatively. What does the "whiteness" chapter say about race? What about Queequeg – what role did he play in the novel?

Yet another part of me rebelled. Hadn't I decided in my thirties that I was sick of the dead white men? As a first-generation college student and omnivorous reader, I'd read largely what was given to me by librarians and English teachers. I had only, in my late twenties, begun to explore the women writers I learned about in college – I knew I loved Marilynne Robinson's *Housekeeping*, Joan Chase's *During the Reign of the Queen of Persia*, Edith Wharton's *Ethan Frome*, Kate Chopin's *The Awakening*. And later, works by Toni Morrison, Isabel Allende, Sandra Cisneros, Julia Alvarez, and Jhumpa Lahiri. My friend Julie, who now worked with Tim, had created and sustained with me, for several years in our thirties, a Women Authors Only book club, in spite of my husband's occasional quips that I was a reverse sexist. In response, I asserted that when a writer like Hemingway presented characters who longed for love and connection, the result was always labelled great literature, but when a woman did the same, her book was merely a domestic tale. A soap opera at worst, a slight domestic tale at best.

What I admired in Melville's *Moby Dick*, was, in fact, the laundry-like exploration and quality of the writing. Details. Of blubber. Of ambergris. Expositions on the differences between the Sperm Whale and the Right Whale.

I wanted to be a woman writer who wrote about important life and world events, but my own life experiences were limited, and I believed in the maxim of writing what I knew. What I knew was family life. Domestic. Real laundry lists, not just metaphoric ones.

I continued to be perplexed by the disconnect I saw between what I'd read over the course of my life and what I wanted to read and write about. I was a woman, and yet the bulk of the books I'd read in my life were by male authors. As I listened now to the CD, it was a male voice that entered my ears, travelled down the auditory canals, and bounced against my two eardrums. While I identified myself as a strong feminist, I was an open-minded strong feminist, and I never outright rejected a man's voice, whether I heard it or read it in print. I always paid attention. But I knew that however much I valued what men said – particularly what my husband, my psychologist (hadn't I come to him in the middle of my life, telling him that after years of seeing women psychologists, I'd decided I needed to work with a man, to make an attempt to value my husband's point of view?), my two sons, a few relatives, a couple of friends, and now my oncologist said – I had a habit of listening to the women in my life when it came to specifics. The maxims I lived by came from women, who gave me their opinions and experiences and helped me guide my life. It was my mother's voice I valued. That of my sisters. My close friends. The wisdom of women came out in astute observations, gathered and reflected upon over time. Women's wisdom often grew from their empathy. Men's wisdom was often about their analysis and what they knew, and however much I might appreciate that analysis or put it to use, I knew it was often both objective and situational — hadn't necessarily been permutated, absorbed by a soul, and lived in a life before being honed. Women's wisdom was hard-fought, from lives lived.

As much as I loved my father's voice, it was the voice of my mother that I'd heeded most when I was young. Always. Consistently. And now I yearned for it. That voice.

Here I was, on the road again, alone. The pavement in front of me white, the flakes and the ice pebbles on my window even whiter. Ishmael was there with Ahab and a boat full of men, and though their mission was so far removed from any pursuit I'd ever endeavored, their communion foreign with its masculine litany of the seafaring, I felt the waves that crashed against the Pequod as it circled in the waters in pursuit of *Moby Dick*, I felt the affection Ishmael had for Queequeg, the frustration and dogged eternal allegiance most of the men displayed toward Ahab, in spite of the sheer folly of their mission.

Henry Adams's Virgin was not so different from Ahab's whale. Yet the object was in the distance, never in the foreground. Henry admired and adored Clover and held her in high esteem. But he failed at bringing her into the grittiness of the real world that he was just beginning to grapple with himself. He stayed too long in his writing room and entertained himself with the world of history and the world of the past in which he was more comfortable, but he left Clover too long alone. Ishmael's world contained all the gritty reality Melville could capture of the whaling industry and the journey of the whalers. He'd romanticized the gritty world, to be sure, but he captured it with more honesty than a previous generation of writers might have captured that natural world. And while the book failed to deal in much detail with the women who remained back in Nantucket while the men sailed, I couldn't fault Melville, whose knowledge of geography, knot-making, and blubber extraction was even now helping me to keep my tires in the beaten tracks of the snow and ice on Pennsylvania and Ohio turnpikes.

One of my psychologist's jobs was to help me remember why I valued my husband's voice. One day he sent me to YouTube for a comic view of how men's brains differed from women's brains. The speaker, Mark Gungor, a man who presented marriage seminars, explained to an audience of men and women that men had multiple boxes in their brains in which to store things separately, and the biggest rule was that the boxes couldn't touch each other. Each box had its limited contents pertaining to one subject only, so the contents were compartmentalized.

Isolated. Women's brains, on the other hand, were made up of a big ball of wire and everything was connected. The speaker made a buzzing noise as if the wires were alert with activity, sizzling. That ball of wire was the Internet Superhighway, and it was called Emotion, he said.

Of course, I agreed with the descriptions. I hadn't read the bestseller, *Men are from Mars, Woman are from Venus*, by John Gray, but I knew that sometimes it really did seem that men and women's perceptions of things were so radically different that they appeared to have distinct and separate origins.

On another day, my psychologist and I returned to a frequent topic – how my brain in times of stress returned to its depressive groove, a groove that my psychologist told me was like one on an old vinyl album we might have played in our adolescence, an album played so often that the grooves became too deeply etched. I thought about myself in dark, negative terms. But he was looking at the newer research, he told me, and it turned out that for some depressed people, not just women, everything really did become connected; many of the prolific associations were hardwired. The neural pathways were like the grooves in the old vinyl, so I might find it more difficult sometimes to keep myself from drifting into the bad grooves.

I liked the associations much of the time. I believed they contributed to my creativity.

But I could see how a life of separate boxes in one's head might feel clean, not messy, the way my head always felt. If that guy was even a little bit right about the boxes, men were so lucky.

As a female, then, I made tons of associations or connections, probably more than the average or typical male. As a female with a history of depression, I probably made additional connections that became embedded in my neural pathways, resulting in the needle getting stuck, riding that same groove over and over again.

In the time I had left, before the cancer cells escaped from their bondage within my Tarceva-protected body, how could I be a woman artist, a wife, and a mother, and live peacefully with the men and women in my family, valuing their voices? How could I keep my ears open and accept what my husband, my sons, and a few other men might say while simultaneously valuing my own reflections and observations and intuitive leaps of knowledge?

Henry Adams valued women's voices. But in spite of his travel, his profound commentary on events of the day, and his social networking, he was more of an observer than an actor. He didn't figure out soon enough how to embrace, how to value, and how to nurture those women's voices he heard. And Clover, unable to find a voice to explain to Henry what she needed or to share her gifts with the world, stopped speaking altogether.

I'd made it to Ohio, a state I knew to be wide with a seemingly endless turnpike. Yet as most east to west travelers know, Ohio is always easier than Pennsylvania, which is always easier than New York. Ohio was much more common ground for me. The digital temperature notation on my central ceiling panel now reflected a colder temperature. The pavement captured by my car's headlights in the early evening appeared to be dry, and I realized the ice had stopped ticking against the roof of the van.

Ahab was in the middle of the Chase. I knew I was near the end of the novel. I knew what happened next, and I wasn't ready to hear that part of the story just yet. I realized that with the weather letting up, I could stop at a rest area and call home to let Nathaniel know where I was on the route. I pushed the power knob on the console, leaving Ahab and Ishmael and Anthony and *Moby Dick* for another day.

But before I reached the sign advertising the next rest area, the phone rang. I picked it up from the cupholder and tapped the "Accept" button. Tim's voice entered the darkness of the van. He was calling from Palm Springs, where he'd flown for a meeting. He explained to me how the hand-off had gone a few days earlier when he left Nathaniel with the Gillespies and their son Forrest, one of Nathaniel's close friends. Nathaniel would be at home, expecting me to arrive, not really waiting but still ready to greet me when I got there.

The voice telling me these things was gravelly and low, the way it sounded when Tim explained things, clarified, reassured. I'd learned since the diagnosis that at times I needed to ignore that voice, along with the other voice I heard in my head. Dismiss it, even. That act struck me as rude, unloving, almost heretical. But when I considered that it was the voice that I heard most often, the voice to which I gave most credence, the voice which spoke an intimate wisdom, one rooted in an intimate wisdom and appreciation of me, I knew that the times of listening and the times of ignoring could live in an equilibrium.

The voice belonged to a living white man. He had to go, but he wished me a safe journey through Ohio and into Michigan. As I put the phone back into the cup holder, I looked into the cold night beyond my windshield. I drove.

MRI, Accompanied by Sufjan Stevens

I sat in front of Connor's rental on Wheaton Street in Kalamazoo, waiting for him to emerge and get in the van so he could start on his coffee and the bagel from Bagel Beanery. When he opened the door and I saw his face, about as scruffy as I expected, I relaxed. He didn't have the somber demeanor that I'd anticipated. He wore a baseball cap, which meant he hadn't taken a shower, but his trademark smile remained intact.

I gave him a choice between the sesame and the asiago bagel. He took asiago. A garbage truck was moving slowly down the street, and we made sure we weren't blocking its path; there were no dumpsters or recyclable containers on the curb next to us. About eight houses ahead of us on our right, a man held a dog on a leash, and we watched as the dog twirled in circles. Connor told me that he had a shift at 10:00 at the Markin Racquet Center. The shift would take three hours out of his already packed day, although he would likely be able to do a bit of writing at work to complete his final exams for the term.

I told him that I needed to come up with a CD to play during the MRI. That I'd wanted to get *Little Women* because the old one I had was scratched, but the bookstore didn't have it, so I'd purchased a Linda Ronstadt album, and the soundtrack to the movie *Once*. Yet when I'd listened to them on the way to the Towne Place Suites the evening before, I hadn't liked either for my purposes. Too jarring.

Connor recommended Sufjan Stevens. I should have thought of it. All three kids had been listening to the album *Carrie and Lowell*. It was about Sufjan Stevens' relationship with his deceased mother, who'd died of cancer. Stevens' music had been introduced to our family first by Rachel's old boyfriend Nando. But I'd learned more about him when

234

the textbook I chose for one of my courses at Oakland included his lyric for "Casimir Pulaski Day" as the only song poem in the book. It turned out that Stevens had gone to Hope College, a Michigan college where the textbook author, Heather Sellers, taught. I'd selected the textbook because of the cross-genre approach that Sellers used, but also because I'd seen her speak before on the topic of why we needed to look at writing as play to de-mystify it. I'd also loved her short story collection *Georgia Under Water*.

The new Sufjan Stevens album would make for a powerful listening experience. My kids, who'd enjoyed his music for years, felt drawn to the story of his complicated relationship with his mother, the time he spent with her, and his grieving process. By playing the CD during my MRI, I would be keeping the three of them close, hearing the music they absorbed each day. In their own ways, they each continued to struggle with how to make sense of my cancer diagnosis and the imprecise information about the amount of time I had left.

But on that day, it felt like Connor was struggling the most, which was why I was in Kalamazoo. The day before, a Sunday, I'd met my friend Sharon in Battle Creek at our usual spot, the Barnes and Noble Bookstore at the Lakeview Mall. But afterwards, instead of going home, I'd gone to Kalamazoo. Tim used his Marriott points to get me a room, and I said that it would be good for me to do some quiet writing before the MRI, but I just wanted to check on Connor because I was worried about him, staying up all night, tired and discouraged by other things that had happened that week with the tennis team. But he'd refused my offer to do a late night run to Taco Bell, told me to go to sleep and he'd be fine, but yes, he'd love it if I could bring him a coffee and a bagel in the morning.

Thus, when I dropped him off at the Markin Tennis Center for his morning shift at the Tennis Desk, I felt a sense of relief that he'd been productive and steady during a dark night. I could head into the MRI challenge carrying just my own anxieties. I had enough time when I got off the expressway back in Lansing to stop at a store and buy the Sufjan CD.

When the MRI technician called me back from the waiting room, I tried to mentally prepare myself for dealing with the small quarters I was about to inhabit. We walked down the wide hallways of the hospital, hallways I'd walked when I came to get my first PET scan and initial MRIs right after I was diagnosed.

I hated MRIs. My stage IV lung cancer diagnosis indicated that I had metastases, and my oncologist had ordered a full slate of MRIs, both with and without contrast, after our initial meeting. I'd tried to do them all in one day, but the overwhelming volume and range of odd noises the machine made – the clacking, pounding, and siren-like blaring – had overwhelmed me, and on the advice of the technicians, I'd asked to return to the hospital the next day in order to get some relief from the sound and the claustrophobic testing environment.

But this time the MRI would be easy. It was just my brain. Maybe forty-five minutes at the most. A piece of cake. And this time, I was prepared, because the information they'd sent me with my appointment confirmation indicated that I could bring my own music to play. I'd been uncharacteristically focused on that task of selecting music.

We walked into the large MRI suite, and the technician gestured toward the changing room. He stepped in and opened a few cupboards, pulling out some scrubs. "Okay," he said. "Just change into those. Take off your jewelry and watch and use the locker to store valuables."

He walked out, and I began to remove my clothes, reaching for the scrubs. I unfolded them and realized there were two pairs of pants. I needed a top. But I could put the pants on first. I began to pull them on and realized right away that they were much too small for my rather large frame. I looked at the label for the other pair, which was marked with the same size. I opened the cupboards and began rifling. Now I needed a shirt AND a pair of pants. I felt guilty for being such a large person. Maybe they trained the technicians to give you a smaller size to make you think about your extra weight.

I tried to hurry because I felt like I'd already taken too much time to undress and figure out the two-pants-no-shirt thing. But I had to try on two more different shirts and pants before I found the right size, and I felt wasteful dumping them in the dirty laundry. But they'd touched my body. Who knew where I'd been and what germs I carried?

I finally made it to the room next door, the office, where the technician needed to interview me about metal I might have in my body or drugs I might be taking. He asked all of his questions, and then I said, "Can I ask the person who reads my MRI to comment on my sinuses? Or will they just look at potential cancer spots because my oncologist is the one who ordered the test?"

"They will comment on whatever is there," he said.

"So there's no point in writing down a specific request about the sinuses?" I said.

He shook his head.

I wanted to be an efficient and thoughtful consumer of health care. If my insurance company was paying for an MRI and that MRI could give me information about my sinuses, information that might help me understand the headaches I'd been having, maybe I should try to seek out that information. But that did not seem to be how diagnostic testing worked.

We went into the big MRI room, and I felt a chill. I knew that I'd been to Sparrow before when they'd covered me with blankets for the testing, but I also had faint memories of the MRI tunnel being warm. Then I remember Sufjan.

"Oh," I said. "I forgot my CD in the changing room. I need to go get it."

"You won't be able to hear it," he said.

I looked at him, uncomprehending.

"The MRI is too loud."

"I know it's loud, but the informational pamphlet they sent said I could bring a CD."

"We can play it if you want us to, but most people find that they just can't hear it."

I almost relented, reluctant to take up any more time, but I decided to honor my gut and get through the experience as comfortably as possible. "I'm going to get it. Just a moment."

He sighed.

I went back to the changing room and used my locker key to get into the locker where the CD waited in a bag. I put everything away, relocked the locker, and scooted back out to the MRI room. "Here," I said, handing him the CD.

And then I hopped on the sliding bed, and they locked me into position and moved me into the tunnel. Once inside, I tried to keep my eyes closed. I remembered that I felt less claustrophobic if I didn't have to see how close the top of the tunnel wall was to my face. I was accustomed to CT scans; the machine used for the CTs had a wide opening, not completely enclosed or as tunnel-like as the MRI. The platform bed that moved in and out of it worked on a similar principle, but the CT scan was more like a ring into which you passed in and out. MRI tunnels were much more claustrophobic with their tight space.

I liked it when the technicians talked to me, telling me how long things would take and asking me if I was doing okay. When I had my first MRI, they were so kind, talking with me often to ease any anxiety I might be feeling. I'd already made the judgment that this MRI technician would not be the warm, fuzzy type. He would not be talking to me regularly.

Then the barrage began. The clacking, like someone had thrown a handful of ball bearings into a blender and left it on, metal fighting metal blades, knocking into the walls of the glass canister. The blaring European ambulance sound. The jackhammer pounding reverberating so loudly that I felt as if I were the one holding the jackhammer, my arms, neck, and head shaking with the drilling force.

And in the middle of it all, off in the distance, a thin strand of music, the finger picked strings of a guitar, the faint Sufjan Stevens voice. I held silent my limbs and breathed my mindful, Jon Kabat-Zinn breaths, focused my attention on the music, teasing out the strands, the repeated pickings, both melodic and percussive, amidst the MRI noises. Breathed in. Breathed out. Breathed in. Breathed out.

A few weeks later, after I'd had the opportunity to listen to the CD more closely, I would tell one of my children how much Sufjan's sad, plaintive music somehow lifted my spirits. How the repeated lyrics in "Fourth of July" – "We're all gonna die. We're all gonna die" – made me giggle out loud with the honest and simple announcement of truth. I felt sacrilegious, like I was dishonoring the music, but I loved the joy that simple repeated line gave me.

As the MRI tech walked me back to the waiting room, he asked me if the music helped. I was eager to tell him that it had; I wanted him to continue offering that option to others, in spite of his skepticism.

"It centers you," I said. "Gives you a focus, a focal point, something to which you can breathe. Like Lamaze for childbirth. Have you ever had a baby?"

He laughed, presumably at gender constraints. "No," he said. "I have never had a baby."

Of course not. How silly of me.

Jeremy's Grave and Dinner with Ryan

When I turned into the entrance of Arbor Crest Cemetery in Ann Arbor, I remembered at once my family's experience in Père Lachaise in France. Yet again I had failed to think about a key cemetery and memorial garden issue – one needs to call ahead to find the location of the specific plot for which one is looking.

But of course, in my rush to leave the house, I'd forgotten that key concept of location. I'd come to see my student Jeremy's grave on this warm day on the first of July. I would be paying my respects a little over a year after his death. I circled around the drives leading to various sections of the cemetery, looking for an office. Several buildings rose up, but none of them looked official in the right sort of way – not ostentatious like a mausoleum or simple and respectful like a chapel. Yet the circular drives in front of me seemed more manageable than Père Lachaise – smaller, more efficient.

Another small building stood tucked away in a corner, and I circled back around to it, my van window open so that as I eyed the building for the presence of a person, I heard the crunch of stone underneath the tires. I was correct in my guess that the building was an office, but unfortunately, it was closed. Not surprising, given that it was the week leading up to July 4, in midsummer, on a hot day. I would indeed need to go hunting for the grave.

Climbing back into my van, I returned to the circles, finding comfort in the gentle rhythm of my car's tires meeting the bumps of the rising ruts. I appeared to be entering the newer part of the cemetery. The markers looked more contemporary, the area more spacious.

I knew which grave belonged to Jeremy even before I arrived at the marker. I'd pulled off to the side of the path in the Garden of Tranquility, spotting a few fresh graves. The location struck me as perfect for Jeremy. This area was situated on one of the rising sections of the cemetery – a "crest" section – and the garden off to the right had a natural barrier on two sides, creating an enclave of sorts. I got out of the car, and the groan and clunk of the van's broken door frame disturbed the quiet.

I saw his face first. Since I wasn't prepared, I stopped. Of course. With so much technology these days, you could etch a face onto a grave-stone just as you could meld a photo's pixels onto the granules of sugar contained within the frosting on top of a birthday cake. I kept approach-ing the marker, and his head and shoulders materialized from the flat surface of the black marble. On the hot day, it was as if a film of heat occupied space in front of me, like a desert mirage, and in that haze, Jeremy's face appeared.

Because of his smile, I wasn't afraid. It was his face, a good likeness. His hair had been a bit different when I'd met him – longer, with more blonde wisps. The smile was lively, expressing his intellect, cynicism, and humor.

I sat down on the ground next to the marker, the way I did at my parents' grave markers in Rochester, not far from where I'd taught Jeremy at Oakland University. My mother had taught me cemetery etiquette long ago, probably at a time when she took me to visit graves whose loca-tions I no longer remembered. My father's parents. Maybe her parents, whose graves she often travelled over an hour to visit on Memorial Days even before I'd left the house. Any of fifty or so relatives, my parents both coming from large families, six siblings each, not counting the ones who'd died as infants.

Etiquette dictated that you walked in between the graves. You never stood on top of them. You left a space, as large as a coffin, from the gravestone down to the spot where your walking would be acceptable, not upon a body buried deep in the earth.

But I'd long ago given up on the etiquette, having travelled and seen many graves mashed together in small spaces and irregular plots, but especially after my mother and father died and had taken up residence in the Christian Memorial Gardens where there were no headstones or monuments, only markers, flush with the ground I liked sitting right on top of the two of them, as if I were just a toddler, snuggled up to talk.

How brilliant his mother, Andie, had been to put the image on the stone so she could face him when she talked to him just as he was that year before he'd died.

I needed to talk to Jeremy and tell him a few things.

I apologized for how long it had taken me to get there. I told him that I was glad he was off in a corner on a hill, so I could see anyone approach and stop talking like a mad woman. But no, really. I loved the space and thought it was perfect for him.

I explained to him that I'd met his mom, finally, in September, on a Saturday, in an Ann Arbor restaurant. She'd told me a bit about the day he died. We sat there, two strangers, eyes glassy with tears, her body holding more pain that I could even begin to imagine.

I apologized, too, for the last day I'd seen him on campus, my last day of teaching at Oakland University. When he asked if I'd be his advisor that day. I should have just said yes, regardless of what I thought or knew about my own health situation, regardless of what little status I had as an adjunct in the department. I told him that I worried, too, that I didn't give his mom what she needed either, when I'd met her in September. She wanted to hear about him. I should have brought her stories. Details. Things he said. I didn't think it through. I just wanted to meet her because I knew from what he'd told me how much he loved her and counted on her, and I knew from her emails during the school year how long she'd fought for him, how long they'd struggled together, those two willful souls.

I explained that even though it didn't make sense, I would always associate his mother with Paris because she was the one who told me about the family trip there, soon after he died, plans established in

242

advance. That I found my own Paris lodging for my family's trip because of what I'd learned from her. That I thought about him while I was there, in Paris, with my family. Even though it was a hot afternoon in July, the wind picked up and breeze filtered through the trees. Around me, the grass had faded to various shades of mid-summer brown. I wanted the grass to be a bit greener, I told him. He deserved that.

I had planned to meet Rachel's boyfriend for dinner at a restaurant in Ann Arbor. I told Jeremy his middle name, Ryan, was Rachel's boy-friend's first name. I promised I would visit again. I rose and took a pic-ture of his face and his corner of the garden.

I walked back to my van, leaving the tranquility of the cemetery, my feet scuffing against the pebbles on the drive.

Ryan and I had planned to meet at Mani Osteria and Bar, at the corner of Liberty and Division streets, just a few blocks from the parking garage. He'd heard about the restaurant but hadn't tried it yet. He'd been in Ann Arbor for about six weeks, working for Judge Judith Ellen Levy, a United States District Court judge appointed by Obama to serve for the Eastern District of Michigan. He would join me after work, and I'd texted him from the cemetery to verify that I was in town now and would see him at Mani soon.

I had asked Rachel ahead of time if it was okay for me to text Ryan with an offer to buy him dinner. I liked to clear things with her, especially now that she was older and out of college with a boyfriend who hadn't spent hours in our house like other boyfriends had. Leery at first, she warmed up to the idea when I reminded her how important it was for me to have a relationship with her significant other and to reach out to him since he was back in Michigan. Rachel had stayed in Philly to work her day job and care for Ryan's dog, Mia, while he did an internship. She had doubts about where they were headed. In fact, she'd texted me at some point during the day and I'd mock chided her for sending me bad vibes on the day I was having dinner with her partner. I didn't want to be prejudiced, didn't want to know or hear any details about their latest disagreement for fear that some small detail could escape in the middle of the conversation and pollute the waters I was, in some odd, indefinite way, testing.

But the two of them were still together, and Rachel knew that one of her qualities I admired most (and questioned from time to time as well) was the amount of effort and energy she devoted to her relationships, whether with friends or significant others. She did not possess a lever which provided for a "let go" or "give up" option. She was like a tenacious bull rider always determined to hang on, no matter how bumpy the ride.

Mani Osteria occupied a sloping corner that provided two separate street levels. Two tiers, each with a separate entrance to the restaurant. The waiter seated me at a table on the second tier right next to a railing overlooking the first. I ordered a glass of wine and took a deep breath. From my vantage point, I could see both doors that led into the building, and it wasn't long before a young man who appeared to be Ryan, nicely suited, came in the door looking confident and professional, if not a bit apprehensive about the hour ahead of him. "When he doesn't know people," Rachel had told me, "he can be quiet. He thinks he's an extrovert," she said, "but sometimes it takes him a while to get talking."

One of the restaurant's featured items was pizza. Ryan suggested that we share one, with simple toppings. Tim was not a big pizza fan but always liked a heavy dose of spicy meats with his pizza when he did order one. I liked the idea of a more exotic, less meat-laden affair.

With our meal order and general pleasantries out of the way, we both settled down to our dinner conversation. He surprised me by bringing up his tense exchange with Rachel via text that day. I'd been planning to feign ignorance, but he seemed to want my input.

"I don't know if Rachel told you about our texting today, but I feel like she's pretty frustrated with me and feeling like I'm not being very supportive."

I didn't confess that she'd texted her beef with him or that I'd told her I didn't want to taint our dinner date with any negativity. I wanted to tell him that she probably respected his privacy more than he even knew – she didn't run to me with every fight they had; in fact, I got the impression that she tried not to bother me with her bigger problems, though at times, she seemed to magnify her smaller problems to make up for her omissions.

Instead of saying those things aloud, I dithered. "Oh," I said. "Oh" was such a noncommittal word. "I guess she did mention something about a little tiff." I didn't like the word "tiff" or "spat," for that matter, but the word "argument" struck me as way too loaded.

He looked a bit sheepish as he picked up his wine glass. "I'm trying to be supportive," he said, "but I do feel guilty about her being there and my being here. With the dog. Even though I know she's made friends at her work."

"Well, I know the arrangements has some complications, but I know she actually likes Mia quite a bit, and I sort of like her having some other living being to come home to at night."

"I just don't know how to talk to her at times. I struggle to find the right thing to say, and then it seems like I say the wrong thing."

"Rachel and I both share this need to sort things out aloud. We're very different in personality, but we both need what I call "oral processing" at times. I often use Tim for my oral processing, but lots of times I talk to friends. I don't think it's a male or female thing, but both Rachel and I have that need. She might just need you to listen more."

"That's what I mean. I do listen okay when I'm there." He paused. "At least I think I do, but when I'm away…." he trailed off.

"You must be pretty busy," I said.

"Well, yes, this internship is important, but Judge Levy is the best boss I've ever had. She says that even though we're supposed to be slaving away on our work, she doesn't really want us to work that hard. She wants us to think, but she wants us to have fun and embrace our time here. She's a family person," he said.

"She sounds great," I said. "And her work lines up so much with your interest in law, right?" Ryan wanted to become a public interest attorney. He was focused on social justice and civil rights issues.

The waiter brought our pizza. As I looked around us, I realized that the restaurant had begun to fill while we were talking. Ryan served us each a couple slices of the pizza. "I don't think I really knew the technical definition for 'social justice' until the last few years," I said. "Yet it's been something I've had an interest in for a while. I just never used those words."

We talked about politics – in particular, Bernie Sanders. I told him I was just learning about him, through my kids, but already I was excited about how much he'd energized the young electorate. "I need to do my research," I said. "I was thinking it was Hillary's turn, but young people seem to love this guy!"

"I was thrilled – stunned, but thrilled – by the Supreme Court ruling," I told Ryan as we discussed the events of the previous week. "I was in my oncologist's office for my quarterly scans, and I started getting texts on the family chat group, telling me that the Supreme Court struck down all state bans on same sex marriage, leaglizing it in all fifty states. And then I got news that my scans were good yet again.

"When I checked out with the receptionist, I told her how happy I was about the ruling, how important it was to me."

I explained that my politics were liberal but "open-minded" – that I'd worked for the Republicans in the Michigan Senate just after Rachel was born when Tim and I had moved back to Michigan, jobless, from Virginia. I told Ryan that I'd valued the people as well as much of what they'd taught me. Many liberals I knew vilified the Republicans. I didn't like to assume that people were "evil" or "heartless" based on their political affiliations.

But I'd always been so strongly focused on civil rights and gay rights, holding beliefs that kept me moving to the left on the political continuum. It was something I'd learned from my parents, who were supportive of my gay cousin in the 1960's and 1970's. My parents weren't perfect role models in the area of civil rights – my dad's father had expressed some racist tendencies in conversation when I was younger, and my mother sometimes said things like, "He's black, but he's a really great guy," the "but" in the sentence revealing the vestiges of her own inherited racism. Yet over the years they'd learned to think about racial injustice and become more tolerant of differences. And they'd wholly embraced my cousin when others shunned her, when others refused to talk openly about homosexuality.

I told him that when I looked back at my life, as cancer patients are wont to do, I could identify a few accomplishments of which I was truly proud. Raising my children. Surviving the death of my parents thirty-six days apart when I thought I'd curl up in a ball and die. Changing the traffic pattern in Nathaniel's middle school parking lot to make morning and afternoon drop-off time safer for the kids darting between the moving cars in the lot. Working with students throughout the years, often on their writing, but sometimes, in my own kids' lives, on theatre productions, or tennis team support, or classroom writing projects. Participating in a group at my church whose goal was to move the congregation toward developing a welcoming statement for gays, bisexuals, and transgendered individuals.

"And years later, years after I worked on that committee, our congregation finally welcomed two gay pastors." I grabbed another piece of pizza from the serving dish and took a deep breath. I hadn't expected to talk so much. "It was so powerful," I continued. "Pastor Sara preached Sunday about the sadness we experienced as Lutherans upon hearing of the shooting in Charleston, South Carolina, in that Episcopal church? The perpetrator was Lutheran. Not my branch of Lutheran, but still. Lutheran.

"Sara said Bishop Elizabeth Eaton, the presiding bishop of the Evangelical Lutheran Church of America, had declared shortly after the shooting occurred that we needed to have a day of repentance and mourning. In a subsequent announcement, she declared that day to be June 28, 2015."

Ryan ate another piece of pizza, listening intently. "And my pastor, Pastor Sara, was very focused on how she would preach on the repentance and mourning, heeding the Bishop's encouragement to deal with the issues of justice and compassion, noting that the Bishop wanted to emphasize the worth of all individuals. The worth, the dignity, the value.

"And then, while she was still working on her sermon, Friday happened. The Supreme Court ruled in favor of marriage equality. And Pastor Sara was able to go with a flock of others to be married to her partner in the State of Michigan. She had experienced this incredible joy in her life over the weekend, but she came to church Sunday morning wanting and needing to honor the day of repentance and mourning.

"I was so glad I was there, because, I don't know if Rachel has told you, but Lutherans aren't committing a sin if we miss church on Sundays. We're not trained to show up in the same way the Catholics are." Ryan laughed. I knew he'd been raised Catholic.

"So, she talked about how the Gospel lesson for the day contained a story within a story, and her own experience of the previous week or so had also contained a story within a story – the story of the marriage equality decision within the story about the Charleston shootings. "And it was such a joyful moment when she said, 'I personally was quite delighted as I now stand before you as a married woman here in the State of Michigan. On Friday, love won – at least the love that can be found between two people regardless of sex.'

"None of us would have blamed her if she'd continued to talk about the Supreme Court ruling. But she didn't. She went on to emphasize that just because some family members of the Charleston victims were able to forgive the shooter, their generosity didn't suggest that systemic racism is in the past and people of color would now be treated as equals. She talked about how we all have a story, many stories, but our stories shouldn't keep us from the communities for which we've been created, just as none of our stories could keep us from God's embrace.

"Rachel said you're agnostic, and I must admit to having my own issues with religion," I said. "But being in that church last Sunday was incredibly rewarding for me. Pastor Sara talked about holding stories in tension with one another, and I realized that I do that so much of the time. I want to figure out what I think about something, but I'll get on a jag where I see the dark side or another jag where I see the bright side. I think it was so helpful for me to feel guilt and sadness about the shooting at the same moment that I felt joy about the ruling."

It was early summer. Outside, the skies still held light, but I looked at my watch and realized I needed to head back home. "I apologize for talking your ear off," I said.

"No, no," he said. "I enjoyed spending time with you."

I settled the bill, telling him not to argue, since he was a couple years from taking the bar, so he wasn't flush yet. We rose from the table, and I gathered my belongings, stashed behind the chair. I looked at his face and smiled, thinking how charming he was, thinking that the evening had gone so much better than I ever could have hoped. We left the restaurant together and parted at an intersection. He was headed off to his summer apartment, and I was driving back to East Lansing. We hugged and talked about meeting when our family visited Philly again. I watched as he turned and headed down the street and I moved in the direction of the parking ramp.

I don't remember if Rachel and I talked that same night or if we waited until the next day. When we did talk, I told her how much fun I had, how much I liked him, how happy I was that I'd made the effort, even if the idea initially made him uncomfortable. "Yeah, he had a good time, too," she said. "I was kind of surprised."

"It was important for me," I said. "I don't know how long I'll be around, and I don't feel like I have to 'approve' or 'approve of' the person you're dating. But I just wanted to know him a bit better and to feel like regardless of whether you stay together or not, he's a good person and your being with him, for however long you're with him, has value and meaning for your life." I laughed. "From my perspective, of course. It's all about me."

Rachel laughed. "I think I get it. I don't want to focus on your future. But I get it. And I'm glad you guys worked it out."

When I drove from Ann Arbor back to East Lansing that night, I thought of Pastor Sara's discussion of how we sometimes held two stories in tension. Two, maybe more. I knew in some ways my life had been a series of moments in which I balanced tensions, feeling inadequate and ill-equipped to handle that balancing act. But I knew how to mourn. And I knew how to feel joy. And maybe knowing how to do both of those things gave me a head start on the balancing.

Death Bed

I could still smell the oil paint. It wasn't as strong as those first days in August when Connor probably had to incorporate the smell into his dreams because of its ubiquity, but it was still there, clinging to the air, especially on those humid days on which everything clung. Paint-by-number sets. I couldn't believe I'd forgotten about them. I'd completed so many throughout my childhood. I loved coloring in the numbers. Pretending I was an artist. Using linseed oil to clean my brushes. What a serious girl I was. Cats. I painted a lot of cats. And horses.

Outside, the leaves were falling from the tree by the road. I needed to figure out what kind of tree that was. I think even if we had the money, we couldn't have the driveway repaved this late in a year when the leaves were falling so fast. The black walnuts, too. The leaves made a drift-twirl pattern. Drift. Twirl. Yellow butterflies caught by gravity, always moving down.

Sanding and painting the single bed stand was my summer accomplishment. The one from my room on Sunderland, the street in Waterford on which I grew up. The room I felt guilty about because my sisters didn't have one; they shared a large area in the basement. It was the same single bed stand I sanded and painted when Rachel grew enough to move into a big girl bed, so that it became her bed stand for so many years in her childhood and then again in college those last two years. Plain, probably cheap, wood. We inherited it from the Galbraith family when they moved back to Texas, back when I was in elementary school.

But after Rachel brought it back from college, we stored it in the basement. Water seeped into the cement walls, came up through the carpet, and damaged the cheap wood, but still I didn't throw it out. I took it to a man who did cheap furniture repair; he glued the layers of lamination back together. Then I sanded it. Painted it with primer. Learned how to use the electric sander, putting on a white dust mask to keep sawdust from my lungs, planing the wood like the men on the floors in the Caillebotte painting, sweeping my finger over the surfaces afterward to feel whether the surface was ready for new paint.

And then, finally, applying the twenty-year old paint, still good according to the women at the ACO hardware desk in Lansing, women who opened up the can and put in a paint stick, and said yes, the paint looks fine and would probably cover the surface, stirring with the stick as if mixing cake batter when the mixer was broken, six hundred strokes by hand. The paint would cover just fine, the women said, no need to buy more.

Then it was just me, back at home, dipping the new brush into the paint, only a half inch or so of white on the faint black hairs of the brush, and then layering paint onto the dry primer coat of white on the wood. Glossy, shiny and wet. Returning to catch drips where the wood hung over makeshift Xerox box sawhorses, makeshift because my father's beat-up sawhorses, inherited the year Connor was born, were too buried behind stuff in our garage to dig out.

We bought the new mattress on sale at the Sleep Store where it lay piled on a stack under a tent (intended to beguile the back-to-school Michigan State student), piled like the mattresses in the princess and the pea story. The mattress sported a padded top and rose so high with its box spring frame that when we finally put the freshly painted and cured-out bed stand together and placed the box spring and mattress on top, there were only a few inches of the freshly painted headboard visible from behind the tall mattresses.

The bed would hang out in Connor's room for a while, so he would have something to sleep on when he came home from college the same time as Rachel, but it was the bed I might want to die in, when the time for dying came around. I'd spruced it up. I was like Darl, making the coffin in front of Addie in *As I Lay Dying*, except I was the one dying, and I wanted to paint that old bed stand myself. Because it would be sort of like coming full circle.

Juglans Nigra
(Eastern Black Walnut)

In Cubing: A Writing Exercise from Cowan and Cowan,* circa University of Virginia Ed School Days, with a Preponderance of Associations and Digressions

Describe it. Look at the subject closely and describe what you see. Colors, shapes, sizes, and so forth.

Green and round, the walnut bore small black spots and fissures, with a slight pebbling of the surface. Light green, the color of new moss. A citrusy smell overpowered with its sweetness. Some unknown external pressure caused this walnut from the driveway to crack, and as I pulled at the jagged edge, more of the scent infused the air. I separated the outer covering to reveal a black sphere, encased almost entirely by a layer of gold. The surface of the walnut gave with pressure from my index finger; I could squeeze it like a grapefruit. I wasn't allowed to eat grapefruit while taking Tarceva, my cancer drug. Something about the citric acid interfered with the pill's properties. Unlike a violated grapefruit, which left only a film of stickiness on the fingers, the violated black walnut stained my fingers yellowish-brown.

Compare it. What is it similar to? What is it different from?

Before the description above existed, before this cubing exercise found its object, I discovered a comparison. Black walnut = tennis ball. Black walnuts dropped every autumn in my driveway and yard; no novelty there. But the other day I looked out at the driveway from an upstairs window and thought I saw a tennis ball, also not a novelty in our house-hold. My sons played tennis, and we'd resurrected their balls when we learned how much our dog Clover enjoyed fetching them with her innate retriever drive and chewing them with her strong oral fixation and need to exercise her jaw. Yet Clover was banished from the front yard and driveway due to the heavy traffic on our busy street.

When I went to investigate the object on the driveway, I realized that what looked like a circular, spongy yellow-green tennis ball was a large black walnut. The largest I'd ever seen. That comparison launched the cubing experience.

From an external visual inspection, the walnut and the tennis ball appeared similar. But I'd watched Clover destroy enough tennis balls with her teeth to know that the inside of the ball was hollow. After she chewed off the soft, fuzzy exterior, she ripped through the spherical material made of some sort of cork or foam. She gnawed it open, revealing empty air.

That citrus smell provoked the grapefruit comparison. But on the inside, the walnut didn't have the circular web or the spoked segments that a grapefruit or an orange had, yet the response of the exterior shell to the pressure of my hand transported me to the breakfast table of my childhood, eating with my father. Back then, as I squeezed a grapefruit half to release the juice, I allowed it to drip into the serving bowl beneath but also into the spoon I held over the bowl. The simple squeezing ritual enabled my younger self to gauge the accuracy of my aim.

Associate it. What does it make you think of? What comes into your mind? It can be similar things, or you can think of different things, different times, places, people. Just let your mind go and see what associations you have for this subject.

My brain had already leapt to association before I finished the comparison. In those early years, I always ate breakfast with my father. Perhaps my mother enjoyed her food at the counter; how could she sit down if she was making breakfast in shifts for her family? Standing over

254

the frying pan, she served as our breakfast slave. Did that realization somehow diminish my memory of eating breakfast with my father?

Eggs, father, spoon, grapefruit half. The painstaking attention my mother paid to the citrus half with the special serrated knife, curving around the circumference of pink flesh to pry grapefruit from the sides, and then entering each segment with the knife's blade, separating it from membrane walls erected between bits of flesh. All that effort to satisfy our taste buds.

I missed grapefruit.

The black of the walnut reminded me of ash from a charcoal fire. Grilling transformed briquettes into small obsidian cubes with graying edges. When walnuts opened, cracked under a car on the driveway, the black material escaped and clumped in dark patches on the asphalt, like flattened briquettes. Or tar. Or a newborn baby's stool – meconium. Chewed tobacco some stranger spat on the blacktopped surface of a parking lot, causing my father to teach me the meaning of "spittoon" and "cuspidor" so he could tell me a bar joke: *One man asks another fellow: How many doors are there in a bar?* Answer: *Three. The front door, the back door, and the cuspidor.*

But when the fellow later repeated the joke, he forgot the fancier word with "dor" at the end and said "spittoon" instead, rendering the joke senseless. Intended to be a joke about meanings and synonyms, cuspidor = spittoon, the riddle cast aspersions on the intellect of the fellow who retold the joke, forgetting the more sophisticated word for the vessel holding spat tobacco. I tried to dismiss any recollection of what ethnic group or nationality my father may have insulted with his relishing of the joke. I tried to dismiss also worries about my own waning intellect, neurons and brain cells polluted with toxic cancer-fighting drugs. How likely would I be to remember "cuspidor" instead of "spittoon?" Even in my earlier years, I rarely told jokes, didn't remember punch lines. I tried to focus on recalling that my father liked bar jokes, beer nuts, and bars in general. Bars in Pontiac, bars in Waterford, bars in Caro.

He inherited black walnut trees years ago at the house up in Caro, Michigan, where I first learned about black walnuts when they fell that season after he purchased the property on East Frank Street.

Analyze it. Tell how it's made. (You don't have to know; you can make it up.)

I possessed little memory of plant reproduction from my high school biology days, though I often told my children I loved biology. The word *cotyledon* came to mind, but I couldn't recall what it meant, couldn't recall a thing about how plants made babies. Yet I could trace origins. The black walnut came from the black walnut tree. A deciduous tree. A hardwood. The grayish bark of the tree was composed of vertical ridges and valleys. Botanists reported that in the fall, the female flowers ripened into fruits (or nuts) with a brownish-green husk and a brown nut. The husk produced a small, hard seed.

The seed was not really a nut, however, but a "drupe." The drupe orbs wore the green, springy, tennis-ball exterior. If you cracked that exterior open, a substance just beneath the surface surrounded an inner hull. Yet black walnuts had a reputation for being difficult to crack. People used car tires to crack those hulls, sometimes creating devices designed to separate nut from hull.

So many of the nuts littered our driveway now, on this day I discovered the large one. More piled up on the side of our lawn next to the O'Lien's house. I should pick them up and bag them. The guy who mowed our lawn, Paul, collected them for us one year. He knew someone who would pay for them, taking them off our hands, but only if we didn't want them.

Since they were green when they first dropped, you didn't realize why they were called black until you cracked them open. The first time Clover came in with the odd sweet-citrus smell and the yellow-brown and black streaked across her white fur, I worried she'd gained access to the Wolverine pipeline that traveled under the ground just south of our yard. But she'd rolled in cracked nuts, the black substance like the tannin in tea keeping patches of her cream-colored fur darkened until Christmas.

Plant biology explained the cycle that deciduous trees went through each year, especially in terms of how they dropped their leaves, yet the dropping of the walnuts became a more significant event largely because of their heft and the sound they made when they landed. Each year we heard them drop from our second-story bedroom window. A tree just above the line of our house bore branches extending out over our sunroom. The sunroom roof sloped down from our rear bedroom window. When the drupes dropped, they thwacked the roof with thunks and then rolled down the slant of the roof to fall into the back yard. Thunk, roll, drop. Thunk, roll, drop. Thunk, roll, drop. The pattern repeated itself during the fall, the timbre of thunks changing only when the drupes hit an intersection of shingles. This year's crop produced full-bodied thunks, the nuts themselves loud in size, like ten-pound babies that surprised petite mothers.

When I researched that process, I learned a technical term for the dropping: "abscission." As I tried to absorb the details of abscission, I saw other words with which I was familiar. Lignin. In elementary school, children learned that lignin helps leaves to drop. Another word appeared – "parenchyma" – one that threatened with its complexity. I associated it with cancer. In plants, parenchyma referred to the soft parts of plants – the leaves, the flowers or berries. In the world of cancer, parenchyma referred to the part of tissue found outside the circulatory system, and the purpose of that portion was to execute special functions of the tissue.

What I learned about cancer was much simpler than anything I absorbed in this black walnut, drupe-dropping process I investigated. Cells multiplied for unknown reasons; they often couldn't be stopped. I could study to discern how things worked, but after a time the words and meanings blurred, and the answer to my questions became a simple repetition of five syllables: *pro-lif-er-a-tion, pro-lif-er-a-tion, pro-lif-er-a-tion.*

Apply it. *Tell what you can do with it, how it can be used.*

Plant it as an ornamental tree in your park or garden. Dye your hair with the black substance. Bake some black walnuts into your nut bread or serve them with your fish or chicken. Build a bookshelf, a floor, a paddle, a gun, or a coffin with the dark rich hardwood.

Some people believed you could make a tincture with the hull of the black walnut to kill off intestinal parasites. Others asserted you could also take the tincture as a cancer cure. (The American Cancer Society doesn't validate this claim. I do not eat black walnuts for my cancer; I drink turmeric tea, and I take my daily oral targeted therapy. Tarceva. Generic name, erlotinib.) Create a three-dimensional pyramid by piling the walnuts atop one another in a corner of your back yard. Select another large walnut to bowl from ten feet away and crash the pyramid.

Sketch with them, as if they were fat stubs of charcoal or charcoal briquettes.

My father used charcoal briquettes and a refrigerator shelf to create the makeshift grill we used to barbecue in the summer during most of my childhood. The last time I ate steak with my dad, Tim and I picked up the meat and cooked it on a similar makeshift grill in the parking lot of his assisted living facility in Clarkston. One of us stayed outside with the steaks and the other one stayed inside to talk to my father. He loved rib-eyes.

Argue for or Against it. *Go ahead and take a stand. Use any kind of reasons you want to — rational, silly, or anywhere in between.*

I wanted to say, "Cut those trees down!" The drupes posed a nuisance, and they contained an insidious poison. These vagabond orbs radiated disappointment. When they were new and green and spongy, they were a novelty, but then they started to get underfoot, easy to trip over, black fissures in the green shell making them unsightly.

That one summer a few years ago, Tim tried to grow tomatoes, like he had when we lived in Virginia, and even though he planted four varieties, none flourished. As vines withered, his sadness expanded. I tried to understand what longing dwelled within him so deeply, what unful-filled desire he wanted to capture and satisfy with the beefsteak or the heirloom.

We'd tried to grow tomatoes on the balcony of our last apartment in Virginia, the apartment we left to move back to Michigan a short month after Rachel arrived. When he stood out on that balcony on the day we left, gazing at the Blue Ridge Mountains in the distance, small tears slipped down his face onto Rachel's head. Tears so quiet I couldn't hear them. Not like when he learned on the phone a few years earlier that his dad had died back in Michigan, when he fell to his knees in the hallway next to the living room, a loud, solitary mangled sob falling onto the carpet with him and the phone.

A few years after Tim's failed tomato yield here in Michigan, I read a John Schneider column in the *Lansing State Journal* about how black walnut trees produced something in the soil that became toxic to certain other plants, especially tomatoes, planted in close proximity. Juglone, it was called. Tim's tomatoes never had a chance.

My father wanted to cut the trees in Caro down. I don't know if he hated the drupes scattered on the two-rut dirt driveway, or if he knew about the toxicity that I learned about only years later. He inherited grape arbors when he bought the house, two of them in the back yard. For a few years, he made red wine with special devices and bottles he stored back in our Waterford basement. Perhaps the grapes didn't grow very well. Perhaps he lost interest or needed to juggle one less ball. He liked to try new ventures, and he'd successfully bought and sold a small house in the community a few years earlier, sprucing up the house, making improvements, and earning a nice profit. He yearned to work through that process again. Revitalize, restore. He aspired to be a flipper, long before reality television existed and popularized the concept and the trade.

But that house on 530 East Frank Street wiped him out. We kids didn't want to move to Caro for our high school years; we didn't want to live in a small, landlocked town in the thumb, even though the two-story house rose majestic to our younger, naïve eyes, larger by far than the one we lived in back in Waterford. We didn't want to relinquish our suburban home on a dirt road because despite its puny size, the house stood in the neighborhood we loved, with a lake just around the block and friends we'd known since birth.

And then there was the divorce. All the while he spent his hard-earned dollars pleading with the workmen to restore this house he loved at 530 East Frank up in Caro while he continued to work at General Motors in Pontiac. Before the fixes happened, he learned about the multiple sclerosis diagnosis and retired on disability, dying just a few years later. The house returned to the state in which he'd purchased it, save the layers of wallpaper we'd peeled from the walls. Replaced by layers of dust and grime, boxes of uninstalled faucets and light fixtures, and swollen window sashes that wouldn't let in the air.

My father had rejoiced when I'd married a handy man, one who could use a drill and saw, climb a ladder. A few weeks after I discovered the mammoth black walnut in the driveway, a soft rain began to pelt our house, and my husband, alerted that a thunderstorm would soon reach our area, carted the extension ladder to the back of the house. As the water drops grew, arriving faster, the wind picking up, spatters becoming slanted sheets, Tim tried to climb the sunroom roof to clean the eaves-troughs. Empty the debris from black walnut tree leaves.

The water trapped in the clogged eavestroughs spilled over the edges of the aluminum and seeped down the sides of the house, creeping into the basement where wet had already taken up residence along with acceptable levels of radon that probably didn't cause my cancer. I opened the back-screen door, stuck my head out into the rain, and called, "Don't be a fucking idiot." Even though he was trained as an adolescent to walk on roofs for his father's roofing business, he'd aged. No one should walk on a roof in the rain, especially if he is the father of three children whose mother is on disability with cancer and can't work.

The morning after the rain, I discovered a dead robin just outside of the window next to Clover's crate in the family room. I pulled some food handling gloves from a kitchen drawer, gloves I'd purchased to protect food from my Tarceva-split fingers in the winter, and went out in the yard to pick the bird up. I transferred the stiffening body to a bag I'd saved from the produce department, one with holes to let the baby Bartlett pears breathe, and then placed the bag on the other side of the yard, far from black walnut trees. Neither Clover nor the black walnut juglone could get to it. I left the top of the bag open on the off chance that the bird was not dead but stunned. Maybe she could extricate herself from the plastic and fly away.

*The text in which the Cubing Exercise appears is *Writing: A Brief Edition*, by Cowan and Cowan. Elizabeth Cowan is now Elizabeth Harper Neeld. Greg Cowan is deceased.

Football Saturday with Clover

Sometimes I likened my first physical movements each morning to the unclenching of a fist. Undertaken slowly and tentatively. In fact, I often discovered my fists clenched when I awoke, like the fists of aged nursing home patients whose bodies prepared to die by assuming the fetal position in their unconscious moments. I wondered if that meant I was closer to death.

When the phlebotomists drew blood every three months at Karmanos Cancer Institute before my CT scans and my visit with Dr. Gadgeel, they had me clench my fist and then unclench it after the first tube started filling with blood. I always unclenched slowly because that's the way I did it each morning, feeling life return to fingers, knuckles, thumbs, and joints.

But sitting in the phlebotomist's chair, I performed the fist unclenching action slowly also because I occasionally had odd *Monty Python and the Holy Grail* visions of unclenching my fist only to see blood spurting out of my veins, exploding and spattering into the technician's face just as the Black Knight's blood springs from his severed limbs when Arthur cuts them off in the movie. Blood spurting because of the sheer power of my rapid unclenching action.

Before I get too far afield here, I should just clarify that, Monty Python aside, the metaphor is pretty simple: fist equals body. My body, not just my fist, now needed unclenching each morning. And some mornings were worse than others. The lung cancer didn't cause a great deal of pain, wherever it was hiding in my body, but I usually struggled with the first breath of the morning because of the amount of air I took in and how it affected the scarring that developed after the original pleural and pericardial effusion surgery. In addition, the part-sclerotic-cancer

262

and part-arthritis spots in my lower spine and hips sometimes gave me trouble. Finally, fibromyalgia, which I might or might not have, provided a couple of achy days a month.

Thus, the body that unfurled itself that Saturday morning in October did not unfurl itself gracefully like a proud American flag or a bolt of satin or crepe. It groaned as it unfolded itself like a cheap, rusted aluminum card table hanging out in a basement corner might complain when pressed into service for an extended family dinner. The body stumbled down the stairs to make coffee and feed Clover. It crawled to the couch and burrowed under an afghan.

An hour later, after a flurry of kitchen activity, Tim and Nathaniel left for our church to park cars before the Michigan State football game. The Spartans were playing the Indiana Hoosiers. Our church was located just a short walk from Spartan Stadium and the Breslin Center, where the Men and Women Spartans played basketball, and because of the prime location, one of our reliable and lucrative fundraisers involved parking cars for Michigan State football and basketball games. The funds supported youth and campus ministry programs. After Tim and Nathaniel finished a two-hour parking stint, they would head to the game, using Tim's mom's tickets. Clover and I would watch the game together, she from the floor, I from the couch.

If I were truthful, I would admit that I felt abandoned. For years, Tim had been able to use some of his mother's season football tickets, inherited from his father, who'd gone to Michigan State on the G.I. bill back in the 50's. I was invited to go in the early days, but as our boys got older, attending football games became the guy thing in the family to do. Which meant that I spent a lot of autumn Saturdays on my own. Tickets were not affordable for the whole family. I'd spent time with Tim during that week – we'd taken a rare mid-week day to visit the Sandhill Cranes on the west side of the state; really I had nothing to complain about, but my aches and pains made me grouchy.

I drank several more cups of coffee and practiced using my muscles in a sedentary sort of way on the couch. But as game time approached,

I realized that I should throw the ball to Clover, to work off some of her energy. Throwing and retrieving the ball were our complementary daily physical tasks, a ritual we performed since I'd learned how to use the Chuckit! Ball Launcher. I secured the perimeter, making sure the three warped and misshapen gates to our back yard were closed. I grabbed the Chuckit! and two specially designed orange fluorescent balls.

I opened the back door and let her fly. Clover was allowed to be off her tie-down in the back yard only when we played ball. Smart and athletic, she could not be trusted to stay inside her boundaries if left unattended.

I had devised a system for our daily ritual, which I'd tried to teach to the men in the family now that Rachel lived in Philly. Thirty balls. At some point, Clover might decide to take a rest, flopping down onto the grass and panting with her enormous tongue, but if I kept sending the two orange balls to the back of the lot, she enjoyed a rigorous, extensive romp, leading to even louder and more saliva-producing panting.

As I stood there, just by the back porch, I began to enjoy the late October day, the marginally warm yet crisp autumn temperature, the sounds of Clover's panting and the low-flying, banner-waving planes circling in the sky near Spartan Stadium. I might have aching muscles and groaning bones, but I was doing a good deed for my dog. She kept her focus on the ball, watching my body intently as I reached out my Chuckit! device after she deposited the ball at my feet and locked the ball into the scooping device to prepare it for another toss. She danced in anticipation on the layer of leaves that covered the grass, her paws crunching against the reds and browns and oranges. I launched the ball and watched her run. In the maple next to me squirrels chittered above, one racing to the far end of the branch, almost teetering due to the thin diameter of the twig, turning back to mock, it seemed, the other squirrel that waited closer to the trunk where the branches were safer, thicker.

The squirrel closest to the trunk scurried back down to ground level and darted to the next tree. Clover had just deposited the umpteenth ball at my feet, and as she panted, she turned her head to watch the squirrel.

Manic, it circled the base of the tree and then scrambled across the yard, scaling the split-rail fence reinforced with chain link.

Clover bolted. Off leash, she couldn't contain her excitement, and she raced away from the bottom of the rise where I stood, that same rise I'd fallen and sprained my ankle on just a few weeks after Clover had joined our family.

She had already reached the side fence, behind which the squirrel had halted in the O'Lien's back yard, and she didn't even stop to think or assess her skills.

She sailed over the fence as if she were a gazelle meant to excel at leaping and flying.

She looked back at me, surprised at her landing.

"Clover!" I wailed. "Come!"

I wanted to sink down to the ground and cry, but with my bones aching like they were, I knew if I hit the ground I'd never get up again. "Clover!" I screeched.

My voice was too high, too panicked. Like our house, the O'Lien's house bordered Lake Lansing Road, a major east-west artery. But unlike our yard, the O'Lien's yard was not fenced in – the fence enclosed only our side of the back yard. Composed of a black webbing of chain link stapled on most sides to an existing, though rotting, split-rail barrier, the fence stood only three feet from the ground. As she'd grown over the first two years of her life, we'd realized that it might be too low for us to let her wander through the yard without a chaperone, especially given her height and the comparative height of the fence.

My worst fear had been realized. Clover had escaped.

She could run into traffic.

I wasn't strong or nimble enough to catch her.

To get her back, I needed to lower my voice. We'd practiced the "Come" calls in dog obedience class a few years earlier, though I hadn't reinforced her learning much in the interim. "Come!" I said, making my voice as low and as dirge-like as possible. "Come!" I growled.

But *how* would she come? I was the one who was enclosed now; she was free, on the other side of the fence. If I moved too forcefully toward her, she'd bolt even further, maybe around the house to the front of the O'Lien's yard, right next to the street. I stepped carefully toward the side gate next to the eavestrough. "Clover, come." I repeated.

Since the treats remained back in the house, I had nothing to offer her. I lifted the U that served as the loop closing the gate entrance and stepped into the side yard, the place where the black walnuts always fell between our yard and the O'Lien's. I felt as though I were tiptoeing, though in fact, she hadn't really taken her eyes off of me, torn as she was between the promise of that frolicking squirrel now active in some other part of the O'Lien's yard and her not very consistent or authoritative master. "Clover," I barked out. "Come!"

And then, emboldened, I marched the last three yards over to where she stood. I grabbed ahold of her collar. "Come," I said, more softly now, and when we made it into our enclosed back yard, I clanged the U of the gate back down, letting it ring into the autumn day, and escorted my dog back into the house.

I fell onto the couch and cried.

"Don't you understand what this means?" I wanted to tell her. "The end of freedom as you know it!" She had many masters, but over time, I'd become the most devoted. Yet I was clearly the weakest, the least able to handle her strength. I knew her leap to freedom meant that I could never leave her off leash in the back yard again.

I texted Rachel and told her that Clover had jumped the fence, and our lives were forever changed. I texted Tim and Nathaniel as well, but I knew the reception in the stadium would be tricky during a game; I didn't expect an answer. My dog was safe in the house, yet I felt overwhelmed with dread. In just over a week, I was leaving for a three-week trip to Georgia to do a writing residency at Hambidge Center for the Arts. I knew I could trust Tim to take care of Nathaniel and Nathaniel to take care of Tim. But I wondered how much attention either of them would pay to the dog. Would they remember to feed her? What if they left her outside overnight, forgetting her after letting her out for her final pee of the night? I couldn't control what happened to her when I was gone.

After a few minutes, I composed myself and went to get Clover her usual post-fetching bowl of water. I would spend the rest of the afternoon on the couch in front of the Michigan State-Indiana game, cursing my husband and Nathaniel for being away at a key moment in Clover's life, cursing them for not understanding how slow I was, how fast I would never be able to run to catch my dog and keep her safe.

In the months to come, Tim and the boys would occasionally take her outside and let her run around fetching balls without wearing a leash or a tether. When I returned from Hambidge, I created a new ball-tossing system for myself to use that involved clipping her to the tie-off and throwing the balls toward the back of the house, on the deck, where her long tie-off tether would allow her to reach. The aluminum siding would now routinely sustain dents and circular dirt marks made by errant balls. Clover adapted rather quickly, learning just how far she could run in any direction before her leash would tug at her neck. Yet I hated that I had to keep her tethered as she chased her balls.

On that afternoon, as the fall weather seeped into the house, and the sounds of football roared from the screen in front of us, Clover remained next to the couch, within hand's reach, docile, even meek. Captive.

Hooking

Green courts with red rectangles. A darkening sky. Crickets. The mesh of the fence making shadow squares on the players' white tennis shorts.

Lights came on in the distance. Light from the right, from The Big House, University of Michigan's football stadium, even though the spectators were long gone. I sat on a small ticking blanket I used for tennis matches, viewing from ground level, not the best place for observing net shots or strokes, but my back was tired of sitting in the deep bucket of the camp chair.

We were at Pioneer High School in Ann Arbor, watching a high school tennis tournament. I was talking to Judy, Grant's mom, about parenting. I turned to finish telling her about how I sometimes looked to not-so-brilliant-but-still-meaningful movies for wisdom and how I frequently thought of Sandra Bullock's earnest face in the movie *Two Weeks' Notice* as she explained to Hugh Grant where she found her moral compass. Whether it was good or bad, she said, her mother's voice was the voice she heard in her head, telling her to do better. Dana Ivey played Bullock's mother, and she scared me with her frank stares and pummeling verbal challenges; I guessed the Hugh Grant character was frightened by her as well.

The question, I explained to Judy, was two-fold: did I want my children to hear my voice in their heads as a source of moral guidance, and if so, how similar to or different from Dana Ivey's voice did I hope my voice would sound?

In front of me, activity intensified. In my distracted state, I'd missed comprehending that Nathaniel and his partner had just lost the second set after winning the first. Because the tournament had started late due to rain, there were no third sets, just a ten-point tie break. I held up my fingers and started the count. I had to count tie breaks on my fingers because I got too excited and couldn't hold the game score in my head as I watched. My son and his partner were always on my dominant hand, the right one. My thumbs came out first, one on each hand, and then an index finger. And then we were up by two, and even though I was sitting close to the ground and couldn't really see the lines and make a guess about whether the balls were in or out, I heard the players call the scores each time they served. I'd watched hours of the U.S. Open on television during previous weeks, studying the player challenges shown to T.V. viewers, where the blue court background showed the white lines of the court, and I could see how the shadow fell above, on, or below the line, the rule always being that it was out only if it was cleanly beyond the line, not touching it, the dark shadow clearly separate from the white of the line.

At some point my fingers uncurled from their awkward, half-clenched, half-extended position, and we were even at 5-all, each team 5 points from a match win at 10 points. Whoever got to 10 first got the win. Earlier in the day, during another tie break, a parent thought I was holding my hands in some sort of prayer. I bit my tongue so I didn't say, "No, I don't believe in a god who picks winners and losers; the boys must win this match on their own." I knew to keep snarky thoughts about prayer to myself. Most of the tennis moms on my son's team had generous hearts.

Points mounted, and now both of my hands were at four fingers stretched again, which meant we were 9-all, and the next point won. I tried to focus on the game, though the light was fading from the sky, and I had difficulty seeing between the links of the fence and the coach from the other team, who decided to stand in front of me, sometimes erect and sometimes in a crouch. Judy, who coached tennis herself, whispered, "Why does she have to stand right there in front of us?" and I whispered something back about maybe she thought it was okay to block our view because she was the coach and more important than we were, although I think she simply didn't notice us.

And then the serve was out, a double-fault by a player on the other team, and our players around the court began to make the sounds of jubilance and victory, because it was, after all, the last match of the day, and Nathaniel and his partner had just won it.

But the coach in front of us said "No! Our point! He moved during the serve!" as she gestured to my son's partner. "Our point!"

And one of our volunteer coaches who has spent his life watching and playing tennis began speaking to her in a voice almost robotic, not unlike that of a police officer. *Step away from the fence. Do not talk to the players. Talk to the tournament director.*

The other team's coach began to argue with him, and our coach barked to the court, "Keep playing." I didn't know if he said it aloud, but the suggestion was there: Ignore her.

But her outrage was lost in the wave that crested next. "Cheater!" A Catholic Central player on the sideline yelled out. "Yeah," another player said. They were standing just feet away from me, calling onto the court where my son stood with his partner. "Cheaters!"

The word reverberated as if it were a score announcement made by one of the play-by-play sportscasters calling the game at the Big House across the street.

"Knock it off, you Catholic boys," Judy called over to them.

But the match was over, the last point replayed, and after shaking hands in a rather amicable way given the intensity of the onlookers' reactions, both teams surge off of the courts to join their teammates moving to the reporting desk almost a football field away where the points would be tallied and winners determined for the days' matches. I heard a Catholic Central player as he walked toward the separate throngs, "Three times they called it out…." I was aghast to realize that they had, all during this tie-breaker, been tallying up wrongs. Their coach's utterance was not something that occurred spontaneously in the moment but instead resulted from the accretion of perceived injustices.

As they trailed behind the others, I remained on the grass. "Both teams played a good match," I said to the last team members from the opposing team as they walked away, emphasizing the word "both." It was the only thing I could think to say.

And then I was alone on the grass, staring at the courts while the voices of four tennis teams wafted back at me.

Hooking in tennis occurs when a player demonstrates a repeated pattern of consistently calling a ball in or out to his own advantage. It is difficult to prove, because the game of tennis is so often regulated by the players themselves and relies on players' judgments and honesty in reporting what they believe they see about where a ball falls with respect to the lines on the court. My son's partner was accused by the other coach not of hooking but of moving into the service box before the ball had been put in motion. Yet the muttering of the players watching the match hinted at a pattern of hooking, making me think that the coach's outrage was focused not on the movement of my son's partner on that particular serve but on a pattern she was watching throughout the match.

I always maintained that I believed in the good side of people and therefore didn't want to believe that players routinely lied about whether the ball was in or out. I did not claim to have the best tennis eye, but I wondered who did in the world of high school tennis. For me, everything came back to the Heisenberg uncertainty principle, and I didn't know if one could really see the truth – wasn't one's vision always colored or altered by some other distraction? The fading light. A call from another court. The honk of a horn across the street.

Cheater. A pronouncement. A judgment. I thought of Oscar Wilde and the slander/libel laws at the turn of the century. My son was almost seventeen, with 20/20 vision, an earnest, ethical sort, yet I knew he would not be able to tell me for sure if his partner had moved. Or had hooked. "Who could say for sure," he would tell me later, "unless someone video-taped the match and played it back." He supported his partner, and that was a trait I admired.

Perhaps I should enter the moral outrage, take sides, and march righteously over to the awards ceremony. But the dusk was settling, the air so sweet with the fading light, and building floodlights illuminated the blue M's on yellow flags hoisted on a few vehicles still parked nearby in the high school parking lot. The crickets talked louder, and red and green court markings made a grid in front of my eyes. I fell back on the grass and looked at the sky.

Appointment with Gadgeel
(October 2, 2015)

I don't remember the details of what preceded the appointment with Gadgeel. We must have been near the tail end of tennis season. Nathaniel's team hoped to make it to the State tournament for our division, and each match drove the team more pointedly in that direction. I was preparing to travel to Georgia for my three-week writing residency, antsy about leaving home during Nate's school year but needing time to work on my writing as well as time to be alone and process my thoughts. Fall always brought complexities, largely because for so many years it heralded the start of the school year for my children and the start of the academic year for me when I taught or advised. This fall represented the second year that I wouldn't be returning to Oakland to teach. The feelings that resulted from acknowledging this fact were mostly those of relief, but I was sad, too, about the loss of that connection to young writers. Janine Novenske Smith, our church choir director, had approached me in the summer with the request that I consider rejoining the choir. Mrs. Smith, as I usually thought of her, had directed Rachel in the church's youth choir from kindergarten through high school; she had been Rachel's director before she'd ever been mine. I'd been in the choir on and off through the last few years, joining and then dropping out when the stress of grading papers kept me from Thursday night practices and Sunday morning singing.

Those practices now served as an incentive, providing me with two fixed events to go out for each week, especially once the tennis season was over – the Thursday practice and the Sunday morning 10:45 service. I loved the people in the choir; they'd come to carol for me and my family that first Christmas, just weeks after I was diagnosed, days after I'd begun my Tarceva regimen. My friend Beth had joined when her daughter went away to college, as we'd discussed and planned when the kids were younger, but she stayed with it. I couldn't.

In addition to providing a community, choir gave me a twice-a-week opportunity to monitor my breathing capabilities. One of the early clues I might have had about my lung cancer in the spring of 2012, nearly six months before I was diagnosed, had I paid attention to it, was my increasing inability to hold a note any longer than six beats at the end of a phrase. Singing a whole phrase was harder; I had to learn to find the oddest place to fit in a breath, avoiding the obvious breaks in a song for which Janine wanted us to keep the line going without a breath. I was surreptitious – in theory, anyway. And I'd actually told her when I rejoined the choir that breathing would be one of my shortcomings. She encouraged me anyway.

Our church was celebrating its 75th anniversary from Fall of 2015 to Fall of 2016, so we had a year full of extra events, one of them a major celebration service with special music and an expanded choir including alumni. Joan, one of the choir's former altos, returned from her new home in the upper part of Michigan's lower peninsula to sing with us. She'd been in the choir for years – I was a relative newbie compared to her, but we'd known each other from our work at LCC. When I first began teaching at the college, Joan's daughter Karen was the key administrative assistant for the Writing Program in which I taught. She left the school long before I did, but I saw her in church occasionally and I knew how she was doing through Joan.

A few years earlier, Karen had died suddenly from an undiagnosed heart issue. Joan was thus no stranger to heartache, but she'd weathered it well, retained the optimism which had carried her through years of running a counseling department at a community college, and she seemed particularly sensitive to life-and-death issues as a result.

She asked me how I was doing health-wise. I gave her my standard truthful but minimalist answer: the last scans I'd had were good; I was still taking my drug Tarceva. Joan said, "It must feel so good to be on this side of things, further away from the event." She made this statement just as we were being called to attention – Janine was at the front of the room in front of the music stand.

No, I thought to myself. It didn't feel good. It felt like time was running out.

The conversation with Joan returned to me several times in the following days, and it was at the forefront of my brain when I arrived at Karmanos in Farmington Hills for my quarterly appointment. I completed my usual routine. Drank the special contrast water. Offered an arm to the lab person so he could suck out my blood. Waited in the lobby for Steve and Donna to make sure my labs were okay. Followed them back to the CT area and held my breath and breathed when the recorded voice told me to. Went back to the lobby and tried to distract myself from guessing about the results. Waited for the summons to the examining rooms, where I would await Kimberly and Dr. Gadgeel.

Gadgeel told me first, as he always did, that the scans looked good. Then he told me that he knew I liked to be a realist, and he appreciated that I had designated an expiration date for myself – December of 2017. That was my five-year mark. I thought I would be insane to hope for much longer than that, so to keep from being disappointed, I'd established an expiration date. The date gave me most of the things I wanted. Seeing Connor graduate from college. Seeing Nathaniel graduate from high school. No grandchildren, but life wasn't perfect.

Gadgeel appreciated my realism, but he wanted me to try. To hope for longer. He wanted me to know that although he could promise me nothing, he didn't view me in the same way that he viewed his other terminal patients. "I don't see you as terminal, like they are." He told me that I was one of the few cancer patients he knew who had no interventions for their cancer other than Tarceva. No chemo. No radiation. I thought to myself that perhaps my pericardial and pleural effusion surgery didn't strike him as an intervention because it was pre-diagnosis, but it certainly registered with me. Since it had taken place before I met him, it was perhaps another era's issue. With each visit and each set of scans, I became stronger and the prognosis became better – even though the cancer was still inside of me, somewhere, my time on the drug counted as some sort of strengthening regimen. A few months later he would tell me he'd heard about a patient from the original study who was still living on Tarceva after twelve years.

He was asking me now to make a shift in my perception of the future. Whether that shift was subtle or seismic, I didn't know. He'd had one patient who'd just waited to die. He didn't want me to do that. "I want you to live your life," he said.

"Okay," I said. "I'll try." I didn't want to be simplistic, or cliché, for that matter, but I thought immediately of the glass half-full/glass half-empty conundrum. When I'd talked to Joan in those few minutes at choir rehearsal, she speculated that I was already living in the glass half-full world. She speculated that I would, like many cancer patients, view each year passing as a flimsy guarantee that my cancer was in remission. But I was stage IV. My cancer had already metastasized to some bones, and even though I was happy that it wasn't in my liver or my brain or any other part of my body, I was still stage IV, which meant I could never be in remission. My cancer was controlled, but it was still there. Hiding.

Yet my doctor wanted me to hope. I'd tried to hope. I'd asked for a section of writing again at Oakland University, against Tim's reservations and his point that the commute for one section of writing, especially a commute in an aging, minimally coddled car, wasn't worth the small amount of income I would make. Also against my psychologist's assertion that I needed to continue to be kind to myself, my brain and my body, and keep alleviating the dangerous stress that often produced dark depression for me, regardless of my cancer's status. I'd also hoped by purchasing a few more items of clothing, some bright things to make me feel better about my appearance. Since the diagnosis, my general practice had

276

been to limit my expenditures on any personal items that might outlive me.

Hoping was complicated. I'd gone to France with my family at the end of 2014, incurring costs that were not in our family budget, knowing I would likely die before the 2020 deadline of my life insurance policy. Hoping meant acknowledging that my family wouldn't get that $100,000 if I lived through the year 2020. It was increasingly unlikely I'd bring in money to justify my existence. I wanted to be worth something monetarily for my family.

I needed a hearing aid. Yet I couldn't imagine myself going to the appointment and pulling out my credit card at the end to pay for the assistive device. It was crazy to purchase a hearing aid when you could keel over any day. And arthritis had crept into my knees and attacked my back. X-rays revealed that I had arthritis in my spine; CT scans revealed I had healing metastases there as well. Which was which? Did the two conditions just commingle there in the open spaces between my vertebrae and my disks?

What would happen, I thought, if I allowed myself to hope and began making plans for my future, spending money on my ailments, and then the bomb dropped, faster than anyone expected, and the cancer reared its head with a maniacal evil creature laugh? I fell so hard when I fell. I'd experienced so many disappointments in my life. I didn't want hope to raise me up to some platform that I would be destined to fall off of not too much later.

"We all fall," Pam, the mom of one of Nathaniel's close friends, told me. Yet why did I sometimes believe that I could prevent myself from falling or soften the blow somehow, coat the cement floor or the jagged cliff with soft fibers?

Could I embrace a glass half-full philosophy toward my cancer?

I would try.

Jean's Trail

I planned to catch the trail just up the road from my cabin, Cove Cottage, where I would head up the narrow ramp-like stretch of gravel and grass leading to Stanton's Trail. I was a writing resident at Hambidge Center for the Creative Arts and Sciences in Rabun Gap, Georgia, just on the border of North Carolina. I had three weeks to work on my parenting-with-cancer memoir before I headed home for Thanksgiving. The detailed map of trails Hambidge provided their guests seduced me into believing that the trek would be easy. For the first time in days, the sun shimmered onto the foliage surrounding my cottage. Rain had pelted softly against the fiberglass skylight each of the last few nights, and when I looked out the window each morning, spoonfuls of water had collected in leaf bowls. Back in Michigan, the weather had already begun its winter dance, so I wanted to enjoy the warmer temperatures here while I wrote.

Upon reaching the beginning of the trail, my body and I recognized the slight incline. I loved trails but did not consider myself a true hiker because I didn't care for inclines. I wasn't fit, and uphill work reinforced that fact. I had walked only 50 yards, yet already the huffs of breath I made aloud drowned out the shush of my feet against the leaves, the volume increasing with each step. When doctors listened to my lungs, they wanted me to exhale loud, deep breaths when they placed the stethoscope on my back.

I breathed out now. I stopped. It was okay to rest. It was okay to breathe loudly. *No one can hear you*, I told myself. I wore my orange vest, recommended in my housing information, because there could be a hunter shooting from a car on one of the roads, even though doing so was unlawful. I carried my cabin key, with its cow bell key chain, designed to startle bears. My accoutrements suggested that I might, in fact, cross paths with someone or something, but I convinced myself that my awkward gasps and huffs would go unheeded.

The map said Stanton's Trail went left, while Anselm's Trail went right. I wanted Stanton's because the map said later it connected to the old logging road and then to Jean's Trail, leading to Patterson Creek. I missed Jean's Trail the other day – walked right by it. I wanted to see the waterfalls on Jean's Trail close up.

The trails were clearly marked, the map said. The light blue rectangle in the key on the right side of the map told me light blue meant Anselm's Trail. On a nearby tree, a small sign with a light blue mark matched the map. I veered left. This spot offered a bit of plateau, affording me the chance to stabilize my breathing.

It was not just the noise of breathing that bothered me. My chest burned. My lungs, I guessed. Because I was out of shape. Or because the cancer was progressing?

We played cards sometimes, my mother and I, during my childhood asthma attacks in the middle of the night. After I woke from a dream – always a detailed dream urging me to wake, a ruse designed by my brain to propel my body into a sitting position so that I could breathe in the real, non-dream world – I would creep past the bathroom door, slightly ajar with light spilling out onto the kitchen linoleum, the light kept on mostly for my benefit. I went through the living room and to my parents' bedroom door, also ajar. *Mom,* I would whisper. *Mom.*

That's all I needed to say. She rose, arching her shoulders to waken her body, and came to the living room, where I waited for her. Turned on the light. And stayed up the rest of the night to watch me breathe.

Watching me breathe meant making decisions about whether to call the doctor in the middle of the night or take me into his office in the morning. She watched the skin covering the trachea at my throat. With bad attacks, the skin would grow tauter at my trachea as I sucked for air on the inhale breath. Sometimes I put my hands on my head, fingers clasped together because latching them and pressing down on my head created more energy to suck in the next breath. As I grew older, I avoided placing my hands on my head, afraid to tip my mother off about how bad the attack was. But if I forgot to hide my distress, or if she saw other signs, she would call Dr. O'Neill from our phone on the kitchen wall. First, she apologized, and then she answered his questions, listening to suggestions he offered based on what she told him we had in the cupboard. Purple and golden liquid medicines sat on the top shelf, along with an envelope or two, one with Pen-G tablets, the other with Prednisone. Years later, Marax tablets would replace the liquid. Then theophylline tablets, theophylline enemas.

For a long and harrowing attack, she woke my father to drive me out into the night air, which we thought helped with the breathing. If he drove me into Pontiac, we meandered through the neighborhoods bordering the hospitals, looping repeatedly down certain streets, our leisurely pace a sham, because really, he remained close to those hospital entrances in case my breathing worsened, propelling us both into the light and warmth of the busy Emergency Departments for an injection of adrenaline, Celestone, Depo-Medrol, Susphrine, the same injection I would receive if I could hold on until we reached the doctor's office the next day.

Sometimes watching me meant making honey, lemon, and whiskey toddies, or, if we had no whiskey, just honey and lemon, so the hot liquid could break up the phlegm in my chest.

But often, as I sipped on my honey and lemon, my mother rubbed my back and shoulders, which were always hunched down with the effort of breathing. Or pounded between my shoulder blades, another strategy to break up the phlegm. If the breathing started to ease, sometimes on its own or sometimes because I'd had some of the medicine from the cupboard, eased enough so that the rattling and wheezing diminished, then she would pull out the cards, because she still needed to watch; neither one of us could rest yet. We would play two-handed Euchre. Or double solitaire.

I continued on Stanton's Trail, heading south. For much of the walk, I'd followed a narrow trail through the forest, but now, as the trees began to open around me, I anticipated the old logging road, which would appear shortly, another left fork ahead.

A loud crackle sounded from the underbrush across the shallow ravine, and I turned in a circle, expecting to see a bear, raising my cottage key chain cow bell. Instead, I saw a tall, thin tree a couple hundred yards away tilt and then fall, landing with a low, raspy crash and the ruffle of dried leaves. I had never seen a tree fall in the middle of the woods. I thought about the old sound riddle; if a tree falls in the forest and there's no one around to hear it, does it make a sound? But *you* were here, my brain reminded me. *You* listened. *You* heard.

A wimpy, neophyte hiker, I was afraid of confronting a snake, or a bear, or a character from James Dickey's *Deliverance* on the trail, yet my exuberance trumped my novice hiker status. I took such pleasure in hearing the wind flick at the edges of the dead leaves, lifting them, allowing them to scrape against fallen trunks. As a silent, grateful observer, I was thankful for both silence and sound. For the proof of existence, with all of its existential possibilities.

I don't know how my mother's level of anxiety fluctuated when she watched me breathe through the night, but she never smoked in the house during my asthma attacks. For intense attacks, ones for which she woke my father, she might take a break from watching me and go into the backyard with a cigarette to look at the sky. Pull the edges of her housecoat closer together, hold them with one fist, and hold the other hand with the cigarette away from her body, the smoke curling up into darkness, disappearing. After such a break, she returned with a smile or a tilt of her eyebrow, a question about whether the breathing had improved. She never fretted in front of me; she remained calm and positive.

The wide swath of the old logging road provided a chance to determine where I stood in relation to Patterson Gap Road, the road off which the Cove and Son House Studios were located, set apart from the larger Hambidge complex on the north side of Betty's Creek and Betty's Creek Road. When I walked and even before that, drove the length of Patterson Gap Road, I missed the entrance to Jean's Trail. As I studied the map, a map revised just two months earlier, I discerned that I should be able to walk across Patterson Gap Road from the logging road and head directly into Jean's Trail. No jags right or left. Yet when I reached the pavement and looked ahead, a dense area of brush greeted me. I refused to accept defeat, and I peered into the spaces between branches, searching for a marker. According to the map, Jean's Trail didn't have a color marker associated with it. But I saw, there in the brush, a bit of orange fluorescent tape.

That's where I picked up Jean's Trail.

I crossed the road and headed into the brush, and almost immediately, I could hear the water. Just those few feet in from the road. The pouring, rushing force of water, falling from a distance. I just stood and listened. And then, I took a few steps and I saw the white froth in movement, behind the bushes. I tried to work my iPhone camera to capture this first small waterfall for my family. It appeared that Jean's Trail headed back north, following both the road and the creek, eventually transporting me to Son House Studio, leaving me with just a brief jaunt over Patterson Gap Road and a large fallen log to my own cabin. I was certain that the short distance of the trail would consist of manageable ground to cover as I finished up my adventure.

Yet I didn't bargain on the slippery moisture of rain that still coated the ground, rocks, bushes, and trees next to the Patterson Creek. This part of the trail didn't get sun. And today, on a gray day, sodden ground, the rain's leftovers, and water from the creek made walking difficult. For the first hundred feet, the walk here was no different from the one earlier on Stanton's Trail. But the trail moved up sharply and then down. My tennis shoes, already slick on the bottom, couldn't gain purchase on the rocks that encroached now on the path.

How foolish to assume I could handle even this modest terrain. My Xgeva injection was supposed to strengthen my bones and keep them strong against invading metastatic cancer, yet one slip here could result in a break. I was angry with myself for not anticipating the weather's effects on the terrain.

I reached an impasse. I needed to jump over a large boulder in front of me. But I was no longer a jumper – I was a scooter. I must grab hold of something to brace myself, but I'd been warned against the poison ivy. When I heard those warnings, I wondered, "Why would anyone purposely step into poison ivy?" Now I understood. There was no *purposely* about it. On a trail, you reached to brace yourself, yet you couldn't always protect yourself from what your desperate hand touched when it reached.

"Up," I told myself. "You must reach up!" That was a partial solution at least, keeping my hands away from the ground cover. I must reach up.

And then, as I stood on Jean's Trail, fear gathering as I contemplated the water on the ground, rocks, tree stumps in front of me, I understood. I must become like Tarzan or Jane.

Because Phil Collins had started singing the *Tarzan* score in my head. I laughed out loud. I reached up, imagining myself swinging on branches through a jungle. Reach up! I chanted in rhythm to Phil Collins music, and I became Jane, reaching up for the vines, not for the poison ivy vines but for the branches that would keep me upright, swinging from one rocky nook of Jean's Trail to the next. Reaching up didn't solve everything, but doing so allowed me to navigate the slippery terrain, the water burbling next to me, disappearing and then bursting into view again.

When the path turned away from the creek and toward the Son House Studio, I was wet and grimy, my thin knit pants soaked with soil and tree fiber. But I hadn't touched poison ivy, and I hadn't broken a leg. I'd danced with Phil Collins in the Georgian rainforest.

As I crossed Patterson Gap Road, ready to stumble over that last fallen tree hurdle before I arrived at Cove Cottage, I heard myself breathing, the sound a bit quieter, but still audible.

During my senior year of high school, after a stressful week of classes, a swine flu shot, and a complicated A.P. Chemistry experiment, I suffered an asthma attack, the worst I'd had since childhood. My pediatrician instructed the hospital to admit me straight to a floor, so I bypassed Emergency, and some bureaucratic glitch on the floor delayed treatment, delayed the delivery of one of those injections I needed to open my airways and help me breathe. Until they finally delivered an injection to the floor, I struggled for each breath. My mother, summoned from work, sat next to my cranked-up hospital bed, the head raised to provide better breathing dynamics. I told her how tired I felt, how hard it was to keep gasping in each breath. She told me to keep going on, just a bit longer. Later, when I said to her, "I think you kept me alive," she told me that she'd never been so worried, that she'd thought for sure I was dying.

When she died, her breathing remained silent until near the end. Small puffs of sound emerged from her lips, like the snore puffs she made on those nights I'd returned from college and lay awake with the hums and creaks of my childhood home. In the hospital, as she lay dying, her brain stem already dead, I couldn't encourage her as she exhaled her last puffs. I just listened.

I extracted the cow bell key from my pocket and entered the cottage to the faint smell of wood smoke from fires the previous resident made. "Living is about the breathing," I might have said to my mother on one of those nights I clambered through an attack. We both knew that. But sometimes it helped to hear things aloud.

Hambidge

In the middle of the quiet, we heard clicking and scratching noises. We sat in the living room of Lucinda's Rockhouse, just next to the dining room where all of us residents ate dinner four nights a week. I was near the end of my second week of a writing residency at Hambidge Center for the Creative Arts and Sciences in Rabun Gap, Georgia, working on my memoir. The noises came from the register on the floor near the lamp. A mouse. A mouse poked its nose out of the register, its whiskers trembling. The woman potter and I laughed aloud, and the mouse ducked its head. Perhaps it smelled the food leftovers packed in my bag next to the chair, ready to go back to my cabin's refrigerator.

Earlier in the week, at dinner, when we talked about the spiders and mice that hung out in various places at Hambidge, I'd told the story of the first mouse of my adult life, how when I'd actually seen it creeping along the wall of the living room in the rented house I shared with my husband and infant daughter, I'd done the most predictable and cartoonish of all things – jumped on a chair and squealed, even though it was six o'clock in the morning and Tim was still asleep in the bedroom and Rachel in her crib.

The woman potter said then that there was a reason responses were stereotypical and fodder for comics. Because they were, in fact, so common and predictable.

I didn't tell the dinner table group about the sound journey that had originally led us to the knowledge of a mouse in our house. I woke several nights in a row hearing a metallic ringing from the bathroom. The sound would reverberate for sixty seconds and then stop, reminding me of kids drinking from real wine glasses for the first time, learning that they could wet an index fingers and glide it along the rim of a glass until it began to vibrate and sing.

The song coming from the bathroom was a solo. A metallic ringing.

I didn't share a lot of stories at the dinner table. As an introvert, I entered group conversation slowly, choosing to listen for a while first.

The potter was a dark-haired beauty, with long, thick hair and a charming space between her front teeth, like that model from my youth, Lauren Hutton. When I came to dinner my first night as a resident at Hambidge, she struck me as the warmest, most vibrant person in the room, asking everyone about his/her day, talking about her own discoveries with pottery that afternoon. She giggled. It was an adult giggle, but so fun and bubbly that it felt child-like. It was her first residency. She'd come from Brooklyn for an entire month.

She was getting ready to start her packing for home. Leaving Sunday morning, stopping in North Carolina. Then on to Brooklyn. The kilns were being opened the next day – first the ANAGAMA kiln in a big ceremony but then the smaller kiln in the Antinori Studio. We hadn't had the chance to share the customary conversations residents shared about work and hopes for the time at Hambidge. And now, with the dishwasher loaded and all of the leftovers divvied up or stored in the refrigerator, most of the residents had returned to their cabins. I remained at the Rockhouse for the WiFi. It was the only place my computer could get an Internet connection and my iPhone a few bars to text Tim and the kids. Though I loved my solitude in Cove Cottage, I wasn't ready yet to go back to my remote cabin for the night.

When she asked me if I wrote for a living, I didn't know what to say. I remember that I didn't want to sound bitter. I have only ever made $5 on my writing, I said. I didn't say that it was from not a whole piece of work but from the first paragraph of a story that Frederick Barthelme had paid for to run in an entire issue of first paragraphs for the *Mississippi Review*. I was largely unsuccessful in the traditional field of book publication, but I'd written my whole life. Published short stories, poems. Still, I told her, it was hard to identify myself as a writer since I'd never gotten that holy grail of book publication. I told her that my residency at Hambidge was my last-ditch effort to get writing out of my system. That I planned to retrain and develop another skill.

She told me I should still consider myself a writer, even if I never made any money. If that's what I did and who I was, I was a writer. "So what is your memoir about?" she asked. It was the innocent question I'd fielded unsuccessfully from others at dinner the first two nights. I'd kicked myself for not thinking through what I'd say. When I'd done my residency at the Vermont Studio Center, I'd just alluded to memoir and family and health, although I revealed a bit more in my reading. When I'd anticipated the work I'd accomplish at Hambidge, the peace and tranquility of the space I'd have and the access to nature, I'd forgotten that I should have a way of conveying a shorthand summary of my work in progress. But I hated talking about the cancer, and it was particularly awkward in large groups. And at dinner.

I told her about my stage IV lung cancer diagnosis and how I was approaching the three-year mark. How my oncologist had told me at my last appointment that he didn't view me as terminal in the same way that he viewed his other stage IV patients as terminal.

"So you might not die of cancer? It might be from something else?" she said. It had been my question, too, though I don't think I'd been as quick to frame it in concrete terms. "Exactly," I said. "What does that mean? He wants me to live my life and plan on living into the future. Maybe I'll die of cancer. But maybe I'll live longer, and someday I'll die of something else. So that's what I'm trying to do. Live my life. Plan on living into the future."

"Wow," she said. "I guess that's where our society is, though, these days. With the cancer, I mean. Where medicine is." She trailed off and sighed. Then she raised her face, her eyes glancing up quickly, and away again. "There are a lot of people here with heavy shit." I nodded. At dinner the night before one of the other artists had talked about caring for a friend with brain cancer, something I'd talked about with her privately on the way to Hambidge, en route from the Atlanta airport.

"And that other new visual artist has cancer, too, I found out last night," I said.

"And the chef's wife just died last month. Just last month."

"And that other resident is making the transition from living in Israel all those years to living in the States."

We were quiet. Even the mouse was quiet. The large cardboard cut-out of Mary Hambidge looked out the window in the corner.

I took a deep breath. "Do you have some heavy shit?" I asked. "You don't have to say if you do. I just wanted to ask."

"Yeah," she said. The room remained quiet.

She told me then that her boyfriend had committed suicide a few weeks before she'd come to Hambidge. He made furniture, and he loved her pottery. But he was feeling pretty sad. And then he killed himself. "So there's not much to say, right? People back in New York didn't know what to say to me. What is there to say?"

I told her I probably had a lot to say, too much, in fact, to say on the subject. I hesitated. I didn't even know her, but I felt I needed to say something.

I told her how sorry I was that he'd committed suicide. That I tried really, really hard not to judge people who committed suicide. That the only time I allowed myself to judge them, and it was only a small bit of judgment that I allowed myself – occurred when I saw the people they left behind, the people who didn't know how to heal from the hurt.

"I find it hard to judge them," I paused and took a deep breath. "Because I have wanted to take my life so many times. I haven't, obviously. I haven't even tried, and sometimes I hate myself for having opinions on suicide when I've never even tried. But I've wanted to so many times, and I've lived in that dark, dark world in which you're sure things will never get better and you'll never stop hating yourself.

"I don't know you," I told her. "I didn't know him. But I have to believe that whatever was going on in his head, it wasn't at all about you; it was about something he was dealing with. Some powerful emotions, and his brain chemistry got all mixed in with his thoughts and his pain.

But he didn't want to hurt you. He just couldn't live with the thoughts anymore. It hurt. It hurt him so much to live with the thoughts. He just wanted to escape from the pain."

"I thought everybody wanted to come to the party," she said. "I didn't realize that some people didn't want to be there. Why don't they want to be there?"

"I can't say for sure. Usually no matter how bad it gets in your head, doctors somewhere have told you not to give in, that it will get better. That it always gets better. And for me, it always does, somehow. But there are cycles, and sometimes it's harder than other times, and sometimes the meds don't work. If you hate yourself enough, you convince yourself that just putting an end to everything is your right." I stopped rambling. "For me, thinking about suicide is a way of having the ultimate control. Believing I can end my life gives me comfort. I know some people think that's sick, but I have to be honest and say that I find comfort in imagining that I have that ultimate control."

My voice was cracking a bit, but I made myself look at her face. "But I'm so sorry that you were in love with someone who needed that control."

I let the silence enter the room, and we sat with it for a while.

The mouse had left us alone. The pilot light in the wall heater remained vigilant to the temperature in the room. The woman potter wiped at the side of her face. "Your children," she said finally. "It would be better for them if you died of cancer than if you died from suicide."

I nodded. "Much better." I tried to remind myself of that, but it was hard. "I don't think I will, now. Things are better. It's getting a bit easier. Dying of cancer is helping me learn how to live with hope."

"Wow," she said. I didn't know if what I said made sense, but it was a bit of the truth.

We talked about her boyfriend's funeral and her lucky fortune at being able to escape to Hambidge to process things, her worries about returning home, wanting the comfort of familiarity but fearing the pain. She told me that I needed to work with clay, even if I thought I wasn't artistic enough. That it wasn't about the product; it was about what you felt with your hands when you molded the clay. I promised her that I would try.

Then we knew we had to go to bed; she had a busy day ahead of her with the kilns and packing up for her departure.

I saw my potter – yes, she is my potter, and she will be with me, like my children, for the rest of my days – the next afternoon at her studio. She showed me some of the pieces she'd pulled from the ANAGAMA kiln that morning, the beautiful gold flecks in some of the bowls she'd made. I rubbed my fingers against the fired surfaces to feel the color. She was exhausted and exhilarated. Ready to be on her way. We hugged, and I walked out of the small studio and across the porch, leaving her with a moment to breathe. Before she headed home.

Visionboard

In my photo of Barb from the Red Dress Exhibit, she wore a red and black dress, a swishy, tiered number, sleeves and bodice of red and white print, like a poster, and a black overlay, almost jumper-like, with smaller straps. She'd crossed her arms in front of her, creating a ledge. Glasses framed her eyes, and she smiled her trademark wide smile, generous, authentic. In the gaze of scrunch-eyed warmth, you could see the barest hint of recognition that yes, this shot was posed. Around her neck she wore a necklace of black ribbon, from which three red daisies hung.

The photo captured the opening reception for the exhibit at Katalyst Art Gallery in Old Town, the place where Lansing, Michigan, claimed its artistry. On the white wall behind her, gilded dragonflies hung in suspension, their wings angled in three-dimensional relief from the wall, as if they were live insects who stopped in for the event. A scattering of gift items created splashes of color in the displays behind her, a mixture of kitchen, art, and personal curiosity wares occupying casual spots for anyone who might come in to shop as the rest of us celebrated Barb's art. Silicone kitchen ware by Joseph Joseph – pasta scoopers, cutting boards, whisks.

Outside the gallery, snow piled up in the streets, so even though we women enjoyed the fig jelly and gluten-free crackers and cookies Barb prepared to create this environment of warm conviviality, we knew too well the cold from which we'd sought refuge, the swirling, heavy flakes that would cover our car windshields before we'd even had a chance to take in two pieces of art hung on the north wall of the gallery in a row of red-dressed wonder.

***

291

My son Connor has captured Barb in video, filmed during the day she took on the artist/teacher role, hosting Rachel, Connor, and me at her house for a Visionboard session. Barb lived in our old Lansing neighborhood, the neighborhood in which my two older children went to the same school, Cumberland Elementary, that Barb's son, Nick, attended. Since Barb and I lived at different ends of the neighborhood, we likely wouldn't have met if it weren't for the school and Barb's role as an involved parent in the Parent Teacher Association. I was an involved parent in the classroom and in the book fair realm, but I shied away from more organized participation. Though Barb and I met at Cumberland Elementary, on the northwest side of Lansing, we cemented our friendship on a bench at the Parkwood YMCA in Haslett, just east of East Lansing, sitting next to the large swimming pool in which Nick and Connor, our two sons, took swimming lessons.

Our family moved from Lansing when Rachel reached middle school age, to a district that offered more services and better extracurriculars. I always felt like a traitor for leaving our Lansing neighborhood behind. Barb and her family stayed in the ailing urban school district; we moved our family out. Although we acclimated to our new home and the new school district, our entire family remained convinced that our Lansing home had more character than the basic colonial we bought in East Lansing, situated on a busy street, a purchase we made because the housing listings offered few options when we searched in the more expensive market.

We'd come to Barb's house for the Visionboard experience for a variety of reasons. I'd always wanted to create one, having a vague idea that the experience clarified decision-making, something I needed help with as I charted two paths, one for living and one for dying. Connor's goals had to do with filming footage for his Senior Individualized Project (SIP) for college. His documentary addressed the concept of how young people determine their directions in life, and while he might benefit most from engaging in the Visionboard process himself, he would film the event. Rachel and I would create the Visionboards. Home for the week from

Philly, Rachel had agreed to be involved in this project that Connor, Barb, and I had concocted.

On Barb's dining room table, an array of supplies awaited us, ready to engage our playful senses. Card stock, markers, glue, piles of magazines, stickers, foam doo-hickeys. Connor set up his camera on the tripod, and Barb prepared herself to speak. The angle Connor chose worked well, because Barb was really speaking to us, but she looked at him, and the lens captured her articulate way of describing a creative process. I watched her face, but at the same time, I ripped pictures out of the magazine in front of me to use on my board.

"It's a process, and we're not worried about it being perfect," Barb said. Rachel and I nodded, pushing aside our perfectionistic selves, hers more artistically talented than mine.

"It's a projection tool, and you don't know what you're projecting until you trust how you feel. It's a way to access your intuition and trust your instinct."

When I closed my eyes, I heard the sound of paper. Barb's voice spoke the melody, but the ripping of paper provided a percussive, rhythmical beat. We ripped photos and words to post on our Visionboards. Connor became silent onlooker, focusing in on the artist.

"Who am I?" Barb said. Then she answered herself. "I'm a work in progress. Think: This is how I want my life to be. Pick a week, a month, a year. It's not just what you're putting down; it's also what you're thinking about and processing."

As a visual artist, Barb possessed skills that I didn't. The ability to draw. Show movement. Use color. Hold and use a brush. My parents thought I might have artistic tendencies as a kid – I was addicted to paint-by-number kits and went through a raft of craft projects each November to find something worthy to create for my aunts for Christmas. By the time I reached my middle school art class, however, it was clear that I had neither talent nor imagination for visual art. I was creative, but not in the area of representation. However, in my conversations with Barb over the years, I realized how alike our brains were, containing the flint for creative sparks but a capacity to analyze as well. We both questioned our creativity, reading it, watching it shape itself, but our analysis made us question things, seek understanding, categorize, discern. My conversations with Barb were not unlike the conversations I'd had with my mother.

***

My Visionboard spanned eighteen inches, landscape view. Barb encouraged us to staple together two sheets of square card stock if we wanted a more rectangular canvas. I stapled together green and white, as if pairing two unmatched socks, just to be different. She said she'd have everything, but we could bring something for the collage if we wanted.

I brought one of my mother's old bras. I'd told only a few people the story about my mother's bras, stored in a lingerie bag buried under some of my old sweaters in the closet. My mother loved perfume and kept her bras, washed as well as unwashed, in a lingerie bag in her dresser drawer, just underneath the dresser top where two or three of her perfumes stood. I took the bras when she died, with my sisters' permission, so I could smell them. I wanted to smell her and her perfumes, powerful elixirs of manufactured scent and body chemistry woven into the fabric of the cotton, polyester, and elastic. I wanted all of my senses to remember her.

On the Visionboard, in the lower right corner, I placed the swatch I'd cut from the bra – the rows of eyes that would match up with hooks, except that I only put the one side on the collage. And next to it the label: Playtex 18-hour. 40B, with the initials E.N. handwritten on the label, faint from so many washes. We labelled her clothes for the facility she went to following her heart attack, a place to be rehabilitated. But her body resisted the rehabilitation.

In addition to the bra swatch, my finished product had eight pictures, eight captions, and a list of nine Latin labels identifying the wildflowers in a photo. On the left I'd placed a photo of large, pinkish-purple flowers, the colors and textures a cross between the lilacs, rhododendrons, and bougainvillea I liked so much, though I might have chosen the photo as much for the word centered above the floral shot: "overachiever." Next to it, I'd placed the word "play" as if I'd immediately diagnosed a flaw and corrected it. Other words: "independent" and "mom."

On the top left, the clipped magazine art I'd selected was an illustration, not an actual photo. Children's legs hung over the edge of a pool, some of the legs extended into the aqua water, fronds of leaves framing the bottom of the illustration, as if this pool were set in some exotic spot in the tropics. Pale blue circles and darker blue swirls mixed with the aqua, suggesting bubbles or depths. Above it, the phrase "Settling In." Yet the phrase seemed to indicate the tenor of adulthood, so at odds with the illustration of childhood and uncertainty that those lower limbs sent into the water. The rich colors of the art stirred in me the recognition that perhaps I'd selected the picture because of Barb herself. It was a link between me and her – between the water I loved so much as an adolescent and the art of my friend.

In the upper center, a much smaller magazine photo rested. A young child sat on a white antiqued bench with a book in his lap. The sun came through the window behind him, bathing his hair with light, creating the sense of wonder and curiosity, highlighting the pursuit of knowledge, or maybe just a thirst for a good story.

What was missing was the lap that held the boy, the body attached to the lap, the gray grandmother hair, bent close to that other, darker, younger hair, the body attached to arms that helped to turn the pages.

This boy was independent, and maybe he didn't even notice the lap that wasn't there, the grandmother who wished to occupy that space, to feel the top of his soft hair brush against her chin, long child legs entangled with her own.

She wanted to read those books to him, smell that sweet child flesh. But she couldn't.

***

Years later, as Rachel approached her 28th birthday, she would say to me, "Do you remember what Barb said to me that day we did Visionboards? That she knew life didn't work the same for everyone, but she'd met a lot of young women who'd found that things come together when they're 28?" She would remind me of Barb's prophecy because she was using new words to describe herself – "happy" and "content."

**

Years later, I would absorb more of Barb's art in an exhibit at the Lansing Art Gallery.

Blue Lagoon. A shock of blue and white like a small mirage ignites the center of the painting, the color luminescent in an otherwise gray landscape of dark, cloudy, smoky, encaustic clouds. The blue resembles a smudge with a surrounding layer of white above and beneath the pink of light from a sun already set, just a hint of yellow to suggest fading rays. Did Barb make the blue so bright, so glowing, because it represents hope or because it is an Erin Brokovich body of water, beautiful in its poison?

Cathedral. Enclave. Created from the flame-shaped intersection of red shrubbery. Red the color of fall, almost magenta, the enclave itself a green-blue flame, the magenta and yellow strokes like two cornstalks bowing together before a dance, tops touching to create in the oval between them a tunneled enclave.

Old Man River. The blurred top third of the canvas demands a closer look. The geography of the bottom two thirds resembles that of a topographical map with textured ravines, craters of space, small holes and indentations the size of pebbles. In the center, the red line. The man? The river? The line starts and continues, dusty quiet path going somewhere.

**

Years later, I would watch my young brother-in-law die of acute liver failure during a surprise turn in his seeming rehabilitation from alcohol abuse, his final hospital bill for a mere two-day death dance paid in large part by a health insurance plan he'd finally enrolled in after friends hounded him.

Years later, I would take a year of classes at the community college where I used to teach and advise, pursuing a certificate in medical insurance billing and coding to secure part-time employment in my home for the purposes of helping my husband pay down our parent loan debt resulting from our children's college educations.

Years later, I would support my youngest son's efforts at campaigning for a progressive Muslim candidate for Governor of Michigan during a democratic primary, a candidate whose platform included universal health care.

Years later, I would learn that two of the women who shared my odd cancer mutation had experienced progression in their cancer, their miracle drugs failing them long before mine began to fail me.

***

During one of my rough periods of juggling that followed our family's move to East Lansing, after I took at full-time job at the community college, I spent a lunch date with Barb itemizing my inadequacies, my intense self-doubt. "The word 'rube' keeps repeating in my head," I told her. "I am a rube. I am a rube. Four syllables over and over again. I'd never even used that word, just saw it in print once or twice. But the definition I found is perfect. 'A country bumpkin.' That's what I feel like. A country bumpkin."

The next time I saw her, or maybe the next time we celebrated my birthday or Christmas, she brought me a gift. Something from her past. "It's just a ring I saw once and saved up for." She gazed at me and spoke emphatically. "You are not a rube. You are a ruby."

"A ruby," I said, looking at the ring, the red stone in the setting.

"A ruby," she repeated.

Tubs

As I pawed through the tubs in my basement, I thought about what kind of mother and housekeeper I'd been. Especially when Connor was a baby. I was a pretty good mother to Rachel, the first child, as evidence from the tubs indicates. It appeared I saved every mark she ever made on a piece of paper, along with many locks of hair. No teeth. They were upstairs in my underwear drawer.

I searched for Connor's masks. The ones he made circa preschool, kindergarten, and first grade, when we lived in our old house on Cumberland. The voice rebuked me: "You saved every single princess drawing Rachel ever drew, and you couldn't even save some of Connor's masks? Bad mom."

The voice was harsh as I searched, but it had easy access to me. I'd entered the basement on a gloomy day. Outside, the skies had darkened, and the wind gusted against the back windows. My soul felt dark as well, even though I often found a way to keep it brighter. I remembered clearly the stack of Rachel's princess drawings. At one point, nearly a hundred of them filled various boxes and folders. I probably went through them one day, trying to winnow the number down. Rachel was obsessed with princesses, like so many other things. Skinny princesses with long arms. Always wearing crowns.

Connor's mask phase was shorter than Rachel's princess phase, but equally intense. He was the child of action figures, Duplos, Legos, and masks. Usually we made the masks with construction paper, and he fashioned the eyeholes. Attaching them to his face and head was always tricky – yarn or rubber bands put too much tension on the paper, but we'd run out of cardboard backing early on, so we had to make do with just the paper. Sometimes the masks would fall apart. I wondered if they simply disintegrated.

I worried that I'd thrown them away. I was a packrat in so many ways, but as I yanked the clear tubs, the blue tubs, the black tubs, and the water-stained Xerox paper boxes off of the shelves, I couldn't find the masks. More artwork by Rachel. Nathaniel's baptismal certificate.

Connor needed the masks for his documentary class project, but he might use them later as well for his SIP. When he returned from his study abroad and decided he would change his major and pursue an English degree and media studies path instead of psychology, I told him that I wanted him to see himself as an artist. I reminded him that he drew striking pencil sketches when he was younger, and one of his high school teachers had even suggested A.P. Studio Art. But he'd sat next to a gifted classmate in one of the requisite beginning classes, and the comparisons he made between himself and his friend and the conclusions he came to discouraged him. Thomas's artwork was better than his in nearly every respect, he felt. If that was the case before he even left high school, why should he bother?

Like me, he sometimes didn't value his talents, and I wanted to find physical, tactile reminders of his artistic nature. I wanted to help him foster his sense of identity as an artist.

Yet I hated going into the basement tubs. Not only did they provide evidence of my oversights and omissions; they contain unfinished business. My past. My parents' pasts. My Aunt Aggie's past. Instead of finding Connor's masks, I found financial aid forms my mother filled out when my older sister and I were in college, along with a letter she wrote to Governor Milliken asking him how she was going to help pay for her children's college educations given recent cuts in college budgets.

Entering my life with my parents made me weepy and angry. Each time I touched the things from their former lives, I revisited how angry I was at their deaths, as well as the timing of them – so close together. And inevitably, I circled back to the struggles I had at the time, with Connor in my womb, travelling to hospitals, funeral homes, graveyards. How neglected he was.

His SIP project was about identity. The masks might be cliché, he said, but the story I told him about his childhood art pursuits had struck a chord. I told him how much I didn't remember from that time right after he was born and his first few years. The time when my grief was so overwhelming that I could barely move through the days. Our best shared memories came from the time after he turned two. The naps we took after his older sister entered school. How I would climb on the couch, and he would climb on top of me, his head resting on my shoulder, an afghan pulled up over my legs. He'd stopped taking naps in his crib much earlier than his sister had, but he could be lulled to sleep by the voice of Bob Ross, an artist making art on a television show, "The Joy of Painting," on WKAR, the public television station. We would drift off to sleep as we listened to the hushed world of color, line, and shading.

My inner voice told me now that I needed to clean up the basement before I died. It was too much paper to leave behind. My sister and I needed to attack the hoards again. But each box or bin or tub had an acuteness that was too powerful to accept in more than small doses. I had already been the child who travelled through my dead parents' homes with my sisters, tidying up their errant papers and throwing away their trash. The mess in my basement came in part from their messes, from my inability to spend time with my own past when tending to theirs.

The tubs were painful not only because of what they reminded me about my dead parents and my children; they also contained notebooks in which I wrote for years. Half-written dialogues. Flash fiction pieces I wrote with students. Drafts of novels and short story collections. Revisions. For much of my life, I'd viewed them as nothing, evidence of my failed life as a writer. The unpublished books. The unfulfilled promise.

But there was so much writing here. A lifetime of it, a progression through the years, sentences, stories, moments. I could reach my hand in any box and pull out some words. Many of which I'd forgotten about. Words that I strung together into sentences and paragraphs. Things that I made. Treasures I could leave behind, for others to discover. Like princesses. And masks.

Afterword

The events in this memoir took place from the time just before my cancer diagnosis in November of 2012 to the end of 2015, when I had lived for three years with my terminal diagnosis. Since that time, I've lived another three years, for which I'm profoundly grateful.

In the fall of 2017, my scans revealed some activity in my lungs, and in February of 2018, just days after we buried Tim's mom's ashes, I underwent stereotactic body radiation therapy (SBRT) at the University of Michigan Rogel Cancer Center in Ann Arbor.

Some would call it miraculous that I lived for five years in a state oncologists call "progression-free survival." I find words related to "miracle" to be borderline offensive at times, especially if the implication is that the miraculous event might have occurred as an act of God's will. As I've mentioned in this book, I refuse to believe in a God who picks winners and losers, and I can be rather curmudgeonly with my opinions on this subject.

I do think the human body is an amazing specimen, capable of many feats our human minds can't even comprehend. I believe, too, in science. I am, oddly enough, a fairly religious and spiritual person who believes that prayer is a powerful force that can bring energy to an individual who feels she is on the receiving end of someone's fervent thoughts and desires. Yet I believe that progression-free survival in my case was not a miracle but the result of a mixture of many factors: plain, dumb luck related to my cancer's genetic mutations, good decisions made by many medical professionals, my oncologist chief among them, and most of all, my husband's health insurance, which is paid for by his employer.

I am alive primarily because my husband has a job with a good health insurance plan that pays for my oral chemotherapy drug, Tarceva, and all the medical expenses that come with my diagnosis and the side effects of cancer. God does not pay for health insurance.

The effort I expended to complete college and graduate school, hold a series of jobs, pay off all of my student loans, and make ends meet had less of an impact on my long-term future than it might have, because at the moment that my cancer was diagnosed, I did not have a job providing me with the health insurance necessary to save my life. Fortunately, my husband did.

If depression hadn't made me feel worthless enough in my life prior to that point, my inability to procure my own health insurance or contribute to its procurement surely made up for it. I am alive today in large part because I married a man thirty some years ago. I feel compelled to note that for a brief time in our early marriage, he benefitted from my health insurance. But that was long ago. I haven't done much for him lately on the money or the health insurance front. I'll admit that I probably wouldn't focus on this fact as much if I'd been raised in a social class different from the working class one in which I grew up.

While I realize that there are other safety nets which might have kicked in had I needed health insurance, such as Medicaid or Medicare, depending on my situation, and while I admit that the pure luck factor affecting my cancer's mutation contributed to the possibility of extending my life this long, I am still chagrined to feel that I failed to support myself economically at the moment I most needed to do so.

When I left the status of progression-free survival some time between the fall of 2017 and February of 2018, I entered a state or status known as oligo-progression. I happened upon this description just days before my mother-in-law's death, just days before I underwent SBRT. I learned about it on my phone while travelling, having Googled lots of terms and concepts to understand what the procedures would be like. As a lover of word parts, I knew that the only word I'd encountered with that piece "oligo" was "oligarchy," and I asked Tim to remind me of its definition as a form of government. "Government by the few," he said. In cancer, oligo-progression refers to a limited progression of the cancer. In my case, the cancer decided to grow after five years, again in my lungs. Thus, my progression-free survival was limited to five years. But oncologists, specifically radiation oncologists, have learned that oligo-progressive cancer can often be addressed by SBRT, along with continued use of the key cancer-fighting oral targeted therapy, in my case, Tarceva.

I know about the terms "progression-free survival" and "oligo-progression" only because I spend time educating myself about my cancer by surfing PubMed, something I learned how to do a few years ago when I worked part-time (without health benefits) for a start-up company. My oncologist, whom I adore, did not share these terms with me, although he was more than willing to comment on them in relation to my health when I asked him. I've also learned from PubMed articles that most people who make it to five years with my diagnosis peter out somewhere in the seventh year. I find this information invaluable in terms of making decisions about my life, and sometimes I'm frustrated that I've had to seek out this information on my own.

I pursued my Certificate in Medical Insurance Billing and Coding from the summer of 2017 through December of 2018 with the idea that if my progression-free survival continued, I would find work of some sort that would allow me to put little bits of money toward the parent loans we've built up sending three kids to college. I don't have a great deal of stamina for standing work. The arenas in which I used to work are no longer available to me. My husband doesn't need money for day-to-day living; it's the massive college loan debt we fret about.

But my health continues to be challenging to decipher. Scans in October revealed new spots in my lungs. Were they shadows? Were they new spots related to the radiation I received? As I write these words, another woman I know with my cancer and its mutation type will be getting a port for her chemotherapy, something I've not yet experienced because of my plain dumb luck with my cancer's mutation and the capricious behavior of the oral targeted therapy drug I take. My heart aches about this new development in this woman's cancer journey.

I worked mightily this past fall to finish my certificate. I took the medical coding test twice, failing the first time, passing the second. I finished my externship, working twenty-one hours a week in a billing office, time spent in front of a computer screen that nearly wiped me out. I loved the people, enjoyed the work, but fretted about whether my brain and my eyes would be able to do such work in the future.

I didn't tell the people in my office about my cancer. The subject didn't come up, but to be honest, I avoided it. If I might be looking for work in the future, why would I tell potential employers that I had cancer? They would never hire me, because why would they hire someone with a terminal disease who might become a burden on their health insurance and a potential problem with respect to workload coverage?

I said above that I was profoundly grateful for my extra time. And yet.

As the pages in this book demonstrate, "grateful" is only one of the many emotions I feel, and it wouldn't be honest of me to pull back now. In addition to feeling grateful, I feel guilty. In the past year, in addition to losing a brother-in-law to alcohol addiction, I observed from afar the deaths of two women from my cancer cohort, both of whom had significantly less time with their families and loved ones than I after their initial diagnoses.

Researchers and doctors and nurses and medical personnel strive every day to help cancer patients deal with their infirmities. Yet their efforts aren't enough to take care of the thousands who are diagnosed with cancer each year.

And cancer isn't the only medical problem facing the country. Depression and suicide have taken their toll on society as record numbers of youth have taken their lives. Each of my children has received news of high school friends who've committed suicide. Last week, I attended a "celebration" of the life of a former student, who took her life at the age of forty-five.

At the end of this month, I will traipse down to the Detroit area to get my MRI and CT scans. The MRI will reveal if there are metastases in my brain; lung cancer often metastasizes to the brain because of the blood brain barrier. The CT scans will reveal whether those odd spots in my two lungs – two lungs, now; it used to be one – are true growths that need attention. And what will that attention be? Will it be more SBRT, which, according to my MyUofMHealth portal, cost $45,821.00 last February, a bill I was privileged not to have to pay because of my husband's excellent health insurance? Will I be switched to another drug, say Keytruda, the one they advertise on television? The newest cancer research, CAR-T, uses the immune system to fight off cancer. Researchers in China are making strides against it with significant clinical trials. I will not be travelling to China, much as I might like to see the country.

Whatever stateside treatment I receive after my next appointment with Dr. Gadgeel, at the end of the month, whether it's a continuation of the Tarceva, a new drug, stereotactic body radiation again, or chemo-therapy, my husband's insurance will pay for it.

At sixty, my husband is nearing retirement. But what if he were to lose his job?

I've had six extra, very expensive years of life since I was diagnosed with terminal cancer. I've had some good years. Shouldn't they just take me out back and shoot me?

My psychologist implores me not to view my value in monetary terms. But in addition to the depression that I've combatted for much of my life, the economic forces leading to the Great Recession and the reliance of the health care system on any potential patient's employment and insurance situation have enabled me to view my value as intrinsically linked with dollar signs. And my net worth, without my husband's earn-ings factored in, is incredibly low.

How many cancer patients can ignore the economic realities of their treatment? How many individuals who suffer from depression, especially those who end up taking their lives, have the ability to take care of their mental health, not to mention their physical health, without worrying about the cost and who pays for it? Those who suffer from alcohol and opioid addiction don't recognize ahead of time that they're travelling down a perilous path; it probably doesn't occur to them to seek a certain level of employment so that they have health insurance when they crash somewhere down the road from a serious medical problem they never anticipated.

I've struggled throughout my life to find my value as a human being, my self-worth. Depression made me de-value my contributions to others' lives; I can't blame cancer for my low self-esteem. And I can't claim to know the answer to the health care/health insurance crisis. But having taken this journey and ended up where I am today, experiencing first-hand the ravages of cancer, the ravages of depression, and the ravages of the Great Recession and the concomitant ageism that infused many employers' hiring practices, I want to gather close my husband, my children, my sisters, my friends, and all of those who have ever questioned their value. I want to tell each of them, as my friend Barb once told me: you are a ruby.

Dawn Newton
East Lansing, Michigan
January 2019

Acknowledgements

How do you thank the village? I am brimming with appreciation for all the individuals who contributed to this moment of validation in my life. I needed this validation before reaching the end, and I feel like a hummingbird, wings whirring, hovering about the nectar, ready to take that sweet sip.

To the friends who have encouraged me in reading and writing habits these many years, including those who learned with me or taught with me, or brainstormed ideas about creating schedules and managing multiple priorities (children and words), thanks for providing the sustenance to feed my writing spirit and intellect: Penny, Marilyn, Polly, Dana, Evan, Bill, Tim, Marie, Mary Kay, Adrienne, Ann, Janet, Ronni, Bob, Kathleen, Julie, Kristen, Barb, Madhu, Sharon, Peg, Beth, Mary, Fred, Dave, Dedria, Dennis, Shashi, Jill, Alison, Jane, and Pam.

To my teachers in universities and various workshop settings who provided me with instruction, wisdom, fun tricks to avoid procrastination, ways to stay in the chair, and brilliant and pithy mantras, please know that your voices enter my head at seemingly random moments when I write, always helping me solve a problem, and I'm thankful that my long-term memory has created a time capsule of your lessons in my brain: Dennis Pace, Katherine Fishburn, Sheila Roberts, Peter Vinten-Johansen, John Barth, George Garrett, Lois Stover, Stuart Dybek, Bonnie Jo Campbell, Valerie Laken, Anne-Marie Oomen, Patricia McNair, and Katey Schultz.

Valerie and Anne-Marie, thanks for helping me battle my way into this book after decades of disappointments. Your wise, evocative teaching and playful prompts at Bear River and Interlochen, respectively, helped me to regroup and refuel.

To my friend Marie, I am profoundly grateful for the words you penned regarding our shared time in Baltimore early in our lives but even more grateful for your long friendship. And my family would join me in thanking you and Bobby for helping me wade through my initial diagnosis information to find my way to Karmanos and Dr. Gadgeel.

To Adrienne, the first reader of a completed draft of this book (outside of my family), thanks for sharing your enthusiastic praise and your steadfast faith in my abilities as a writer after time had worn my ego thin. Your praise transformed itself into a big boost of energy that launched me into the sky.

To Mary Kay, another comrade from the Hopkins years, thanks for your encouragement and your willingness to rendezvous in Michigan and to host my family in D.C. for a fabulous dinner during a sweltering power outage. Your suggestion to revisit Vivian Gornick's *The Situation and The Story* came at the exact moment I needed it.

To Kathleen Pfeiffer, the chair of my English Department at Oakland University during the time of my diagnosis, thanks for helping me out when I got into tough corners during that year I taught nearly full time. Thanks for encouraging me from afar.

I will always be most grateful to Elizabeth Cowan Harper Neeld for creating, along with Gregory Cowan, one of the prompts – Cubing – that I used consistently over thirty years of teaching with students at all age levels and abilities. Thanks to Lacy Johnson for nominating me for an Honorable Mention in Gulf Coast's 2018 Nonfiction Prize Contest, for my essay using the Cubing prompt. Thanks to Gulf Coast for the prize money and thanks to *Carolina Quarterly* for publishing the essay.

I have enjoyed more residencies and writers' conferences than I thought possible during my years as a writer. Thanks to the staff members and my residency colleagues at Ragdale, the Kimmel Harding Nelson Center for the Arts, the Vermont Studio Center, Hambidge Center for the Arts and Sciences, River Teeth, Bear River Writers' Conference, and

Interlochen. I am thankful to the residency sponsors and staff for the time and space to pursue my work. Fellow residents, I loved meeting you and learning your stories. I hear your voices, too, and being blessed with a visual memory, I see your faces, and I am so very pleased that I had a chance to share space with each of you.

To my former students, I can barely find the words. You enriched my life in ways you can never fully fathom or understand. There are so many of you, ranging from the Blue Ridge Mountains and the Shenandoah Valley (Prospect Heights Middle School and James Madison University) to the campus of Dickinson College (Hopkins Summer CTY programs) to downtown Lansing (Lansing Community College and the Gifted and Talented Education Program) to the rolling hills of Rochester, Michigan at Oakland University. And to the families I tutored – Heashin, Min, and Yong Yun and Amrita and Priya Karve, thanks for letting me come into your homes during your adolescent learning years. I felt enriched by the education you gave to me.

And to the community of East Lansing, in which I got to play writer in the schools at so many grade levels and even at the Public Library, thanks for giving me the gift of spirited learners.

To the people who cared for my children on and off when they were young and I did part-time writing gigs and jobs, thank you for helping me feel safe and secure about leaving my kids. I promised myself I would list your names when I got my first novel published, but that was so long ago, I'm sure I'll forget. Still, I want to articulate those names I remember: Denise, Lauren, Renee, Chelsea, Taylor, Cassie, Beth, Filomena, and of course, Homa Khodadoost, the angel who entered Rachel's life after my parents died. Caregivers are nearly always underpaid. Please know I valued every minute you spent with my children; we are all better people for your efforts.

To Sue Butler and my coding cohort at Lansing Community College, please accept my deep thanks for allowing me to be a learner in your midst. I fretted about the power of my brain after so many years on a cancer drug, but you buoyed me up with your stick-to-it attitudes, and I experienced sheer joy in learning new subject matter. Thanks to Cindy, Marina, Rose, Kimberly, and Zarina for befriending me when I tried to stay aloof and hide my cancer. You helped me remember that I love to learn in a community as much as in solitude.

To Wendy and Lisa, thanks for helping me manage the hairs on my head and face. Thanks for listening and sharing the glories of parenting with me.

To Joan Sirigiri, thanks for hanging out with me and delving into my life of too many words and too much stuff! Your generous and nurturing nature, your sense of humor and wit, and your keen intelligence have enabled me to clear the cobwebs out of my brain, my environment, and my life. Every cancer-ridden hoarder with a tendency toward depression needs a Joan in her life, and I am thankful you are in mine.

To the doctors, nurses, physicians' assistants, techs, and schedulers who worked with me through these years to solve the big and little problems, thanks for answering my interminable questions and calming my fears. I owe Dr. Gadgeel and the staff at Karmanos Cancer Center in Farmington Hills a huge thank you for making my first years with cancer so easy. When I left Karmanos with Dr. Gadgeel as he transferred to the University of Michigan, I was sad to say goodbye to the team there, but I have come to appreciate all the good qualities of the University of Michigan's Health Care System, something that lifelong Michigan State Spartans are not always able to do. My internist, Regina McGill, my obstetrician, Maude Guerin, and my psychiatrist, Andy Homa, all helped me figure out the intricacies of complicated health diagnoses. Nicki, Dr. Homa's nurse, served as my lifeline. Thanks also to George Varughese, who took me on as a patient when Gina retired.

To Tim Goth-Owens, my psychologist, please accept my eternal appreciation for helping me to recognize the voice of depression in my head in its many iterations and to establish strategies to keep it in its place. As we both know, the voice is the jack-in-the-box that keeps popping up, but I'm closer to nirvana than I used to be, and I have valued your lessons and wisdom. Thanks also for supporting my kids.

To Christine Reppucci, my Virginia psychologist from nearly three decades ago, thanks for helping me understand in my twenties that my depression was a force to be reckoned with, one that would invade all aspects of my life, but one that I could master with the right drugs and tremendous effort. For years after we returned to Michigan, I kept your list of reminders on that folded piece of paper in my purse, your handwriting a soothing reminder of our time together.

To my church, University Lutheran, and its staff and members, thanks for being a place that I could come back to again and again with my grumpy, challenging faith. My parents chose to baptize me as a Lutheran before I had a mind of my own, but when I grew into adulthood, I was overjoyed to find in my inclusive church a philosophy that matched up with my ecumenical, mystical, pantheistic view of a God whom I often call Mother. Thanks also to the members of the church who sustained my children over the years with their spotty attendance at Sunday School, and thanks to Janine and Kristie for giving Rachel and me so many years of powerful musical opportunities. Thanks to the range of pastors who served in our church over the decades. I listened to your words. I heard your voices. I take your counsel when I can. Thanks to Sara Cogsil for preaching the sermon that provided me with an opportunity to hold mourning and rejoicing in my heart simultaneously.

I would like to thank all my children's friends over the years for coming into my messy house, enjoying and entertaining my children, and never saying in a loud voice, "Don't your parents ever clean?"

To the Apprentice House staff, namely Kevin Atticks, Communications Professor and Apprentice House Director, and students Paula-Yuan Gregory, Julia Trinkoff, and Miranda Nolan, thanks for putting so much work into the project of me and my book. Thanks for reading my sometimes delayed, sometimes alarmed, always too long emails with too many questions. I like to think that a bit of each of you peeks out of the pages.

To the extended Newton, Moritz, Dalton, and Kennedy clans, thanks to you all for being part of this larger thing I call family. I know I haven't always appreciated you as a group since big social gatherings are often challenging for me. But I remember the jokes, the stories that got retold, and the special dishes that arrived with each holiday; thank you for your gracious selves.

To Jean and Terry, please know that your recent passings changed us all. We keep you with us. I beg your forgiveness for the wrongs I may have done against you in the name of whatever I thought was right at the time. I don't create scenarios in my head any more about what heaven might be like. But if the idea of a big party with lots of laughing and good food is the image I should hold, and I gain admittance to that party, I'm counting on standing rib roast. Jean, let Terry take it out of the oven when he wants; I'll gladly eat the rare meat if it means I get to see you both again and make Terry do the dishes.

To Kari and the Reps, thanks for bringing joy to Jean and Terry in their final days.

To Linda and Lori, I want you to know how happy I am when I think of our time back in Waterford – our imperfect perfect childhoods. Even when our parents were struggling with the possibility of divorce, we found ways to come together as a family. When we lost them in 1993, I was so thankful for the two of you and our burgeoning families. We did the best we could, raising the Newton grandchildren – Rachel, Devon, Colin, Connor, Emelia, Griffin, and Nathaniel – without the presence of Grandma and Grandpa Newton, and my children have always valued the time spent with their aunts, uncles, and cousins. Thank you for being the sisters who know my flaws and weaknesses, recognize them, ignore them, and forgive me for them. And thanks for being part of the musical fabric of my life.

Clover, your capacity for empathy and delight never ceases to amaze me.

To Rachel, Connor, and Nathaniel, my three favorite children. Before I became a parent, I feared that I could never be as natural of a mom for the three of you as my mother was for me. As an extrovert, she was nearly my opposite in many ways, but as a nurturer, she was my anchor. I feared that I would never have her patience, her flexibility, or her ability to let go of the small things. But you are all almost grown now, and however much I may have screwed you up, I see signs that you are mostly healthy, capable of deep love, and thoughtful in more ways than I ever could have envisioned. Tim Goth-Owens says the nature-nurture argument about the effect parents have on their children is still largely a draw, so I won't take any credit for your strengths, but I thank you for allowing me to see your growth, for growing in front of me instead of running away and hiding, returning only as fully formed adults. Thanks for letting me stand closer to you than most kids allow their parents to stand, for letting me hold you right up in front of my face so I could breathe the air from your souls. So sweet, that air. No mother could be as lucky as I.

To my husband Tim, thanks for your steadfast presence and your willingness to let me serve as the catalyst for so many events in our lives. Thanks for listening, hour after patient hour, to my oral processing during those times when I needed it most. You have been my most trusted reader of nearly every word I've written in my life, and I value your honesty and diplomacy; I know it's not easy to provide critiques for someone who often suffers from depression! Thanks, too, for your many years of patience with my passionate way of arguing. You were the boy I wanted, I pursued you relentlessly (in my very low-key, Midwestern shy girl, unassuming way), but when I got what I wanted, I didn't trust it. I know my relentless and whipsawed emotions sometimes contributed to misunderstandings that begat misunderstandings even after an argument was settled. You still are the boy that I want, still the most handsome with the striking blue eyes, and even though I said I'd struggle if you chose to marry after my death (not something for which you've asked or advocated), I really just want to make sure you get a pre-nup so you can be sure to save some retirement money to help the kids with those student loans.

To anyone I may have forgotten to name, thank you. My long-term memory is better than the short-term memory, and chances are I've thought of you in the last year or so, feeling gratitude that once upon a time we shared a sidewalk, a book, or a story.

Permissions Acknowledgments

Grateful acknowledgement is made to the following publications, in which portions of this book first appeared: *1966: A Journal of Creative Nonfiction,* "Her Skin"; *Conquer: The Patient Voice,* "CT Scans"; *The Carolina Quarterly,* "Juglans Nigra"; *Months to Years,* "Jean's Trail"; and *Scope* (Stanford Medical Blog) "Breathing: A reflection on living with asthma".

Grateful acknowledgement is also made for permission to reprint the "Cubing Exercise" instructions which appear in "Juglans Nigra." From *Writing, Brief Edition* by Elizabeth Cowan, copyright © 1983 by Scott, Foresman and Company. Permission granted by Elizabeth Harper Neeld, PhD (also known as Elizabeth Cowan), www.elizabethharperneeld.com @elizabethneeld

Grateful acknowledgement is also made to Pastor Sara Cogsil for the words from her sermon at University Lutheran Church, East Lansing, MI, in July of 2015.

.

About the Author

Dawn Newton has spent her life with words. A first-generation college student, she attended Michigan State University and subsequently earned a fellowship to attend the Johns Hopkins University, where she received her M.A. in Fiction. Shortly after she was diagnosed with stage IV lung cancer in November of 2012, she learned that her cancer had the vulnerable EGFR mutation. When not attending doctors' appointments, she fills her days with writing, researching, and texting with her husband, Tim Dalton, and three grown children – Rachel, Connor, and Nathaniel. Her rambunctious dog, Clover, keeps her honest.

Apprentice
House Press
Loyola University Maryland

Apprentice House is the country's only campus-based, student-staffed book publishing company. Directed by professors and industry professionals, it is a nonprofit activity of the Communication Department at Loyola University Maryland.

Using state-of-the-art technology and an experiential learning model of education, Apprentice House publishes books in untraditional ways. This dual responsibility as publishers and educators creates an unprecedented collaborative environment among faculty and students, while teaching tomorrow's editors, designers, and marketers.

Outside of class, progress on book projects is carried forth by the AH Book Publishing Club, a co-curricular campus organization supported by Loyola University Maryland's Office of Student Activities.

Eclectic and provocative, Apprentice House titles intend to entertain as well as spark dialogue on a variety of topics. Financial contributions to sustain the press's work are welcomed. Contributions are tax deductible to the fullest extent allowed by the IRS.

To learn more about Apprentice House books or to obtain submission guidelines, please visit www.apprenticehouse.com.

Apprentice House
Communication Department
Loyola University Maryland
4501 N. Charles Street
Baltimore, MD 21210
Ph: 410-617-5265 • Fax: 410-617-2198
info@apprenticehouse.com • www.apprenticehouse.com

CPSIA information can be obtained
at www.ICGtesting.com
Printed in the USA
FFHW011319110919
54908526-60599FF

9 781627 202459